The Scandal of Sacramentality

The Scandal of Sacramentality

The Eucharist in Literary and Theological Perspectives

BRANNON HANCOCK

Forewords by
ANN LOADES and DAVID JASPER

PICKWICK *Publications* · Eugene, Oregon

THE SCANDAL OF SACRAMENTALITY
The Eucharist in Literary and Theological Perspectives

Pickwick Publications
An Imprint of Wipf and Stock Publishers
199 W. 8th Ave., Suite 3
Eugene, OR 97401

www.wipfandstock.com

ISBN 13: 978-1-62032-632-9

Cataloguing-in-Publication Data

Hancock, Brannon

The scandal of sacramentality : the Eucharist in literary and theological perspectives / Brannon Hancock, with forewords by Ann Loades and David Jasper

xxviii + 204 p. ; 23 cm. Includes bibliographical references.

ISBN 13: 978-1-62032-632-9

1. Lord's Supper. 2. Christianity and Literature. 3. Human body—Religious aspects. 4. Christianity and the Arts. I. Loades, Ann. II. Jasper, David. III. Title.

BV825.3 H152 2013

Manufactured in the USA

Cover image: Friedrich Herlin's *Schmerzensmann* (Man of Sorrows), *Epitaph des Paul Strauss*, (1469), reproduced with kind permission from Stadtmuseum Nördlingen, Germany.

For Gloria

Contents

Foreword

THEOLOGIANS WRITING ON THE long, prodigal, and contentious tradition of reflection on the "sacrament" of the Eucharist are in for some surprises as they read this book! Artists of many kinds resist having their insights regarded as merely "illustrative" of what theologians supposedly already "know." Some writers have been gripped by the "scandal" (1 Cor 1:23) of the Eucharist, of the relation of language to flesh, the profane to the sacred, the erotic and destabilising "grace" of its mystery. For Dr. Hancock to have included Graham Greene's *Monsignor Quixote* was perhaps predictable, but not so the other half a dozen or so voices he argues that theologians cannot afford to ignore. Some of them require a strong stomach to read, but all of them subvert any sense we may have of certainty and possession in thinking or about or experiencing Eucharistic devotion in the supposed comfort of an ecclesial body. Dr. Hancock's approach is challenging, disturbing, eminently readable, and should be taken to heart.

> —Ann Loades CBE
> Professor Emerita of Divinity, University of Durham; Honorary Professorial Fellow of St. Chad's College, University of Durham; and Honorary Professor in the Divinity School at the University of St. Andrews.

Foreword

The sacramental life of the Christian Church has, from the very earliest times, been acquainted with scandal. There is reason to think that the celebration of the Eucharist, in some form, predates even the canonical Gospels, and by the end of the second century of the Christian era, Tertullian was grimly satirizing those outside the Church who clearly thought that the sacrament was shocking in the extreme and beyond what was tolerable. "We are accused," he wrote, "of observing a sacred ritual in which we kill a little child and eat it." He goes on to describe this action in graphic detail: "Come, plunge your knife into the infant. . . . Take the fresh young blood, saturate your bread with it, and eat freely." For St. Paul, a hundred or so years earlier than Tertullian, in his first letter to the Corinthians, "Christ crucified" is a stumbling block, or more precisely a "scandal" to the Jews and foolishness to Greeks. Scandal, it seems, was never far from the early Church, and most especially in it liturgical practices and the sacrament of the Eucharist.

In this new book, Brannon Hancock explores this theme of the scandalous sacrament in the context of our current Western culture, which some would describe as "post-Christian," and where, for the most part at the very least, the Christian churches that hold the sacramental life as central to their faith are in decline. Yet the scandal and the life of the sacrament continue in our society in literature and film, often in graphic and shocking forms that match the language of Tertullian, and, it is suggested, the life of the eucharistic community continues, perhaps impossibly, even beyond the boundaries of the Church itself.

But Aristotle observed that, in literature and art "a likely impossibility is always preferable to an unconvincing possibility." In the texts of literature may be embraced, then, the scandal that has survived for so long in the rituals of Christendom and its aftermath in the Reformation West, finding its power, and perhaps even its "truth" in the postmodern scandals of brokenness and fragmentation. And if Christianity has for so long been, at best, cautious about the human body and its energies, at the heart of the sacrament there is no such tendency to prudishness, and in literature this is even less the case. In the texts addressed by Hancock here we return to the body in all its messy complexity, and therefore to the mystery that lies at the very heart of the incarnation, the Word made flesh. Here are bodies, broken, consumed, penetrated—as was (and is) the body of Christ at the Passion, on the cross and by the spear.

For some this may seem a profane book—but it is in its heart deeply sacramental and, perhaps, even devout. Yet it is timely and challenging, a reminder that religion, and the Christian sacramental tradition, remains a central part of our world and our experience of what it is to be human.

—David Jasper
Professor of Literature and Theology, University of Glasgow

Acknowledgments

This work, far from being the product of an individual mind, was truly brought to birth by a community, a kind of *corpus mysticum* transcending time and place, of those whose lives have touched mine over the past decade or more. I am grateful to all those without whose gracious hospitality and friendship I would have had no place to lay my laptop, much less my head, especially Andrew and Elma Young, Mattias and Sara Martinson, and Brian and Luanne Stahl. A special thanks to the Community of the Transfiguration in Cincinnati, Ohio, for welcoming me into your library, your liturgical life, and the joy of your *simplicitas*.

I have been eternally blessed by the worshipping communities that I have called "home," and which have claimed me as their own, during this research and writing—Nashville Bethel Church of the Nazarene, Hart Memorial Church of the Nazarene, St. Mary's Scottish Episcopal Cathedral, and Xenia Church of the Nazarene—thank you for giving me a Body with and within which to pray, to serve, to celebrate, and to participate in the ecclesial and sacramental bodies of the Risen One. Amongst all the faithful of these four churches, I am especially grateful to Robert and Carol White, Caroline MacKillop, Frikki Walker and family, Chris and Sarah Hampson, the St. Mary's Choir and Compline group, Mark Cummings, Jerry Gardner, and Mark Atherton.

I am thankful for friends who have shaped and continue to shape my life through communion and conversation: Schuy and Felicia Weishaar, Joseph Wood, David Belcher, Andrew Brower-Latz, Joe Gunby, Doug Van Nest, Brent Peterson, and my fellow "Sacramental Nazarenes." Thank you to all those who, in a variety of ways, encouraged or enabled our migration to Glasgow to pursue this dream, especially Steve Fountain and Rob Blann.

My life has been enriched by many fellow sojourners on the unpredictable path of interdisciplinary theological thinking, including all those who sat with me around the table at the University of Glasgow's Literature,

Theology and the Arts postgraduate seminar, especially Doug Gay, Brad Johnson, Jeff Keuss, Brad and Kara Pickens, Andrew Hass, and Mark Godin—you have provided the intellectual community, conversation, challenge, and kinship that energized my thinking, and this project, from beginning to end.

David Jasper is for me a model of the scholarly and priestly vocations cohabiting a fulfilled, fruitful life. Thank you, David, for your support, kindness, inspiration, and mentorship. Michael and Julia DeLashmutt, thank you for our shared life and inseparable familial bond. Thank you, Troy Carter, for the confidence, pastoral care, theological dialogue and, above all, friendship that you have given and continue to give me.

To my family, especially my parents, Michael and Rebecca Hancock— thank you for raising me to love adventures, words, people, Jesus, and his Body called Church. Thank you to my in-laws, Allen and Charlotte Barrett, for allowing me to whisk your daughter off to Scotland for four years, and for never flagging in your belief in me that I could and would finish this thing! To my kids, Andrew, Joseph, and Cecilia—thank you for loving your daddy, putting up with his frequent absences, and providing him with motivation and immeasurable joy. Finally and most significantly, my deepest debt of gratitude is to my wife, Gloria, who is to me a daily embodiment of sacrament—thank you, my love, for everything.

Introduction

Our contemporary fascination with presence . . . is based on a long-ing for presence that in the contemporary context can only be satis-fied in conditions of extreme temporal fragmentation.[1]

THINKING "SACRAMENT"

This book is an interdisciplinary inquiry into the nature of sacrament and into the relationship between the Eucharist—the ritual partaking of the body and blood of Christ in the symbols of bread and wine—as the sacrament *par excellence*, and sacramental themes or "traces" of sacramentality that appear in contemporary fictional narratives. In a "post-Christian" (or at the very least "post-ecclesial") age characterized by waning participation in traditional Christian practices,[2] a surprising persistence and relevance of sacramental themes and eucharistic allusions may be observed within contemporary literature and the creative arts more broadly. One wonders, then—apart from the legitimizing role of the Church in her theology and liturgy—from whence the Eucharist, or even a more vague concept of "sacramentality," derives any meaning. In seeking to understand why the sacramental/eucharistic continues to capture the contemporary imagination, this project pursues several questions: What is a sacrament? Why has Christian theology found sacrament to be such a contentious concept? How has the notion of sacrament, most fully realized in the celebration of the Eucharist, both defined and been defined by the Church? How is sacrament related to language and the body? How is the notion of a sacramental or eucharistic "real presence" figured within contemporary postmodern narratives and practices? And what new insights into traditional Christian sacramental

1. Gumbrecht, *Production,* 20.
2. See, e.g., Bruce, *God is Dead*; Brown, *Christian Britain*; Davie, *Religion in Britain*.

and liturgical practice might contemporary literature and the arts provide, and what impact might this in turn have on Christian faith and practice?

While they have, at least since the Enlightenment, enjoyed a certain freedom from the liturgical and theological constraints of the Church, throughout history the creative arts have maintained a complicated relationship to Christianity, and Christian worship in particular. The arts have of course been employed in Christian worship as supplemental or illustrative tools—as, so to speak, a "handmaiden" to the aims of theology and liturgy—but the arts also offer a unique perspective on the scandalous and subversive implications of the Christian faith; thus we might call the relationship between the arts and Christian ritual a "deconstructive" relationship. The arts seem to understand and wrestle with the profanity inherent to the sacred in a way that theology is rarely, if ever, capable of. This essay's central thesis is that literature and the arts are able to "think through" the deconstructive core of the Eucharist in ways that theology undertakes only at its own peril. That is to say, theology takes seriously this deconstruction—which we will develop according to the theme of *scandal*[3] (Gk. *skandalon*, literally "stumbling block")—only by risking the stability of the eucharistic community itself: the Church, under the headship of the Christ represented in the eucharistic celebration, which may be understood as the Church's "constitutive action." Yet the Eucharist itself, which simultaneously (de)stabilizes and (con)founds the Church and her theology, demands, and indeed enacts, this risk. In other words, on one level, the Eucharist "guarantees" God's grace[4] and Christ's presence to the Church, while simultaneously

3. While we have developed this heuristic to meet the demands of this project, several other thinkers deserve credit for providing the useful theme of scandal/*skandalon*: Prof. David Jasper first pointed out that the Pauline concept "stumbling block" was the Gk. term *skandalon,* and he has utilized the theme of scandal in his recent study *The Sacred Body,* e.g., "the scandal of the crucified" (33). Nathan Mitchell points in this direction, e.g., "On the cross, God subverts all we know of "God." Such a searing scandal cannot be grasped *conceptually*" (*Meeting Mystery,* 37). See also Westhelle, *Scandalous God.* In all these examples, as in St. Paul's usage, the *skandalon* is the crucified Christ. The only precedent we know of for relating sacrament directly to *skandalon* in the Pauline sense is Louis-Marie Chauvet's *Symbol and Sacrament,* which is foundational to this thesis in many ways, e.g., "The Sacramental Stumbling Block" (153–54), "For this true scandal is that God . . . continues to raise up for himself a body in the world" (187), "there is something particularly scandalous about the Eucharistic presence of Christ" (383 and *passim*). Finally, while we will disagree with him on certain points, we must cite the influence of Graham Ward's discussion of "the ontological scandal" of the eucharistic "is" ("this is my body") in relation to Christ's "displaced body" and the "broken bodies of postmodernity" in chapters 3–4 of *Cities* (81–116).

4. Following Chauvet, *grace* from the standpoint of Christian sacramentality implies *graciousness* as well as *gratuitousness,* i.e., that which is beyond economy and utility; see *Symbol and Sacrament,* 108–9.

problematizing and unsettling *every* foundation. The effort to "found" the Church upon Christ's eucharistic presence, then, results in the "foundering" of the Church itself; for Christ's body—both historical and eucharistic—refuses to be "nailed down."[5]

This book proposes to undertake an interpretation of the Church's eucharistic practice as inherently and irreducibly *scandalous*, as demonstrated in the literary and artistic explorations to which we will attend; and then to apply the implications of this scandal to the liturgical and sacramental practices of the Church today, as well as to the secular cultural context that the Church inhabits. This will require close readings of a variety of texts: liturgical, theological, and historical sources, as well literary and artistic texts which illuminate the questions at hand. What will emerge is a reimagining of the Eucharist as participation in this *skandalon*, and of the eucharistic community as an assembly (*ecclesia*), a gathering, which is *con-voked*, called together, by this scandal, even as it is torn asunder by it. In this sense, the Church (or any assembly which might be described as eucharistic) is a community founded upon a scandal, and it is this scandal which necessarily un-founds and up-roots this community. A community that is properly called eucharistic is not one which *possesses* the Eucharist, but one which is *possessed by* the Eucharist. This possession *by* the Eucharist is a *dis*-possession of every possession, a risk that can never be fully avoided, the same risk God ultimately undertook in the incarnation of Christ: the risk of death, that is, the absolute loss of self.

Even prior to the cross, the central symbol of the eucharistic community is the broken body of the Crucified One. It is this symbol of brokenness that unites the Church, and has done so throughout the ages. The loss of the centrality of this symbol is nothing less than the loss of the Church-as-Church. But we can understand this only by understanding the Church as a community that interprets death—a particular death—as its very *life* and reason for being. The Church, then, has an entirely different perspective than the world, one that understands death-as-presence (and correspondingly, resurrection-as-absence), as we shall see in our examination of biblical sources. This is the scandal of the Eucharist today, a scandal that has typically been domesticated by the Church, but which, we argue, must be continually sought and upheld as essential to the very be(com)ing of the Church as the Body-of-Christ broken for the life of the world.

5. See Moore, *God's Gym*, 37–39.

THE EUCHARIST IN THEOLOGY AND LITERATURE

The problem with the Eucharist has always been primarily a problem of interpretation; indeed, we might propose that the attempt to interpret the Eucharist is an exercise in futility from the outset. The Reformation debates about how the Eucharist "works"—how Christ's real presence is manifest in the present, whether according to notions of transubstantiation, consubstantiation, commemoration, or otherwise—simply brought to a climax the Church's ongoing attempt to understand and articulate the meaning of Christ's declaration "this [bread] is my body . . . this [cup] is my blood" (Mark 14:22–24), and what, if any, direct relationship those identifications have to the Church's *leitourgia*.

Long before they were inscribed in the writings that would comprise the New Testament, Jesus' words and actions at the Last Supper were repeated by those followers who believed in his bodily resurrection from the dead. From their first repetition began a ritual tradition and with it the project of interpreting these words and actions. David Power is clear on this point: "tradition is first and foremost the transmission of life in Christ and the Spirit, down through time and across cultures. This has its doctrinal, theological . . . devotional, and sacramental expressions. As far as these are concerned, the action of tradition involves a constant process of interpretation."[6] So we ask, what did Jesus mean by "this is my body . . . this is my blood"? By "do this" (*touto poieite*)? By "remembrance" (*anamnēsin*)? What did Jesus mean for them, and us, to "do," and what did he mean for us to understand by it?

These are significant and in some ways irresolvable questions; and yet, in an important sense, *understanding* is not the point of the Eucharist at all. Christ does not instruct his followers to *comprehend* or *explain* or *interpret* the mystical action, but rather simply to *do* it. Theology, however, has never quite been able to cope with such an apophatic posture toward the mystery. David Jasper puts it thus:

> In this lack of a beyond, utterly immanent yet wholly transcendent, lies the sacramental heart of the insistent "real presence" of the Eucharist in which, even from the time of St. Paul, the followers of Christ took the intolerable flesh into their own bodies in the Eucharist even as they were consumed by it. Yet the oblivion of theology itself has tended to obliterate this scandal,

---

6. Power, *Sacrament*, 39. For a more detailed account of Power's hermeneutical approach to sacraments as "language" (drawing upon the work of David Tracy), see 48–49 of the same work.

the scandal of the crucified, unwatchable body, the body in hell,
that yet we take into ourselves.[7]

Indeed, theo-*logy*'s task is necessarily iterative; it is to reason or speak a
word (*logos*) about God (*theos*). Theology, it would seem, is genetically pre-
disposed to resist silence and absence. And while theology has always left a
little room for the apophatic way of the *via negativa*, its dominant mode is to
speak and reason endlessly about those divine matters that are its concern.

Literature, on the other hand, and the arts more broadly, is able to
cope with silence and absence, even when attempting to inscribe it into
its own narrative. Where theologians have often sought to overcome or
explain away the divine *mystērion*, the work of artists and writers have been
able to sustain the mystery, albeit in obscured, inverted, subverted, perverted, and otherwise scandalous and scandalizing ways.[8] Theology seeks to
define, in the service of ecclesiastical doctrine, and to construct speculative
systems that "make sense" of the complex interrelationship between God,
humankind, creation, sin, Scripture, and so on; such delineation tends to
limit the scope of its subject matter. Art (literary or otherwise), on the other
hand, seeks to "make sense" (i.e., create meaning) as well, not by delineating
but by *transgressing* boundaries, by *de*-limiting in a less or even un-system-
atic mode. Art does not serve doctrine or dogma, or else it ceases to be
art, and instead becomes propaganda; its "narratives," such as they may be
called, do not seek to construct intellectual systems but to deconstruct rigid
patterns of thought and action so as to open new pathways and possibilities
for human thinking and being.

In this sense, literature and the arts pick up where theology leaves off.
While this is an "interdisciplinary" study, one cannot act as theologian and
literary critic in equal-but-autonomous measure. While this essay might
blur them on occasion, the boundaries between these disciplines remain
intact.[9] The underlying concerns and driving motivations for this project

7. Jasper, *Sacred Body*, 33.

8. See Schwartz, *Sacramental Poetics*. Very near to our own thesis, Schwartz's suggests that the Reformers' rejection of the doctrine of transubstantiation enables (even
forces?) the sacramental to spill over into poetry, the arts, culture, etc: "Aspects of the
Eucharist began showing up in the poetry of the Reformation, albeit in completely
unorthodox ways" (7–8). Her last statement is key—this displacement of sacramental
presence results in *unorthodox* expressions of sacramentality—expressions that scan-
dalize and subvert traditional, orthodox understandings of the Eucharist.

9. This would be impossible anyway, as literary critic Stanley Fish has pointed out in
his essay "Being Interdisciplinary Is So Very Hard to Do" (in *Free Speech*). Of interdisciplinary studies, he posits "either they are engaging in straightforwardly disciplinary
tasks that require for their completion information and techniques on loan from other
disciplines, or they are working within a particular discipline at a moment when it is

are theological, and indeed, insofar as they concern Christian liturgy and sacrament, ecclesial and ecclesiological. Our engagements with literature are not undertaken simply for the sake of adding another page to the volumes of secondary criticism on the works treated herein. Rather, they seek to open possibilities for theological thinking that theology has either forgotten or never fully known.[10] Furthermore, in an era that has been described as "post-secular," "post-Christian," and even "post-atheist,"[11] the theological discipline seems to have become uncertain as to whether or not it still exists to serve the Church at all (so long as churches linger), or whether it must refigure its purpose as purely academic, whether that means being swallowed up under the canopy of "religious studies" or "sociology of religion," or as a substrata of the humanities. On a kind of meta-level, therefore, this project is an attempt to confront theology with the delusion of its own self-sufficiency,[12] exposing it to a method of theological thinking that may reinvigorate or even reinvent it to address the changing cultural and intellectual landscape into which it desires to speak.

To summarize, then: this project explores the possibility of sacramentality, based upon eucharistic theology, which takes seriously the

---

expanding into territories hitherto marked as belonging to someone else . . . or they are in the process of establishing a new discipline, one that takes as its task the analysis of disciplines, the charting of their history and of their ambitions. . . . Nor is there anything reprehensible about these activities. Depending on one's own interests and sense of what the situation requires, the imperial ambitions of a particular discipline may be just what the doctors ordered; and it may equally well be the case that, from a certain point of view, the traditional disciplines have played themselves out and it is time to fashion a new one" (242).

10. Without being presumptuous, it is our guess that the present work corresponds most closely to Fish's second possibility: indeed, we are working within the theological discipline, and pursuing theological questions, at a point when the parameters of what theology *means* and *does* are expanding (or perhaps vanishing). As students of the interdisciplinary study of literature, theology, and the arts continue to develop hermeneutical tools that allows these discourses to be engaged simultaneously, a new discipline altogether has begun to emerge, wherein, for example, theological writing may be regarded as a form of literary or poetic discourse, and literature and the arts may be recognized as valid expressions of theology. Following Carl Raschke and David Jasper, we prefer to describe such interdisciplinary work as "theological thinking"; see Raschke, *Theological Thinking*, and Jasper, "From Theology to Theological Thinking."

11. See Blond, *Post–Secular Philosophy*; Vahanian, *Death of God*; and Marsh, *Post–Atheist Age*.

12. Contra the theological program known as Radical Orthodoxy which seeks to subjugate every other discipline to the meta–narrative of Christian theology; for the most complete development of this thesis, see Milbank, *Theology and Social Theory*, esp. his final chapter (382–442). Cf. Milbank, John, et al., *Radical Orthodoxy*, for a representative collection of essays by many scholars whose subsequent work extends this agenda.

contribution postmodern literature and culture, which challenges contemporary Christian theology and liturgy to risk its own stability—and indeed to understand this instability as *grace* itself—while also calling attention to the sacramental and even specifically eucharistic traces that appear in contemporary literature, arts, and culture. It is precisely this scandalizing *risk*—this unavoidable (self-)deconstruction that yet clears the way for new constructions, uncharted possibilities—that fascinates us. It is a risk that, we assert, must be taken. As they endeavor to think what is for theology unthinkable, Christian theologians cannot afford to ignore the prophetic voices of literature and the arts, even to the point of allowing those voices to challenge theology's basic assumptions and expose its scandalous, de/constructive core.[13]

To be clear, we highlight this inherent scandal not to undermine the validity of Christian theology and/or liturgy—this is not self-indulgent iconoclasm—but to reveal the cracks and fissures that always already exist in the foundation; to unsettle false and unexamined certainties about Christian thought and practice; and to clear the way for the kind of thinking (and the kind of worship) that is truly constituted by the Christian virtues of faith, hope, and love. In short, we hope to expose Christian faith and practice to some of its tendency toward idol-worship—the idols of knowledge, power, and possession—and to point instead toward the "more excellent way" (1 Cor 13:1) enfleshed in the Christ event and re-presented in the Church's eucharistic action.

THE TWO-FOLD SCANDAL OF SACRAMENTALITY: AN OVERVIEW

According to the writer of the Fourth Gospel, "the Word became flesh and made his dwelling among us" (John 1:14). Acknowledging the postmodern fixation on language and the body, we have chosen to explore the scandal of sacramentality according to a two-pronged thematic: that of the *word* and the *flesh*, of language and the body.[14] By no means do we pit these two terms

13. In *The Puppet and the Dwarf*, Slavoj Žižek unveils a similar hidden "core," which he calls "perverse"; namely, an "internal gap" within Godself, exemplified in God–in–Christ's self–abandonment on Calvary. As it relates to the present work, we would argue that Žižek's "perverse core of Christianity" is given concrete form within sacrament, and is enacted within the symbolic matrix of the Church's eucharistic celebration.

14. What we are calling the *two–fold scandal of sacramentality*—that of language and that of the body—is a heuristic at which we have arrived as a result of the influence of (at least) two key sources. The first is Louis-Marie Chauvet's *Symbol and Sacrament*, whose postmodern sacramental theology has perhaps influenced this project

against one another; indeed, the overcoming of the dualisms and opposing binaries of *logocentrism* is central to postmodern thought. Rather, these two concepts represent distinct but parallel modes of the symbolic operation of the Christian notion of sacrament, exemplified by the Eucharist. Returning to John 1, the Christ event encapsulates the collision of word and flesh, the creative logos of God becoming incarnate within the created order spoken into being by that selfsame Word. The Eucharist, therefore, which points to the Word-made-flesh, Christ the "primordial sacrament,"[15] makes present the co-incidence or con-fusion of word and flesh: of language taking on a body; of the immaterial entering into and taking on materiality; of the sacred coming to inhabit the profane. So, not as a dualism but as a coincidence of opposites (*coincidentia oppositorum* is the Cusan term),[16] we shall explore the Eucharist and the notion of sacrament(ality), along these two trajectories, each of which are of central concern to postmodern thought.

This study is organized in two parts. Part One, "The Scandal of Sacramentality," articulates the theoretical framework upon which the interdisciplinary explorations of Part Two rely. Three chapters comprise Part One. Chapter 1 ("*Skandalon*: Stumbling over Sacrament") examines the concepts of sacrament and sacramentality, highlighting the inherent difficulty of defining these terms. In seeking to understand what a sacrament *is*, we shall look to sources ancient (Augustine) and modern (Tillich) to relate sacrament to both sign and symbol. In dialogue with theologians of the East (Zizioulas) and West (Rahner, de Lubac), we shall establish the centrality of Christ and describe sacrament as that which simultaneously *makes* and *breaks* the Church.

---

more than any other single work. Chauvet deals extensively with language as mediation (84–109) as well as the relationship between symbol and body (110–55). The other key text is Pickstock, *After Writing*, in which the author seeks to establish the "co–primacy of sign and body" in her account of the liturgy and the liturgical subject. She posits that "the coincidence of sign and body is most manifest in the event of the Eucharist" (xv).

15. See Schillebeeckx, *Christ the Sacrament*, especially §1.2, "Christ the Primordial Sacrament" (13–39). He writes: "Consequently if the human love and all the human acts of Jesus possess a divine saving power, then the realization in human shape of this saving power necessarily includes as one of its aspects the manifestation of salvation: includes, in other words, sacramentality. The man Jesus, as the personal visible realization of the divine grace of redemption, is *the* sacrament, the primordial sacrament, because this man, the Son of God himself, is intended by the Father to be in his humanity the only way to the actuality of redemption" (15). Like his contemporary Karl Rahner, Schillebeeckx also regards the Church as the "Sacrament of the Risen Christ" (see chapter 2, 47–89).

16. "On Learned Ignorance" (*De docta ignorantia*, 1440) describes Nicholas of Cusa's notion of the coincidence of opposites (*coincidentia oppositorum*); in Bond, *Nicholas of Cusa*, 87–206. See Bond's "Introduction" (19–36) for a helpful synopsis.

In chapter 2 (*"The Word . . .*: The Problem of Language") we shall consider the scandal of sacramentality in relation to the basic problem of language, so thoroughly critiqued in post-structuralist and postmodern thought. The Eucharist originates with the symbolic and metaphoric speech of Jesus; is inscribed within the narrative and epistolary texts of the New Testament; and has been and is disseminated through the liturgical books and actions of the Church throughout history. Therefore, the *skandalon* of sacramentality is, on the one hand, a linguistic scandal. We shall think through the impact of postmodern shifts in our understanding of language and textuality upon the Eucharist in particular, attending to poststructuralism (Derrida), the radical theology of the "death of God" movement (Altizer), and the liturgical reforms of the Second Vatican Council, at the heart of all of which resides an anxiety about the ability of language to convey meaning. Guided by Catholic theologian David Power's description of sacrament as "the *language* of God's giving,"[17] we shall relate sacrament to metaphor (Ricoeur) and arrive at what we wish to call the "de/constructive core" of sacramentality.

To restate, the idea of sacrament is, on the one hand, a language problem. On the other hand, an extension of the creation and the incarnation, sacraments convey spiritual presence to human bodies via the material elements such as the bread and wine. Thus the Christian conception of sacrament is also a *corporeal* or bodily scandal. This is the focus of chapter 3 (". . . *Made Flesh*: The Problem of the Body"). The discussion shifts toward the issue of the Eucharist as embodied performance, as physical/bodily liturgical action; as well as the physical ritual instantiation of *God's* body in the incarnate and crucified Christ, made mystically but no less *real*-ly present in the sacramental act. According to the narratives and creeds of Christianity, God first *speaks* creation into being, and then in the ultimate redemptive act, the Divine becomes enfleshed in the body of a woman; enters the world in the body of an infant; grows into the body of a carpenter from Nazareth called Jesus, whose body is executed on a cross and buried in a tomb. After that lifeless body is found missing from the tomb, it appears resurrected to hundreds of followers before ascending to the Father. The Church is described as the Body of Christ, a lingering physical presence of the ascended Christ within human history. In the Eucharist, the Church's "quintessential sacrament,"[18] the bread is transfigured as Christ's body and the wine as his blood. The participation of Christ's ecclesial body in his sacramental body constitutes the Church *as* the body of Christ, drawing individual members

17. Power, *Sacrament* (italics added).
18. Schwartz, *Sacramental Poetics*, 7.

into the communion of Christ's body. To paraphrase Augustine's famous phrase, in the sacrament, the Church receives that which it is.

Hence, the body is of particular significance. Divinity wrapped in a body is not only difficult to conceive of but difficult to cope with as well; for where there is a body, there is pleasure and pain; hunger, eating, drinking and excreting; sensuality and sexuality. None of this sits easily with our common notions of the Divine or the Sacred. In addition to Jesus' words in John 6:63—"It is the spirit that gives life; the flesh is useless"—and certain writings of St. Paul (e.g., Phil 3:3), our Platonic inheritance (which, it must be said, is not necessarily indigenous to the biblical witness, but has held considerable influence over the Christian faith) has led us to polarize flesh against spirit in such a way. But we must confront the truth that sacraments are, in Louis-Marie Chauvet's potent phrase, "the word of God at the mercy of the body."[19] By the end of Part One, it should be clear that this two-pronged conception of language and body actually reveals itself to be an interconnected matrix of significance, such that the body-of-the-text and the text-of-the-body may be conceived as inextricably related; the "problem" or *skandalon* of sacramentality comes down to the (im)possibility of grasping the Body-Language of God.

Part Two ("The Eucharist in Literary and Theological Perspectives") undertakes a practical application of the theoretical framework outlined in Part One by engaging in close readings of select literary and artistic texts which demonstrate a theological thinking about sacrament and sacramentality, and about the Eucharist in particular. Some of these texts explore the Eucharist and/or sacramentality in fairly traditional ways (indeed, several of the authors have a literary imagination profoundly shaped by Catholicism), and others in a decisively *un*-orthodox, and hence scandalous and scandalizing, ways. We have found it useful to organize these explorations thematically. Chapter 4 ("Fracturing: Brokenness and Sacrament") considers the sacramentality of broken and wounded bodies in three novels, Graham Greene's *Monsignor Quixote*, Ron Hansen's *Mariette in Ecstasy* and Chuck Palahniuk's *Fight Club*. Mikhail Bakhtin's characterization of the degradation of the body in his study of Rabelais' grotesque realist fiction provides additional theoretical support for our suggestions about the sacramentality of the body broken.

---

19. Chauvet, *Sacraments*. This work's subtitle in the original French is "*parole de Dieu au Risque du corps*"—literally "the word of God at the *risk* (or *hazard*) of the Body." It would seem, therefore, that Chauvet is keenly aware of the scandalizing role the body plays in sacrament. Also note the dual meaning of the French *corps* as both *body* and *corpse*.

Chapter 5 ("Consuming: Cannibalism and Sacrament") turns toward the virtually universal cultural taboo of cannibalism. Of course, cannibalism is something Christians have been accused of and the Eucharist has been confused with since its earliest practice, as witnessed it the writings of Justin Martyr and Tertullian. However, this aspect of the sacrament's symbolic matrix—eating the body of God—must be fully confronted, not avoided or simply dismissed as ignorance or misperception. Two novels in particular, Patrick White's *A Fringe of Leaves* and Patrick Süskind's *Perfume: The Story of a Murderer*, depict cannibalistic acts in a sacramental light, whether implicitly or explicitly, serving as a reminder that this connotation, however taboo, is in fact an irreducible feature of eucharistic thought and practice, as evinced by Jesus "bread of life" discourse in John 6.

Süskind's novel describes the closing scene of bodily consumption as an act of "Love"; chapter 6 ("Penetrating: Eroticism and Sacrament") explores this transgressive theme further into the domain of the erotic.[20] There is a clear tradition within Christian history, especially amongst the writings of female mystics, of ecstatic and even amorous attachments to the Eucharist. The connotations of communing bodily with Christ—of ingesting him, taking him into oneself, being interpenetrated by him—are not hidden very far beneath the surface of the Eucharist's symbolic matrix. We look to Aidan Mathews' novella *Lipstick on the Host* as a literary examination of the sacramentality of sex, and the sensuality of the sacrament. However, a more deeply profane examination of the erotic is also close at hand. J. G. Ballard's apocalyptic novel *Crash*, as well as the work of Georges Bataille, particularly *The Story of the Eye*, provide the literary resources for this final avenue of exploration. Here the collision of language and the body is most fully probed. Both authors are interested in the limits of language and story to communicate erotic experience; both seek a language by which to discuss the relationship between sexual and religious experience; eroticism and death; sacrality and profanity, pleasure and pain, presence and absence, brokenness and wholeness, beauty and the grotesque. We will assert this "erotics" to be the unvanquishable *skandalon* of the Eucharist, the a/theological, unthought and unthinkable de-stabilizing "other" of Christian sacramentality.

---

20. Jean-Luc Marion's recent study of the erotic lends legitimacy to this avenue of exploration; see Marion, *Erotic Phenomenon*.

A METHODOLOGICAL NOTE: INTERPRETING SACRAMENT

This interdisciplinary project, which transgresses the boundaries of theology, philosophy, and literature, ultimately reveals itself to be an experiment in "sacramental hermeneutics." *Hermeneutics,* the name given to the art or theory of interpretation, alludes to the Greek god Hermes, who moved fluidly between the divine and human spheres to deliver messages from one to the other. But as Joyce Zimmerman points out, Hermes, who on one hand enables communication between gods and mortals, "is also a thief and a trickster and patron of bargainers; he is the guide of souls to the underworld . . . [and] the wayfinder for travelers. All these images suggest to us that the art of interpretation is a tricky, multifaceted journey."[21] Considering these various faces of Hermes helps us to see that the basic problem is that of communication itself.

Communication, to which *communion* (and hence sacrament, Eucharist) is closely linked, only occurs by mediation. Hermes conveys the messages of Zeus, his father, to the mortals down below, and relays their response to the heavenly realms. Without the correspondent, the word of one interlocutor to the other would never meet its mark. In other words, Hermes' job is the *translation* ("to carry across") of messages across an otherwise uncrossable barrier. However, this translation is also *transgression* ("to travel or move across"), and Hermes is guilty of transgressions as well. Communication is tricky business wherever Hermes is involved. Messages might be lost or stolen along the way, or become tangled and twisted.

Further, and in keeping with Hermes' many faces, communication is based upon a bargain between the parties involved, an agreement that words and messages will mean what they are intended to mean. This bargain, like all bargains, places a bet on the truthfulness of the interlocutor, and trusts that the linguistic or symbolic conventions established by previous experience will hold true once again. All communication is founded upon this extension of trust, and therefore entails a fundamental risk that trust will be broken and truth will be distorted.

Zimmerman offers another less commonly noted insight into the task of hermeneutics. She observes that Hermes' name derives from the root word *herm,* "a square, stone post."[22] In noting this etymology, Zimmerman emphasizes the dialectical character of interpretation, namely that the stable, steadfast *herm* stands in stark contrast to the winged Hermes, always

---

21. Zimmerman, *Liturgy and Hermeneutics,* 5.

22. Ibid., 5.

in motion. However, and in keeping with these multiplicitous meanings, might not this square stone *herm* also be construed as the *skandalon*, the stumbling block that obstructs one's journey or trips one up as she goes on her way? In other words, just as Christ is described as the "stone that the builders rejected, which has become the cornerstone" (Ps 118:22; Mark 12:10) as well as the *skandalon* or stumbling block to faith (1 Cor 1:23); that very thing which one might trust for surety and stability—the foundational post we can build on—might also de-stabilize, unfound, and cause one to stumble. Our assertion *viz.* sacrament is that the Eucharist fully and authentically re-presents Christ in precisely this paradoxical manner, as both cornerstone and stumbling block. And while this study makes the claim more by implication and interpretation than by irrefutable, empirical analysis, we shall conclude with the suggestion that, similarly, the arts—including but not limited to literature—have a similar function in their relationship to theology: one which de/constructs and destabilizes the foundational discourses of the Christian faith by providing a voice that theology simply cannot afford to ignore.

PART ONE

The Scandal of Sacramentality

1

Skandalon
Stumbling over Sacrament

One stumbles, then, on the sacrament, as one stumbles on the body, as one stumbles on the institution, as one stumbles on the letter of the Scriptures—if at least one respects it in its historical and empirical materiality. One stumbles against these because one harbors a nostalgia for an ideal and immediate presence to oneself, to others, and to God. Now, in forcing us back to our corporality, the sacraments shatter such dreams.[1]

WHAT IS A SACRAMENT?

Before we are able to discuss sacrament as a linguistic or a corporeal scandal, we must have a basic understanding of what a sacrament *is*. In this chapter, we will establish what we mean by *sacrament* and *sacramentality*, and examine the reasons this concept has been a stumbling-block to Christian theology and liturgy. Any understanding of sacrament must be tethered closely to the entire Christ event, to the biblical witness concerning the person of Jesus Christ and the sacred meal he instituted in the Last Supper. However, sacraments must also be understood as cultural artifacts of a sort; indeed the Christian concept of sacrament derives directly from an existing concept found with the surrounding Roman cultural context. We must take

1. Chauvet, *Symbol and Sacrament*, 154.

3

this into account as well. Finally, sacrament must be understood in relation to signs and symbols. The writings of St. Augustine and Paul Tillich will assist us in understanding the characteristics of sacrament as a unique species of religious symbol.

Once this is established, we will turn our attention to the relationship of the sacraments, and the Eucharist in particular, to the Church.[2] Any Christian concept of sacrament is meaningless apart from the person and work of Christ, and indeed from its inception the Eucharist has been regarded as the Body and Blood of Christ. But the Church is also understood to be the Body of Christ, a designation that derives directly from the eucharistic action of the Church. Therefore, we must determine how the Church is *constituted as Church* by the Eucharist—how the Eucharist *makes the Church*. Yet inherent to the scandal of sacramentality is the tendency to both stabilize and de-stabilize, or as David Power has observed of all rites, to both gather and scatter.[3] That which provides the Church with her very being and identity, her sacramental function and form, is also that which strips the Church of every possession, power, and authority, calling her to be broken and poured out, like the eucharistic elements and the body and blood of Christ they represent. In this way, the Eucharist simultaneously *makes* and *breaks* the Church.

The word *sacrament* comes from the Latin word *sacramentum*, which, along with *mysterium*, was used to transcribe the Greek term *mystērion* or "mystery" in Latin translations of the New Testament.[4] Henri de Lubac points out that in the "language of the liturgy, as with that of exegesis,

2. A more precise definition of "Church" is required here. We have taken a deliberately eclectic, wide-angle approach to ecclesiastical and doctrinal history, attending variously the Roman Catholic, Anglican and Eastern Orthodox traditions as we have found them most useful to the discussion at hand, while acknowledging the differences between these traditions in ecclesiology, theology and liturgy. We use "Church" (capitalized) to refer in the broadest sense to the Church universal/catholic, as a kind of trans-historical and pan-ecclesial, yet always thoroughly contextual and this-worldly entity. While acknowledging the legitimacy of a "cosmic" or mystical conception of the Church as the Body of Christ, our interest never strays from the particularity of the Church as both an expression of and reaction to its given historical and cultural context. Wherever it appears, "church" is used in reference to a specific local church or the traditions/denominations that comprise the Church.

3. Power, *Sacrament*, 94.

4. It is noteworthy that these scriptural instances of even the Gk. term *mystērion*, later translated *sacramentum* in the Vulgate, do not refer directly to the Lord's supper or any ritual act, but simply to a *mystery* or in some modern translations, a *secret*; e.g., Mark 4:11 (KJV), "And he said unto them, Unto you it is given to know the mystery of the kingdom of God"; Rom 16:25 (KJV), "Now to him that is of power to stablish you according to my gospel, and the preaching of Jesus Christ, according to the revelation of the mystery, which was kept secret since the world began."

mystery and *sacrament* are often used interchangeably. The Latin version of the New Testament translate *mystērion* equally by either word."[5] As de Lubac has demonstrated in detail, the phrase "mystical body" (*corpus mysticum*) of Christ was first applied to the Eucharist—that is, Christ's *sacramental* body which mediates his *historical* body—but the phrase was gradually detached from the Eucharist and transposed into an exclusive link with Christ's *ecclesial* body, the Church.[6] This shift represents a significant step in an incremental departure from the mysterious and mystical nature of sacraments in Western Christianity in particular, and by extension in Western thought in general.[7] By making this point, we wish to highlight the fundamental *mystery* of the Christian sacraments, which were and still are referred to as *mysteries* in Eastern Christianity. This mystical and mysterious quality must not be forgotten or neglected, for it is an even more originary concept to the meaning ascribed to the ancient Christian rituals commonly called sacraments.

Sacramentum was borrowed from the surrounding Roman cultural context, where it might refer to a ritual oath sworn by a Roman soldier in allegiance to the emperor, or more generically to something set aside for sacred or religious uses. The term is not adopted in Christian theology to describe various rites of Christian worship until its usage by Tertullian near the end of the second century. One of the struggles of the early church was against persecution by a surrounding culture which did not recognize Christianity as an acceptable religion. In fact, after Justin Martyr, Tertullian is one of the earliest apologists for the societal legitimacy of Christianity. With this struggle emerges the inevitable but somewhat problematic tendency to define Christian faith and practice according to extant religious traditions already deemed acceptable by the surrounding culture. And so, in their effort to defend themselves as good citizens and harmless practitioners

---

5. De Lubac, *Corpus Mysticum*, 45.

6. Ibid., 13–119.

7. It is not far-fetched to suggest that the de-mystification of the "sacred mysteries" of the church is in fact a central chapter in the entire narrative of secularization. In *The Legitimacy of the Modern Age*, Hans Blumenberg points out that the entire concept of secularization only makes sense when approached with certain theological presuppositions: "Early Christianity found itself in what was, in view of its foundational documents, the difficult position of having to demonstrate the trustworthiness of its God to an unbelieving surrounding world not by the fulfillment of His promises but by the postponement of this fulfillment. . . . In order to demonstrate its usefulness to the surrounding world, which, while it is a source of affliction, is also itself afflicted, the ancient Church 'secularizes' itself into (takes on the worldly role of) a stabilizing factor" (44). For similar readings of secularization, cf. Vattimo, *After Christianity* and Schwartz, *Sacramental Poetics*.

of their faith, the apologists borrowed concepts like "mystery" or "sacrament" from the surrounding culture to explain their own practices. In the long-term, this tactic would shape Christianity's understanding of its own rites in significant and lasting ways.

However, this is not a point to be passed over too quickly, for it proves central to the argument we offer here. We contend that to formulate any meaningful understanding of sacrament in a postmodern milieu, one *must* look to corresponding traces from the surrounding culture, for in such a way, the Christian notion of sacrament came into being in the first place. The sacred meal in which the early Christians partook of the bread and the cup as a "sharing" (1 Cor 10:16)[8] in the body and blood of Christ pre-dates any application of the concepts *mystērion* or *sacramentum* to this ritual. As Christian faith and practice expanded and became more codified over time, these concepts from the broader (pagan or "secular") culture were usefully appropriated to explain the significance of what appeared to the uninitiated to be at best secretive and at worst criminal religious rituals. Over time, these initially foreign concepts became indispensable to the Christian understanding of their own sacred rites. This observation is by no means a deconstruction of the primacy or integrity of the Eucharist or the theology of the sacraments—for indeed, the ritual predates the terminology and theology later applied to it—but rather demonstrates that to approach the notion of sacrament in the first instance, one is already firmly within the realm of hermeneutics, for to refer to the Lord's Supper as a *sacrament* is to have already performed an act of interpretation or translation, the "carrying across" of meaning from one concept to another.[9]

We have discussed the origins of the term *sacrament* and how it came to be applied to the Christian ritual partaking of the Lord's Supper. We must extend this understanding by tracing the Lord's Supper, through Scripture and the earliest Christian practice, to the institution of the Eucharist at the Last Supper and ultimately to the entire Christ event encompassing the incarnation, life, death, resurrection and ascension of Jesus Christ. But before we proceed to these theological connections, we must continue to pursue

8. The NRSV translates the Gk. *koinōnia* as "sharing"; other translations include "participation" (NIV) and "communion" (KJV). In *Corpus Mysticum*, de Lubac remarks that "in Christian antiquity . . . *communion*—together with the Greek *koinōnia*—implies no other idea except that of the reception of the sacrament" (18).

9. cf. Power, *Sacrament*: "Sacraments have to be interpreted as liturgical celebrations. . . . Interpretations of the sacraments have to face the diverse character of the scriptural texts proclaimed in their celebration and of the rites celebrated. They cannot reduce the texts to a single grand narrative or overarching symbolism, nor the rites to a clearly demarked essence of matter and form. Interpretation respects the pluriformity of faith in Christ already evident in the New Testament . . ." (48–49).

the question *what is a sacrament?* by considering the concept of sacrament in relation to the broader categories of sign and symbol.

SIGN, SYMBOL, AND SACRAMENT

Looking back across Christian history, sacraments have been described variously as "sacred signs," "means of grace," "visible words," and especially in Protestant thought, as "symbols." We shall address all of these descriptions in due course, but to begin with, we will examine sacraments as signs, and then sacraments as symbols. A sacrament is a unique type of religious symbol, and a symbol, whether religious or not, is a special type of sign. Therefore, any discussion of sacrament or sacramentality, and hence any sacramental theology, must begin with an understanding of the nature of sign systems and the processes of signification, as well as symbol and the symbolic matrix according to which sacraments derive their unique form and function.

St. Augustine is the first Christian thinker to clearly differentiate between the sign and that which the sign signifies. In Book II of *On Christian Teaching*, Augustine writes that at the most fundamental level, "a sign is a thing which of itself makes some other thing come to mind, besides the impression that it presents to the senses."[10] A sign, in other words, points beyond itself to something besides the sensory reception (as a sound, shape, color, etc) of the sign itself. A sign "calls to mind" something other than itself, and is thus different from that which it represents. Augustine thus establishes the relationship between the sign and the thing signified as a relationship characterized by *difference* or (dis)continuity, we might say, by placing the interpreter of the sign at a distance from that which the sign represents.[11]

According to Augustine, there are "natural" signs, which signify "without a wish or any urge to signify," and with which Augustine is not particularly interested (e.g., animal tracks; smoke). Far more interesting to Augustine are "given" signs (which might be better understood in contemporary parlance as *symbols*), which begins to approach the even more exclusive concept of sacrament. Given signs are exchanged between "living

10. Augustine, *Christian Teaching*, 30. Augustine's examples include a footprint being a sign of the creature that left it, and smoke signifying the presence of a fire.

11. While this *distance* or *difference* is not fully developed in Augustine's semiotic theory, it will be of significant interest to postmodern thought, leading such contemporary thinkers as John Caputo to read Augustine as something of a proto–postmodern thinker; cf. Caputo and Scanlon, *Augustine and Postmodernism*, and Dodaro, "Loose Canons."

things" to convey that which is invisible or un-depictable, namely emotions, feelings, knowledge, and so on. He explains: "There is no reason for us to signify something (that is, to give a sign) except to express and transmit to another's mind what is in the mind of the person who gives the sign."[12] Signs of this kind, therefore, require interpretation—and so again, we cannot avoid hermeneutics, the art of interpretation, which involves a wrestling with the text (sign). This wrestling *renders* or brings forth the meaning of the sign. However, as the very presence of the sign itself emphasizes the distance between the interpreter and the thing interpreted, this wrestling also *rends* and creates tears in the fabric of signification, by delineating this gap.[13]

This image of *wrestling* is not inappropriate, for as Augustine points out, "it is much more pleasant to learn lessons presented through imagery, and much more rewarding to discover meanings that are won only with difficulty."[14] This calls to mind Jesus' teachings, specifically about his body and blood, which the disciples describe as "hard teachings" (John 6:60); however difficult, the interpreter will be rewarded with pleasure when meaning is discovered. We will return more comprehensively to the themes of tearing, disruption, and pleasure in Part Two, but for now let us only briefly allude to Karmen MacKendrick's observation that "Pleasure is destabilizing and threatening not only to the political and cultural orders but to all manner of orders."[15] Certainly the pleasure of sacramentality, closely linked with the erotic nature of sacramental participation and interpenetration, is part of sacrament's risky and destabilizing scandal.

Sacraments are not merely signs, but are symbols, and specifically symbols of a religious nature. *Symbol* comes from the Greek term *symbolon* meaning "token" or "watchword," which was first used by Cyprian of Carthage (c. 250) to describe the Apostles' Creed as the distinguishing mark of a Christian. Etymologically, a symbol is something *thrown* or *cast together*: sym- ("together") + bole (from *ballein*, "to throw").[16] In the ancient context, a symbol could be a physical token, such as a coin, something cast as an integrous whole, which would be broken in two and given to two people, so that the authenticity of an agreement, relationship, or other claim could

12. Augustine, *Christian Teaching*, 30.

13. In chapter 2, we will further pursue this notion of the gap between the signifier and the signified in our discussion of the problem of language, especially as it is expounded upon by Saussure and Derrida.

14. Augustine, *Christian Teaching*, 33.

15. MacKendrick, *Counterpleasures*, 6.

16. See "symbol" in *Online Etymology Dictionary* <http://www.etymonline.com/index.php?term=symbol> accessed 8 March 2010.

later be established by the coming together of the two halves of the symbol. Chauvet explains:

> The ancient *symbolon* is precisely an object cut in two, one part of which is retained by each partner in a contract. Each half evidently has no value in itself and thus could imaginatively signify anything; its symbolic power is due only to its connection with the other half. When, years or even generations later, the partners or their descendants come together again to "symbolize" their two portions by joining them together, they recognize this act as the expression of the same contract, of the same alliance. It is thus the agreement between the two partners which establishes the symbol; it is the *expression of a social pact based on mutual recognition* and, hence, is a *mediator of identity*.[17]

This ancient understanding undergirds later developments in the theory of symbols. Chauvet's analysis is incredibly detailed, and merits consideration beyond the scope of this project, but apropos to our purposes, he demonstrates that "symbol, and especially ritual symbol, is the very epiphany of mediation in its most contingent and most culturally determined aspects."[18] Further, this understanding of symbol reveals "the tear, the 'fissure' that splits *every* symbol, that belongs to the very definition of symbols. Symbols crack; that is ultimately the source of their power."[19]

In his essay "The Meaning and Justification of Religious Symbols," Paul Tillich constructs a theory of religious symbols beginning with five characteristics of all representative symbols. First, in accordance with St. Augustine's understanding of signs, he notes that, like signs, it is "the character of all symbols to point beyond themselves . . . to something which cannot be grasped directly but must be expressed indirectly, namely, through the symbolic material."[20] Second, unlike signs, all symbols "participate in the reality of that which they represent. . . . It radiates the power of being and meaning

17. Chauvet, *Symbol and Sacrament*, 112. In chapter 4 ("Symbol and Body"), Chauvet presents a rich analysis of symbol and symbolization in relation to Christian sacramentality (see 110–55).

18. Ibid., 110–11. Chauvet's study eventually leads us "from the symbol to the body . . . [as] the primordial and arch-symbolic form of mediation" (111); we will postpone this discussion until chapter 3.

19. Mitchell, *Meeting Mystery*, 52. This characteristic of symbol will be more fully explored in chapter 2.

20. Tillich, "Religious Symbols," 165. Klemm's introduction to Tillich's essay is extremely helpful. See also Tillich's similar discussion of the meaning of symbols in *Dynamics of Faith*, 41–43 (reprinted as "The Meaning of Symbol" in Church, *The Essential Tillich*, 41–43).

of that for which it stands."[21] Samuel Taylor Coleridge's description is unsurpassed in its richness: "a symbol is characterized by a . . . translucence of the eternal through and in the temporal. It always partakes of the reality which it renders intelligible; and while it enunciates the whole, abides itself as a living part in that unity of which it is the representative."[22]

A third characteristic Tillich observes is that, unlike signs, which can be created and replaced as necessary, symbols cannot "be created at will. It is not a matter of expediency and convention, as signs are."[23] Even where individual creative talent is responsible for bringing a symbol to birth—as with the design of a flag, or a photograph, or work of art that becomes iconic to a social body—it is only by virtue of its acceptance by a larger group that an image or object becomes truly symbolic. In other words, in a certain sense symbols require the ratification of a community. Fourth, representative symbols have the "power of opening up dimensions of reality" otherwise inaccessible or inarticulable. And fifth, symbols have an "integrating and disintegrating power" to both individuals and groups. Tillich contrasts the "elevating, quieting, and stabilizing power of religious symbols" and "the 'healing' power of religious symbols" with what he calls the "disintegrating effect: causing restlessness, producing depression, anxiety, fanaticism, etc."[24] Thus, according to Tillich, symbols comport a "tremendous power of creation and destruction. By no means are they harmless semantic expressions."[25] In this final characterization, Tillich hints at the *dangerous*, risky, and destabilizing power of symbols—an idea to which we have alluded already, and which shall continue to surface. These are the characteristics of all representative symbols, and as sacraments are representative symbols, these characteristics apply to their definition as well. However, sacraments are *religious* symbols, which requires unique characterization.

Later in the same essay, Tillich declares that "Nothing is prevented from becoming a sacred thing. Only historical contingencies prevent it."[26] Subtly, Tillich is pointing us toward a kind of inherent sacrality that pervades "everything that is," a sacra(menta)lity inescapable in the human experience of the created, material order. According to Tillich, the "authenticity" of all symbols, including religious symbols, is determined according

---

21. Tillich, "Religious Symbols," 166.

22. Coleridge, *Statesman's Manual*; in Richards, *Portable Coleridge*, 388.

23. Tillich, "Religious Symbols," 166.

24. Ibid., 166. Cf., Tillich's essay "Religious Language," in which he refers to the "ambiguity" of religion in general, and by extension, religious language and symbols: "meaning that it is creative and destructive at the same time" (50).

25. Tillich, "Religious Symbols," 167.

26. Ibid., 168.

to their "adequacy" to that which they express—so, for religious symbols, we are interested in their adequacy to express *religious experience*. Authentic symbols exist in contrast to "nonauthentic" symbols "which have lost their experiential basis, but which are still used for reasons of tradition or because of their aesthetic value."[27] But there is more to it than this: the "truth" of a religious symbol is distinct from its authenticity. Rather a religious symbol's *truth* is "the degree to which [the particular symbol] reaches the referent of all religious symbols."[28] This is a complex notion, for it seems to suggest that all religious symbols share, at least on one level, a common referent (the Sacred; in Tillich's perspective, "Ultimate Concern"). So while on the one hand, we have the religious symbol in its "self-negation and transparency to the referent for which it stands"—this Tillich calls "the negative quality," the degree to which the symbol annuls or empties itself on behalf of its referent. And on the other hand we must consider "the value of the symbolic material used in [the symbol]," which is "the positive quality which determines the truth of a religious symbol."[29] To give a concrete example, from a Tillichean framework it is viable to suggest that bread is both more *authentic* and *truthful* a symbol for Christ's body than, for instance, meat or cheese, because the significance of bread as a basic unit of human subsistence transcends history, geography, religion, and culture. Bread is a recurring theme in the biblical witness, specifically in direct association with *life itself*, life in-the-body, which of necessity requires nourishment.[30] As David Klemm has observed, "Bread and wine are symbols of fundamental or essential human activity.

27. Ibid., 168. Closely related is Paul Ricoeur conception of metaphor's passage from "living" (authentic) to "dead": "In the metaphorical statement (we will not speak any longer of metaphor as word, but of metaphor as statement), the contextual action creates a new meaning, which truly has the status of event since it exists only in the present context. At the same time, however, it can be reidentified as the same, since its construction can be repeated. In this way, the innovation of an emergent meaning can be taken as a linguistic creation. And if it is adopted by a significant part of the linguistic community, it in turn can become a common meaning and add to the polysemy of lexical entities, thus contributing to the history of the language as code or system. But at this final stage, where the meaning-effect we call metaphor has become this shift of meaning that increases polysemy, the metaphor is then no longer living, but a dead metaphor. Only authentic metaphors, that is, living metaphors, are at once meaning and event." See Ricoeur, *Rule of Metaphor* 115. We will return to Ricoeur's theory of metaphor in chapter 2.

28. Tillich, "Religious Symbols," 170.

29. Ibid.

30. E.g., manna in the OT (Exod 16); Jesus' miraculous feedings (Luke 9:10–17; Matt 14:13–21; Mark 6:30–44; John 6:1–14); Jesus' "Bread of Life" discourse (John 6:22–65). The same could be said, with some limitation, for wine, e.g., Jesus' first miracle at the wedding at Cana (John 2:1–11) and his self-identification as the "vine" (John 15:1–8)

They represent in great simplicity the fruits of human labor in dwelling on earth and the basic sources of human nourishment"; additionally, "Bread and wine symbolize the capacity for human fellowship."[31] For these reasons, bread and wine occupy a privileged place over other possible symbols for Christ's physical body and blood in the celebration of the Eucharist.

This brings us to *sacrament*. St. Augustine also gave us one of the most enduring definitions of *sacraments* when he described them as visible signs of an invisible reality.[32] De Lubac notes that "the classical definitions of a St. Augustine or a St. Isidore of Seville are well known and have been endlessly repeated. The word *sacramentum* essentially means a sign. . . .St. Augustine insists on using its first adjective *sacred*, which brings it near to *sacrifice*: *sacrifice, as if made sacred*; . . . Isidore underlines its second adjective, *secret*, which makes it look more intimately akin to *mystery*. Already in St. Cyprian both senses can be found."[33]

This is the basis of the common definition of sacrament, set forth by the Council of Trent, of sacrament as an outward and visible sign of an inward and spiritual grace.[34]

Most doctrinal and catechetical definitions of sacrament follow this formula. For instance, the Anglican Articles of Religion state that "Sacraments ordained of Christ be not only badges or tokens of Christian men's [sic] profession, but rather they be certain sure witnesses, and effectual signs of grace, and God's good will towards us, by the which he doth work invisibly in us, and doth not only quicken, but also strengthen and confirm our Faith in him."[35] This is consistent with St. Thomas Aquinas, whose

31. Klemm, "This is My Body," 294.

32. This idea is present in several places in Augustine's writings, e.g., *De Civitate Dei*, Book 10, chapter 5: "A sacrifice, therefore, is the visible sacrament or sacred sign of an invisible sacrifice"; cf. *De Catechizandis Rudibus* ("On the Catechising of the Uninstructed"), § 26.50: "On the subject of the sacrament, indeed, which he receives, it is first to be well impressed upon his notice that the signs of divine things are, it is true, *things visible*, but that the *invisible things themselves are also honored in them*" (italics added); Augustine's definition is foundational to Aquinas's thorough examination of sacrament in questions 60–65 of the *Summa Theologica*, Part III, especially Q. 60 "What is a sacrament?"

33. De Lubac, *Corpus Mysticum*, 45.

34. Session XIII of the Council of Trent (1551) addresses sacraments, and the Eucharist in particular. De Lubac also notes the subtle difference between *mystery* and *sacrament* in ancient Christian thought, quoting Algerius of Liège (*De Sacramentis*): "*A sacrament and a mystery differ in this respect that sacrament is a visible sign signifying something, while a mystery is something hidden that it signifies. However one can be used for the other . . . with the consequence that a mystery is both concealing and concealed, and a sacrament both signifying and signified*" (49, italics in original).

35. Art. XXV, *BCP*, 872.

description of sacrament as "causes" of grace draws attention to another unique feature of that differentiates *sacrament* from other signs; namely, that sacraments do not simply *mean* something but in fact *do* something. Like all signs, they *re-present* that which they signify, but they also *effect* the grace contained within that which they signify.[36] Sacraments, then, are not simply signs but "*effectual signs*." To borrow Samuel Taylor Coleridge's conception of language itself, they are "living Things," "*Spirits* and *Living Agents*," and "living educts of the Imagination."[37] These are not "mere signs" but rather signs which accomplish something: namely, the bestowal of God's grace upon the participant.

To cite another modern Anglican source, the catechism of the Episcopal Church (USA) answers the question "What are the sacraments?" thus: "The sacraments are outward and visible signs of inward and spiritual grace, given by Christ as sure and certain means by which we receive that grace."[38] This well-established doctrinal and catechetical definition goes on to clarify that "God does not limit himself to these rites; they are patterns of countless ways by which God uses material things to reach out to us."[39] Sacraments, therefore, according to Christian teaching, are more than mere "reminders" or mundane "signs" of grace, but are the medium or *means* by which that grace is given and made manifest.[40] In this way the Eucharist, as the

36. Aquinas, *ST* III.62.1: "only God can cause grace, for grace is no other than a participation in the divine nature . . . in this way the sacraments of the New Law cause grace, for they are instituted by God to be used for the giving of grace." Clark, *An Aquinas Reader*, 485.

37. David Jasper highlights these phrases from Coleridge in *The Sacred Body* (121, 158, citing the original sources in his endnotes). Interestingly, by the modern era, Romantic thinkers such as Coleridge consider this effectual/"living" quality hitherto unique to sacrament as applicable to all language, as though with the collapse of the "liturgical city" of the high medieval era (cf. Pickstock, *After Writing*, 135–58), the sacramentality of the Christian rites becomes diffused and disseminated into the world itself, which is accessible to us in any meaningful way only through language. Regina Schwartz draws similar conclusions in *Sacramental Poetics*, focusing in on the literature of the early Reformation.

38. *BCP*, 857. Of course, it would be virtually impossible to catalogue every doctrinal statement on *sacrament* in the contemporary Christian context, especially with so many independent churches having drafted their own unique statements and articles of faith. While our selection of sources is admittedly idiosyncratic, we will most often look to the doctrine of the Western Catholic and Anglican traditions.

39. *BCP*, 861. Aquinas lies behind this understanding as well: "man's salvation . . . must be brought to spiritual and intelligible reality through corporeal and sensible things . . . sinning subjected him to corporeal things by his affections. But any healing remedy must be given to man so as to reach the part affected by the disease" (*ST* III.61.1).

40. We recognize that many Protestant churches, especially in the North American

sacrament of God's redemption of the world by Christ's broken body and shed blood upon Calvary, may indeed be said to re-present—literally, *make present again*—Christ's gracious giving of himself for the life of the world.

This definition also includes a vital caveat that the Eucharist in particular, or the sacraments in general, are by no means the *only* manner by which God's grace is conveyed. However, the sacraments make clear that God's grace comes to us *through materiality*, through the physical matter of the created order. They are, in Chauvet's phrase, "the grace of God at the mercy of the body," or in David Power's phrase, "the language of God's giving"—two key phrases which will guide the next two chapters' exploration of sacrament as a scandal of language and of the body. As regards the Divine, sacraments are an acknowledgment of the Creator's relationship to and participation in the creation. As regards the human, to quote David Brown, sacraments "guarantee the believer's continuing engagement with Christ's humanity."[41] Therefore, it must not be overlooked that, while never limiting or confining the gracious action of God, sacraments provide a glimpse into the ways in which God works graciously through and within material reality.

Tillich holds such a robust or high view of symbol that it is difficult to identify how he distinguishes between symbol and sacrament. Sacraments *are* symbols, although not all symbols are sacraments, but at times it seems that, for Tillich (as for Coleridge), all symbols possess a sacramental or sacrament-like quality. Tillich notes that, like symbols, "Sacraments cannot be created arbitrarily; they originate only by virtue of historical fate. All sacramental realities depend upon a tradition which cannot be abandoned

---

context, reject this understanding of sacrament; indeed, many reject the language of "sacrament" altogether and hold Baptism and the Lord's Supper to be "ordinances" instituted by Christ, which the Scriptures command us to obey. However, we argue that our conception of the Church and of sacramentality still includes such "non-sacramental" traditions because it is demonstrably true that these churches hold a view of the Bible, of the "conversion experience," and in some cases, of the "gifts" or manifestations of the Holy Spirit (speaking in tongues, words of prophecy, etc.) that is unmistakably "sacramental," in spite of the rejection of this language. Furthermore, it could be argued that the priority given to the Eucharist (or Communion or the Lord's Supper, as it is called in many Protestant churches) in our study excludes churches like the Salvation Army or the Society of Friends (Quakers), which do not partake of bread and wine/ grape juice as a remembrance of Christ's broken body and shed blood. However, it is noteworthy that neither of these ecclesial bodies employ the term "church" in their self-description: one is an "army," the other is a "society." In any case, our earlier claim holds true of these churches as well: while they may reject the idea of sacrament, and even the Eucharist, they are not without a sense of the sacramental, even if it has been displaced by other symbols and experiential practices of the faith.

41. Brown, *God and Grace*, 390.

arbitrarily or exchanged with some other tradition."[42] It appears, then, that sacraments differ from symbols in that sacraments are not merely conventional, like symbols, but are traditioned, and tradition-bound. While symbols may be abandoned when they have outlived their usefulness, sacraments have a staying power that comes from outside the sacrament itself; this "outside" is not simply the ratification of the community that has elevated these particular symbols to the level of sacrament—though a sacrament could not exist without this—but is some real and active participation in the Holy itself. So symbols *may* be abandoned or exchanged arbitrarily, while sacraments cannot. However, sacraments are not immune from what Tillich calls "prophetic criticism,"[43] which speaks or acts on behalf of the Divine and can therefore call for the creation or destruction of sacraments.

In addition, it is not the "literal" but precisely the *symbolic* character of the sacramental that makes it significant—that makes it "true" in the Tillichean sense. For "the literal is not more but less than symbolic. . . . The sacrament is *not only a sign*."[44] Tillich cites the very real and lasting differences between the sacramental thought of Luther, who affirmed that the materiality of the eucharistic elements participate "really" (that is, "symbolically") in the reality of Christ's body and blood, and Zwingli, who reduced the sacramental materials to the status of "mere" symbol. Tillich remarks, "Even in that period there was semantic confusion. And let us not be misled by this. In the real sense of symbol, the sacramental materials are symbols. But if the symbol is used as *only* symbol (i.e., only signs), then of course the sacramental materials are more than this."[45] What should be evident by this point is the observation that these terms—*sign, symbol, sacrament*—are highly ambiguous; clear, nuanced definitions require us to bracket the rather careless manner in which they are employed in common usage. Still, following Tillich, one may assert a clear progression, beginning with *sign* as the broadest and most inclusive, but also the most mundane category; followed by *symbol* as a more restrictive and specialized type of sign; culminating finally in *sacrament*, as an exclusive type of *religious* symbol which bears a particular connection to the Holy and allows the Holy to be made uniquely and materially present in physical, tangible form.

This *material* and immanent plane of religious symbols is precisely the domain of *the sacramental*, which "is nothing else than some reality becoming

42. Tillich, "Nature and Sacrament," 94.

43. Ibid.

44. Tillich, "Religious Language," 54 (italics added).

45. Ibid., 54. Cf. "Literature differs from history as fiction differs from fact. . . . History and literature are equally modes of dealing with, of finding language for, *reality*" (Templeton, *True Fiction*, 305).

the bearer of the Holy in a special way and under special circumstances."[46] However, this symbolic connection between the sacramental and the Holy is by no means infallible: "It is the danger and an almost unavoidable pitfall of all religious symbols"—including but not limited to sacraments—"that they bring about a confusion between themselves and that to which they point. In religious language this is called idolatry."[47] In other words, we must not mistake the symbol for its referent, or allow the two to be identified so closely that it becomes difficult or impossible to differentiate between them, for "participation is not identity; [religious symbols] are not themselves *the* Holy."[48] Tillich's observation here is prescient: sacraments are not immune to idolization, precisely because they are *this-worldly* artifacts. Like every element of the created order, they may be used or abused. They may be means of grace, or they may become demonic, for as Tillich observes, "In all sacramental activities of religion, in all holy objects, holy books, holy doctrines, holy rites, you find this danger which we will call 'demonization.' They become demonic at the moment in which they become elevated to the unconditional and ultimate character of the Holy itself."[49] The difference is perspectival, as the same artifact may function as sacramental or demonic, depending on the orientation or vantage point of the practitioner (viewer/recipient).[50] This characteristic is not inherent to the religious symbol or sacrament, although, to return to Tillich's conception of the "authenticity" and "truth" of symbols, the capacity for sacrament to point toward not only

46. Tillich, "Religious Language," 54.

47. Tillich, "Religious Symbols," 170. Tillich explains further: "[Symbols] always have the tendency (in the human mind, of course) to replace that to which they are supposed to point, and to become ultimate in themselves . . . they become idols. All idolatry is nothing else than the absolutizing of symbols of the Holy, and making them identical with the Holy itself" ("Religious Language," 50).

48. Tillich, "Religious Language," 49.

49. Ibid., 50–51. It is noteworthy that in this essay, Tillich draws a clear connection between liturgical and poetic language: "There are words in every language which are more than this [i.e., arbitrary and discontinuous signs], and in the moment in which they get connotations which go beyond some thing to which they point as signs, then they can become symbols. . . . [In] liturgical or poetic language . . . words have a power through centuries, or more than centuries. They have connotations in situations in which they appear so that they cannot be replaced. They have become not only signs pointing to a meaning which is defined, but also symbols standing in for a reality in the power of which they participate" (ibid., 46).

50. In this regard Tillich might be seen as prefiguring the work of Jean-Luc Marion on the difference between the icon and the idol. For Marion, the icon diverts the "gaze" of the viewer away from itself toward the unrepresentable which lies beyond its frame, beyond its material depiction, while the idol freezes or fixes the gaze upon the "envisagable," that is, material symbol itself. See Marion, *Idol and Distance*, especially chapter 1.

its referent but to the referent of all religious symbols is the measure of its authenticity, or, we may say, it's "sacramentality"—the truth-quality of the sacrament which makes it appropriate to regard it as a sacrament.

Having considered Augustine and Tillich, and consulted briefly with catechetical literature on the topic, we can now assert that according to this perspective, sacraments are *more than* mere signs or symbols; cannot be created, but arise from and are dependent upon tradition; cannot be abandoned, but may be subject to prophetic critique; make present the Holy/divine/sacred under special circumstances; participate in the reality they represent, yet remain distinct from it; derive their "truth" not from their literal but rather from their symbolic (or we might say *literary* or *aesthetic*) quality; and are susceptible to a dangerous, even demonic, tendency to supplant or become confused with that for which they stand in (i.e., idolatry).

SACRAMENTAL(S) AND SACRAMENTALITY

Some comment should be made on two variations of the root word *sacrament* which shall appear throughout this essay. In our discussion of sacraments, we will employ the terms *sacramental* and *sacramentality* in specific ways. The Second Vatican Council's "Constitution on the Sacred Liturgy" (discussed further in chapter 2) addresses *sacramentals* in articles 60 and 61, stating they are

> *sacred signs* by which, *somewhat after the manner of sacraments,* effects of a spiritual nature, especially, are symbolized and are obtained through the church's intercession. By them, people are made ready to receive the much greater effect of the sacraments, and various occasions in life are rendered holy. Thus, for well-disposed members of the faithful, the liturgy of the sacraments and sacramentals sanctifies almost every event of their lives with the divine grace which flows from the paschal mystery of the passion, death and resurrection of Christ. From this source all the sacraments and sacramentals draw their power. *There is scarcely any proper use of material things which cannot thus be directed toward people's sanctification and the praise of God.*[51]

From this statement it is clear that as early as 1963, the Catholic understanding of sacramentals was rather fluid: they are "sacred signs . . . somewhat after the manner of sacraments," which are "directed toward people's sanctification." Liturgical dictionaries often include a separate entry for

51. Flannery, *Vatican II,* "Sacred Liturgy," 139.

sacramentals, referring to sacred actions, instituted by the Church (in contrast to the dominical institution of Christ), which are not sacraments in the proper sense, but are usually but not exclusively employed within liturgical celebrations of the sacraments and which "make explicit the meaning of the sacramental action although they are by no means indispensable to it."[52] However, a more recent definition admits that "any theology of sacramentals must run parallel to an emerging theology of sacraments, *at times with no meaningful distinction between the two*[;] . . . today an understanding of sacramentals is very open-ended."[53] While this latter definition is nearer to the our understanding, *sacramentals* in its noun form will not play a role in the present work. We shall, however, utilize the adjectival form *sacramental*, as employed by Tillich, as a descriptor for anything that exhibits "sacrament-like" qualities and might therefore be appropriately described as sacramental.

Returning momentarily to Tillich's broader notion, we agree that "Any object or event is sacramental in which the transcendent is perceived to be present."[54] The implication of Tillich's assertion is that the number of things—objects, events, but also people, experiences, texts—which might be regarded as "sacramental" is virtually without limit. The key criterion for Tillich is individual perception, which does differentiate this view from traditional conceptions of the sacraments proper; in this view, the biblical ordinance of Christ, nor the acting authority of the Church, necessarily determines what is or is not "sacramental"—the final determination rests on the experience and perception of the individual participant. However, "there can be no sacramental object apart from the faith that grasps it. Apart from the correlation between faith and sacrament, there can be no sacrament."[55] In other words, that which might be perceived as sacramental or as a sacrament proper might also be perceived as perfectly mundane and religiously neutral by those without eyes of faith—and not faith in a generic sense, but the specific, traditioned faith according to which a sacrament is accepted as sacrament. Tillich understands that the *ability* to perceive life as sacramental is indeed itself an act of faith. In fact, "Faith," writes Nathan Mitchell, "is desire for that *utterly* Other, desire whose goal is not possession (grasping God on *our* terms) but dispossession."[56] And so the sacramental,

52. "Sacramentals" in Davies, *NDLW*, 473. This definition goes on to note the triple immersion in baptism, the sign of the cross, the kiss of peace at the Eucharist, the blessing of palms or the consecration of a church as examples of sacramentals.

53. Osborne, "Sacramentals," Bradshaw, *NWDLW*, 417.

54. Tillich, "Nature and Sacrament," 91.

55. Ibid., 93.

56. Mitchell, *Meeting Mystery*, 69.

and the faith required to experience the sacramental, is at its core "not *grasping* something . . . but *letting oneself be grasped*."[57] In this sense, it is wholly other; it does not come from within the Self, but comes from beyond as the gratuitous gift of grace.

Finally, we shall frequently employ the term *sacramentality* to refer to the distinctive character or quality of sacrament *qua* sacrament. In other words, just as persons have and are defined by their *personality*, and texts operate according to an inherent *textuality*, so sacraments exhibit an intrinsic *sacramentality* which in turn assists us in defining what is meant by *sacrament* in the broadest sense. It should be noted that we have not coined this term. To consider one recent example, while we generally accept his premise, Kevin Irwin's use of *sacramentality* appears slightly more restrictive than ours: "signs of what is both human and divine"; he goes on to write of "the broad meaning of sacramentality, namely that God is disclosed and discovered here and now on earth and in human life is the ground on which sacraments per se are based."[58] However, his use of the term *sacramental* more nearly approaches ours when he writes: "By 'sacramental' I want to underscore . . . the unity of both the divine and human and the sacred and the secular. By 'sacramental' I also mean that God is both revealed and yet also remains hidden . . . all sacramentality both reveals and hides the complete reality of God."[59] Irwin emphasizes, as does this essay, the *paradoxical* quality of sacrament, which simultaneously veils and unveils the Divine within the realm of human experience. That which deserves to be called *sacramental* confuses and confounds the tidy distinctions between such binary opposites as immanence and transcendence, the material and the spiritual, the sacred and the secular/profane, and so on.

This paradox is central to the scandal of sacramentality. As Catholic theologian Karl Rahner writes, "The grace of God no longer comes (when it does come) steeply down from on high, from a God absolutely transcending the world, and in a manner that is without history, purely episodic; it is *permanently in the world* in tangible historical form, established in the flesh of Christ as a part of the world, of humanity and of its very history."[60] Rahner is one of the most influential Roman Catholic theologians of the twentieth century and a key contributor to the liturgical reforms of Vatican II. In this quotation, he asserts in no uncertain terms the "this-worldliness" and historicity of the grace of God. The "worldliness" of God's grace is, to

---

57. Ibid., 68.

58. Irwin, "Sacramental World," 201.

59. Ibid., 202.

60. Rahner, *Church and Sacraments*, 15 (italics added).

reiterate, "established in the flesh of Christ." Rahner is making the radical claim that grace does not reside outwith the world, (e.g., in heaven) and then come into the world "from on high," but rather is *in* the world, *part of* the created order. This is all due to the kenosis of the enfleshed, incarnate Christ, who "poured himself out" (*ekenōsen*; Phil 2:7) to take on humanity. So we can say that grace is *present* in the world. And yet, as the great creeds of the Church profess, the resurrected, bodily Christ "ascended into heaven and is seated at the right hand of the Father." Thus the question of *presence* and *absence* is brought to the fore. How is Christ "present" in the world via the Church and the sacraments?

THE CENTRALITY OF CHRIST

The Christ event is, in our estimation, a crisis or scandal in the life of God, a scandal which then infuses the Christian faith and is expressed, however covertly, in Christian sacramental worship. Reflecting on Jacob's wrestling with the angel/God in Genesis 32, Geoffrey Wainwright employs similar language: "The 'scandal of God's *defeat*' . . . points, theologically, to the 'scandalous' divine self-giving represented first by creation and then by the cross."[61] In both cases, the out-pouring of God in creation and in the Christ event, the creative *Logos* of God is the principle actor. It appears that, by the incarnation of God in Christ, God is scandalized. One thing must be made clear: this scandalous characteristic of sacrament we are tracing is only inherent to sacrament insofar as sacrament itself, the Eucharist in particular, is rooted in the Christ event.[62] Jesus' life, death, and resurrection are the apex of the out-pouring (*kenosis*) of God which begins with creation

61. Wainwright, *Doxology*, 44.

62. By "Christ event," we intend to encompass entire narrative of the incarnation, life, death, resurrection, and ascension of God in the historical figure Jesus of Nazareth. Behind this historical figure lies the theological doctrine of the co-eternal second person of the Trinity, God-the-Son, the creative *Logos* of the Father, etc.; and in front of this lies the continued spatio-temporal presence of Christ in the Church (as the Body of Christ); but neither of these implications are intended when we use the term "Christ event." To be clear, we are not interested in what may or may not lie "behind the text," for we take seriously the poststructuralist critiques, namely Jacques Derrida's assertion that "There is nothing outside of the text" (see Derrida, *Of Grammatology*, 158). We are interested in the Christ event as re-presented in the literary narratives of the New Testament and in the "texts" of the Church's liturgical celebrations throughout history. This is in no way to diminish the "truth" of these literary instantiations, but rather to clearly focus on the irreducible "textuality" of the Christ event, of the Eucharist, and by extension, of sacramentality in general.

and culminates in the eschatological reconciliation of the entire created order to God.

As Tillich affirms, "No sacrament, in Christian thought, can be understood apart from its relation to the new being in Jesus as the Christ."[63] To pursue this christological basis of sacramentality, let us further examine Karl Rahner's sacramental thinking. Rahner refers to Christ as the "primal sacramental word of God" and the Church as "the abiding presence of that sacramental word of definitive grace"; therefore "the Church is truly the fundamental sacrament, the well-spring of the sacraments in the strict sense. From Christ the Church has an intrinsically sacramental structure."[64] In Rahner's conception, a hierarchy of the sacramental mediation of the Divine is established: The Godhead > The incarnate Christ (primal sacrament of God) > The Church / Body of Christ (fundamental sacrament of Christ). The Church is in fact "the source of redemptive grace."[65] Rahner claims his understanding of the Church-as-fundamental-sacrament is derived not "by a vague borrowing from the concept of sacrament known to us already from the current teaching about the sacraments" but rather "from Christology" itself.[66] This is consistent with our assertion that the sacraments, and the Eucharist in particular, point back first and most significantly to the person and work of Jesus Christ: the entire narrative of his incarnation, life, ministry, death, resurrection, ascension, and his sending of the Holy Spirit. But Rahner enters into the equation the necessity of the Church, as Christ's Body on earth to whom the administration of the sacraments has been entrusted. The Church is therefore considered the fundamental sacrament; "custodian" and even "source" of the sacraments, by virtue of an authority derived from Christ himself. Rahner upholds the primacy of the Church, and the centrality of the sacraments to the Church's identification as the vehicle of God's redemptive activity:

> But when the Church in her official, organized, public capacity precisely *as the source of redemptive grace* meets the individual in the actual ultimate accomplishment of her nature, there we have sacraments *in the proper sense*, and they can be seen to be the essential functions that bring into activity the very essence of the Church herself. For in them she herself attains the highest degree of actualization of what she always is: the presence of redemptive grace for men, historically visible and manifest as

63. Tillich, "Nature and Sacrament," 90.
64. Rahner, *Church and Sacraments*, 18.
65. Ibid., 22.
66. Ibid., 23.

the sign of the eschatologically victorious grace of God in the world.[67]

In other words, the Church in the world, by way of her sacramental activity, becomes both *sign* and *source* of redemptive grace—a reminder that signs, symbols, and therefore sacraments participate in the reality of and indeed *effect* that to which they refer.

Rahner continues to work out his definition of sacrament: "the sacraments precisely as signs are causes of grace[,] . . . causation by symbols."[68] In an effort to follow this train of thought, let us reword Rahner's statement slightly, recollecting Aquinas's formulation:[69] the sacraments *cause* grace. As signs/symbols, they are not merely means, channels, or conduits for grace to be transmitted, but they are in fact the indispensable source of grace. It is precisely *as* signs or symbols that sacraments are causes of grace. Yet does Rahner's definition open up the possibility that the converse could be true: that in fact those signs or symbols which cause grace are appropriately called *sacraments*? If a sacrament is a sign or symbol that causes grace, then could we not also say that any sign or symbol that effects grace is a sacrament? In seeking to understand how grace is caused by symbols, is it appropriate to begin with a theological concept of sacrament, or should we rather arrive at a concept of sacrament by understanding and experiencing grace via signs or symbols? And historically, and even scripturally, which would be the more sound understanding? It occurs to us that although Rahner's proposal goes no further than the former, the latter—by giving primacy to *grace* (rather than *sacrament*), and by acknowledging the utter contingency of *all* signs and symbols—is the more appropriate conclusion. Rather than beginning with a theological definition of sacrament in the sense of limited, identifiable, liturgically instantiated means of grace, we should begin with the understanding that a sign/symbol which causes or mediates grace[70] is that which deserves to be called a *sacrament*. As Schillebeeckx asserts, "every supernatural reality which is realized historically in our lives is sacramental."[71] It is plausible, then, to assert that the Church cannot ultimately constrain the notion of *sacrament* on the basis of its rubrics and formulae (although we are at the same time reminded of the "traditioned" and tradition-bound character of all religious symbols, including sacraments). If Christ is the

---

67. Ibid., 22 (italics added).

68. Ibid., 37.

69. Aquinas, *ST* III.62.1

70. Any distinction between *causality* and *mediation*, we contend, is practically as well as experientially irrelevant.

71. Schillebeeckx, *Christ the Sacrament*, 5.

ultimate referent of the sacraments, the Church—however true it may be that she is custodian of and charged with the right administration of the sacraments—must be seen as deriving her identity as the Body of Christ first *from Christ* and then only by extension from her participation in the sacraments. It is the grace of God, supremely manifest in Christ, made available in the Eucharist, which *makes the Church.*

THE EUCHARIST MAKES THE CHURCH[72]

The earliest cultic practice of the Christian faith, which Scripture affirms included the breaking of bread (cf. Acts 2:42), took place in absence of textual recollection or written liturgical instruction. Yet liturgy, as text *and* performance, and as the original context for eucharistic action, precisely embodies the root hermeneutical ambiguity we face. We often associate "a liturgy" with a textual artifact, something bound within a prayer book or ecclesiastical manual of some kind. Liturgies "script" our worship. Today, if one asks if a given church has a "liturgy," what is invariably meant is, does the church worship according to a script or text that provides the words and prayers by which sacraments are "guaranteed" to be biblically and theologically sound. In short, liturgical worship is worship "by the book." But it is a mistake to associate liturgy only with the textual guide or formula for worship, for the work of the people only authentically occurs in the actual performance—local yet universal—of the liturgical text or rite. In this sense, Christian liturgy, at the center of which lies the Eucharist, is irreducibly performative: the bodily senses are engaged by word, gesture, song, movement, food. Bodies interact with one another in the liturgy. A community is formed around the Word and the sacrament. These bodily individuals who make up the *ecclesia*, both constitute and are constituted by the eucharistic action that makes the Church the Church. It is in this communion that the Eucharist and the Church are each given its highest expression.

In *Being as Communion*, Orthodox theologian John Zizioulas seeks to construct a Christian ontology based upon the Eucharist. Zizioulas asserts, as implied in his title, that true being is only found in communion with God and neighbor (all humankind). Zizioulas distinguishes between *personality* and *personhood*, or in Greek terms, *hypostasis* and *persona*. To

---

72. The phrase belongs to de Lubac: "Literally speaking, therefore, the Eucharist makes the Church. It makes of it an inner reality. By its hidden power, the members of the body come to unite themselves by becoming more fully members of Christ, and their unity with one another is part and parcel of their unity with the one single Head" (*Corpus Mysticum*, 88). It is used by Paul McPartlan as the title of his study *The Eucharist Makes the Church*.

attain true being, one must move beyond the *individuality* of personality into personhood and *community* through relationship to the "other." According to Zizioulas, "A human being left to himself cannot be a person."[73] For Zizioulas, God is the "other" in relation to whom our being is grounded. However, this in no way negates the necessity of human relationships, for one may only commune with God *communally*. As God has been revealed as the communion of the Trinity—Father, Son, and Holy Spirit—it follows that "the being of God could be known only through personal relationships and personal love. Being means life, and life means *communion*."[74] Neither does this relationality negate difference: "The mystery of being a person lies in the fact that here otherness and communion are not in contradiction but coincide. Truth as communion does not lead to the dissolving of the diversity of beings into one vast ocean of being, but to the affirmation of otherness in and through love."[75] Ultimately, for Zizioulas, authentic being means participation in the life of God, which is only possible through the incarnation of Christ. Since "Christ Himself becomes revealed as truth not *in* a community, but *as* a community,"[76] (i.e., the Church), it follows that "[the] eucharistic community is the Body of Christ *par excellence* simply because it incarnates and realizes our communion within the very life and communion of the Trinity."[77]

Therefore, it is only through the communion of the Church, conceived as the "eucharistic community," that individuals may become *persons*. Via the Eucharist, Christian persons are made into a community called Church. A rich passage from de Lubac helps articulate this:

> For, in the same way that sacramental communion (*communion in the body and the blood*) is always at the same time an ecclesial communion (*communion within the Church, of the Church, for the Church . . .*), so also ecclesial communion always includes, in its fulfillment, sacramental communion. Being in communion with someone means to receive the body of the Lord with them. Being united with the saints in the Church and participating in the Eucharist, being part of the common Kingdom, and sharing in the holy mysteries go together in tandem and it can be said

---

73. Zizioulas, *Being as Communion*, 107. Martin Buber makes a similar observation in *I and Thou*: "Individuality neither shares in nor obtains any reality" (64).

74. Zizioulas, *Being as Communion*, 16.

75. Ibid., 106.

76. Ibid., 115.

77. Ibid., 114.

that they are one and the same thing. It is what will later be suc-
cinctly expressed in the formulation: *Christian communion.*[78]

Clearly, the sacramental and ecclesial bodies of Christ cannot be separated. This communion runs deeper still, for according to Zizioulas, "The
eucharist is the only historical context of human existence where the terms
'father,' 'brother,' etc., lose their biological exclusiveness and reveal, as we
have seen, relationships of free and universal love."[79] As we welcome the
replacement of our biological or "natural-born" hypostasis with a new *ecclesial* identity based on love without exclusion, it becomes clear that "[it] is in
the Eucharist, understood properly as a community and not as a 'thing,' that
Christ is present here and now."[80]

Zizioulas demonstrates that "*To be* and *to be in relation* becomes identical. . . . Here is certainly an ontology derived from the being of God."[81]
As true being requires the integration of the one into the many, it follows
that this same ontology applies to the relationship of local Churches to *the*
Church. "Thus the Church becomes Christ Himself in human existence,"
just as "every member of the Church becomes Christ and Church."[82] Local congregations acquire authentic being as the Church in communion.
As "the Church has bound every one of her acts to the Eucharist,"[83] it is the
Eucharist that creates the Church, and makes the Church *catholic*.

Thus far Zizioulas has provided us with a concept of Church as the
eucharistic community, and of being that requires relationship to God via
the eucharistic community, as it is the Eucharist itself that makes individual
personalities into *persons*, and makes the Church (into) the body of Christ.
As such, we agree with Zizioulas when he writes that "the eucharist *constituted* the Church's being."[84] From a Western perspective, Rahner put it
thus: "She [the Church] is most manifest and in the most intensive form,
she attains the highest actuality of her own nature, when she celebrates the
Eucharist."[85] And in *The Shape of the Liturgy*, Anglican monk and liturgical scholar Gregory Dix traces the evolution of the Eucharist beginning
with Christ's last supper with the twelve and in the life of the early church,

78. de Lubac, *Corpus Mysticum*, 21.

79. Zizioulas, *Being as Communion*, 60.

80. Ibid., 213–14.

81. Ibid., 88.

82. Ibid., 58.

83. Ibid., 61.

84. Ibid., 21.

85. Rahner, *Church and Sacraments*, 84. He states elsewhere that the Eucharist "the
highest actual fulfilment of her [the Church's] own being" (66).

concluding that "the primitive church did not create the Eucharist. It would be less untrue to say that the Eucharist created that primitive church which preached the paradox of 'Messiah crucified.'"[86] In this history, Christ's exhortation is that the breaking of bread and sharing of the cup—a fellowship meal quite familiar to his disciples—would from this time on be done "in remembrance" of him, of his broken body and shed blood. Through the early Church's keeping of this command to remembrance, the Eucharist develops into a distinctive and definitive event in Christian worship. The emerging ritual will eventually settle into a "four-action" shape, in which the sacred elements are taken (offertory), blessed (consecration), broken (fracture), and given (distribution or communion). This liturgical embodiment of Christ's redemptive death and resurrection by the eucharistic community is intrinsic to the Church's identity.

In this way, the Eucharist is always the activity of the *whole church*, with Christ as its head. In doing so we "become what we are," for as Dix asserts, "It is by the sacraments that you receive 'what you are,' your true christian being; it is by your life that you must 'become' what they convey. . . . The church is in the sight of God the Body of Christ; at the Eucharist and by the Eucharist for a moment it truly fulfils this, its eternal being; it becomes what it is."[87] Furthermore, it is never *a* Eucharist we celebrate, but always *the* Eucharist—one ritual, infinitely repeated—for when we experience *anamnēsis*, we are transported into "something altogether beyond time, which yet 'comes' into time—the Kingdom of God."[88] This is "eucharistic time," wherein "there is no room for the slightest distinction between the worshipping eucharistic community on earth and the actual worship in front of God's throne."[89] The Church's present communion also includes both past and future, gathering together Christ and the twelve at the last supper along with the *eschaton*, the assembly of all humankind at Christ's feet, in the single moment of the eucharistic event. Hence, Dix reminds us that "all eucharistic worship is of necessity and by intention a *corporate action—'Do* this' (*poieite*, plural)."[90] Furthermore, the "doing" of the Eucharist is not an act of cognition or feeling, but the action of a community that

---

86. Dix, *Shape of the Liturgy*, 77.

87. Ibid., 267. Cf. Augustine's statement from Sermon 7 on the New Testament: "by being digested into his body and turned into his members we *may be what we receive*" (§7, italics added). Augustine makes this point again in Sermon 227, an Easter homily for the newly baptized, when he writes of the eucharistic elements, "If you receive them well, you are yourselves what you receive" (Cummings, *Eucharistic Doctors*, 77).

88. Zizioulas, *Being as Communion*, 75.

89. Ibid., 233.

90. Dix, *Shape of the Liturgy*, 1.

knows where its real life is found. The eucharistic community, therefore, is a representation of the life of God in Christ, and is rightly called "eucharistic" not simply because it gathers as a community around the sacramental celebration, but because it is *constituted as a community*, as a *people*, in the first instance, by participation in the communal life of the Triune God. Communion is the expression that the life of God is personal, relational. Here we begin to understand that nothing exists without sharing in the life of the God who loves in freedom. As God is love, and being is grounded on communion with God, Zizioulas is right to ultimately conclude that "Being depends on love."[91]

THE EUCHARIST BREAKS THE CHURCH

We have seen how the Eucharist makes the Church: how in her eucharistic action, the Church receives not only the means of grace but her very *being* from Christ himself. We have also seen, in our consideration of Rahner, that the Church-*as-Church* has both a sacramental function and a sacramental form—it is the foundational sacrament, following the primordial sacrament, the incarnate Christ. D. M. Baillie calls the mystery of the Incarnation "the climax of all the Christian paradoxes."[92] Correspondingly, as the incarnate Christ is both subject and object of liturgical celebration,[93] "the very act of worship, particularly corporate worship, involves the use of words and thoughts about God, and to think or speak of God at all is to run into antinomy, dialectical contradiction, paradox."[94] This observation suggests that every aspect of the Christian faith, be it spiritual, liturgical, or theological, is riddled with paradox. This is not to the discredit of the Christian faith. To be clear, by "paradoxical" we refer to those tensions within Christian thought and practice, those seeming contradictions which arise from an honest interpretation of the incarnation of God in Jesus of Nazareth. These tensions must not be smoothed over or entirely explained away; they must be held together and maintained.

From its earliest enactment the Eucharist paradoxically both sustains and scandalizes the Church. The tendency of the sacrament to

91. Zizioulas, *Being as Communion*, 97. However, as Jean-Luc Marion has shown, the God whose Being is Love *empties Godself* of Being in the outpouring of that Love, first in the eternal *perichoresis* of the Triune Godhead, and then in creation; hence God is "without Being" in being given to and for an other (cf. *God without Being*, 45–49)

92. Baillie, *God Was in Christ*, 110.

93. Cf. Torrance, *Worship, Community*.

94. Baillie, *God Was in Christ*, 108.

simultaneously establish and disestablish the *ecclesia,* to simultaneously
manifest the real presence of the Divine by making possible a participation
in Divine *absence,* is evident from the very beginning, even within the narrative into which the Eucharist is inscribed.[95] This dialectical characteristic
is definitive of sacrament in such a way that has been overlooked or even
deliberately repressed in the history of Christian sacramental theology and
practice. So let us return to Rahner's conception of the sacramental structure of the Church. For Rahner, the Church is a sign, but a sign that appears
to be exempt from one universal characteristic of signs, per our Tillichean
model—the susceptibility to change: "because the Church is the sign of the
grace of God definitively triumphant in the world in Christ, this sign can
never—as a real possibility—become a meaningless symbol. As an historical
and social entity, the Church is always unchangeably the sign which brings
with it always and inseparably what it signifies."[96] This thinking requires a
leap of faith, for if the Church can never become a meaningless symbol, as
Rahner asserts, then it is inappropriate to regard it as either a symbol or
a sign. According to the understanding of signs considered above, it is a
structural feature of the sign to remain open to the possibility of change,
and according to Tillich, even to the possibility of becoming meaningless,
because the significance of the sign is always based upon convention or social agreement, and it always remains at a *distance* from what it signifies.
Furthermore, as Rahner acknowledges, the Church receives its nature as a
sign of the grace of God from Christ himself, who as the Word (*Logos*) is
also the *sign* of God. Therefore, to deny the possibility of change (or even
disappearance; dissolution into meaninglessness) in the case of the Church
is to alter the basic understanding of the necessary *mediation* of the grace
of God, and perhaps even to deny the totality of the incarnation of God in
Christ.

We find that Chauvet provides a useful corrective here to Rahner's
triumphalist conception of the Church:

> those who live too comfortably in the Church also misunder-
> stand it: they are then in danger of forgetting that the Church is
> not Christ and that if, in faith, it is recognized as the privileged
> place of his presence, it is also, in this same faith, the most radi-
> cal mediation of his absence. This is why to consent to the sacra-
> mental mediation of the Church is to consent to . . . *the presence
> of the absence of God.* The Church radicalizes the vacancy of

95. E.g., the two travelers' encounter with the risen Christ along the Emmaus road,
and the meal that followed (Luke 24). We will return to the Emmaus narrative in chapter 3.

96. Rahner, *Church and Sacraments,* 18–19.

this place of God. To accept its mediation is to agree that this vacancy will never be filled. . . . *Those who kill this sense of the absence of Christ make Christ a corpse again.*[97]

In this rich passage, which merits further unpacking, Chauvet makes the point that the Church, as a sign or symbol of the grace of God, is unique in that it mediates the presence of Christ, without becoming identical with Christ, while paradoxically and radically demarcating the location of his *absence* or *vacancy*. With this correction, we can say with Rahner that "the Church is always unchangeably the sign which brings with it always and inseparably what it signifies," because what it signifies is "*the presence of the absence of God*" (Chauvet), the paradox of the God who is fully disclosed in the crucified, resurrected, and ascended Christ and yet whose absence is (re)narrated in the Church's sacramental celebration as presence.

Rahner seems to allow for a more radical sense of the Church when he concedes that a trace of sacramentality exists within gracious action even outwith the *ecclesia*. He suggests that "any grace-giving event has a quasi-sacramental structure and shares in Christ's character as both divine and human."[98] By distinguishing between "quasi-sacramental" events and "sacraments in the proper sense," Rahner acknowledges that the line between the two is, for him, nothing more or less than the boundary between the Church and everything else. This slipperiness is telling, in fact, for such a strong assertion of this boundary indicates that its integrity is in question, just as the need to differentiate "proper" sacraments from quasi-sacramental grace-giving events at the very least reveals a kind of theological anxiety that the distinction between ecclesially "sanctioned" and "unsanctioned" sacramental experiences of grace might become blurred. Also, this reference to "sacraments *in the proper sense*" implies that the sacraments *proper* are the property or possession of the Church, which flies in the face of Nathan Mitchell's assertion that sacraments are less about possession and propriety and more about dispossession or being possessed by the grace of God.[99] The economy is, and must be, that of the gift, gratuitously given without limit or condition.

Rahner calls the Eucharist "the highest actual fulfilment of [the Church's] own being."[100] But what is that being? Rahner goes on to suggest that "the moment when this community grasps her own innermost nature, in the ritual celebration of that death which is her true life. That is the

97. Chauvet, *Symbol and Sacrament*, 177–78 [italics in original].

98. Rahner, *Church and Sacraments*, 22.

99. Mitchell, *Meeting Mystery*, op cit.

100. Rahner, *Church and Sacraments*, 66.

Eucharist."[101] It is a *coincidentia oppositorum*, a conjoining of life and death, of presence and absence, of the material and the spiritual, of humanity and divinity, of heaven and earth. What we have begun is a radical reinterpretation of the Eucharist as irreducibly scandalous, and of the eucharistic community as an assembly (*ecclesia*), a gathering, which is con-voked, called together, by this scandal. In this sense, the Church, or any assembly which might be interpreted as eucharistic, is a community founded upon a scandal, and it is this scandal which necessarily un-founds and up-roots this community. A community that is properly called eucharistic is not one which possesses the Eucharist, but one which is *possessed by* the Eucharist, which is consumed by Christ even as it consumes his body and blood. This possession necessarily entails a risk that can never be avoided, a risk of abandonment and irrevocable loss, of being offered up to be broken and poured-out so as to be *given* to and for an/Other. Indeed, the central symbol of the eucharistic community is not first and foremost the cross, but rather is the broken body of the Crucified One. It is this symbol of brokenness which unites the Church,[102] as it has done so throughout the ages, and by which the Church is called, in like manner to Christ, to empty itself for the life of the world, emptying itself of every vestige of power and possession. This "dispossession" is nothing less than *the loss or "letting-go" of the Church* as an institution of power and authority.[103] But we can understand this only by understanding the Church as a community that grounds its very being in *death*—a very particular death. The Church, then, has an entirely different perspective than the world, one that understands death-as-presence and resurrection-as-absence. This is the scandal of the Eucharist today, a scandal which has been repeatedly domesticated by the Church, but which must be continually sought and upheld as essential to the very be(com)ing of the Church as the Body-of-Christ in the world.

---

101. Ibid., 79.

102. The 1982 liturgy of the Scottish Episcopal Church encapsulates this in the words spoken by priest and congregation at the moment of the fracture:
(celebrant) "The Living Bread is broken for the life of the world."
(congregation) "Lord, unite us in this sign" (see chapter 4),

103. We are indebted here to J. David Belcher's unpublished master's thesis "Baptism into the Poor Body of Christ," provided to us by the author, which examines the sacrament of baptism according to the theme of dispossession. David Jasper also briefly attends to this theme in the final chapter of *The Sacred Body*, exploring the possibility of "liturgical living" as "dwelling"; he writes, "To dwell ascetically with nonpossession is to subvert the "natural" tendency to acquire and, above all, to acquire power for the self. . . . To abandon all totalitarian tendencies is to find freedom in the most deeply human encounter with the Absolute" (178).

SACRAMENT AS GOD'S BODY/LANGUAGE

As we have sought to show in this chapter, the concept of sacrament must be understood against the backdrop of the broader categories of sign and symbol. Christian sacraments must also be understood as pointing ultimately to the entirety of the Christ event, from whence they are given their meaning. The Church as the Body of Christ must be seen as deriving her identity, and her sacramental form and function, from Christ himself, specifically through participation in the sacrament of his broken body and shed blood. As such, the Church is both founded and unfounded—both made and broken—in her eucharistic celebration. In this way, the Eucharist has both a stabilizing and de-stabilizing effect on the recipient, both individually and corporately.

In the two chapters to come, we will attend to the scandal of sacramentality as a dual scandal of language and of the body. David Power articulates this well when he writes, "Word and thing merge in sacrament."[104] Thus far we have begun to glimpse the confluence of these two themes. Sacraments are signs/symbols which embody the real presence of God in Christ; yet sacraments come to us via language, in both the narratives of Scripture and in the creative Word (*Logos*) of God, by which creation was spoken into being—the Word that became Flesh in the person of Jesus Christ. We continue, then, to wrestle with sacramentality as the very challenge to theological thinking posed by the Body/Language of God.

---

104. Power, *Sacrament*, 57.

2

"The Word . . ."
The Problem of Language

*The Christ event being necessarily present in the manner of histori-
cally conditioned symbol (word and sign) is not present in itself,
but in a variety of historically conditioned symbolizations. It is thus
absent, even in its being present.*[1]

*Words fail, always fail, for they inscribe the absence they seek to
erase.*[2]

MEDIATION AND LANGUAGE

In the previous chapter, we have shown that the scandal of sacramentality
derives first from Christ himself, the Word of God made flesh, crucified on
Calvary, which St. Paul calls a "stumbling-block" (*skandalon*). Sacraments
are visible and tangible, yet they mediate to us the invisible and intangible
saving grace of God, which is resident within the material, created order
precisely because of the incarnation of God in Christ Jesus, the Word of
God made flesh. Through participation in this mediation, the ecclesial community is both constituted, *made into* the body of Christ called Church,
and unmade: fractured, broken, de-stabilized, and stripped of any power

1. Power, *Sacrament*, 58.
2. Taylor, "Unending Strokes," 142.

or possession it might hold as a body politic. Thus sacrament is a scandal to faith and practice, theology and Church. As God's body/language, sacraments call for participation and must be entered into via language and the body.

In this chapter, we shall begin by establishing sacramental signs/symbols as both part of language—that is, part of the system(s) of signification by which meaning is conveyed—and as the particular language of God's saving grace. An assessment of the relationship between language and sacramental theology would be incomplete without attending to the liturgical movement leading up to and encompassing the reforms of the Second Vatican Council, which implicitly wrestles with some of the same concerns about language that captivate postmodern thought. In what may at first seem a strange maneuver, we will consider the "death of God" theology of Thomas Altizer alongside the critiques of language which emerge from poststructuralist and postmodern thought, exemplified for us by Jacques Derrida.[3] In their own ways, both of these intellectual trends point to the absence of any transcendent guarantee of linguistic meaning. Then, guided by Paul Ricoeur's theory of metaphor, we will demonstrate that the struggle with sacramental language stems at least in significant part from Jesus' instituting words at the Last Supper, his metaphoric speech which ruptures semantic associations and confounds interpretation. This eruptive tendency, which breaks open a plurality of meanings, we call the "de/constructive core" of sacramentality, the "/" indicating a simultaneously de-constructive and constructive movement or tendency.[4]

3. To be clear, we are not attempting to draw a direct connection between Altizer's "death of God" and the crisis of signification characterized by Derrida as the death of the "transcendental signified," nor trace them to some common source or catalyst (though Nietzsche could be cited as a common influence). However, we suggest that these two intellectual impulses, emerging around the same time, share a more or less theological concern for language and the problem of signification.

4. Our point of reference for this use of the "/" (which can be written but not spoken) is Mark C. Taylor's use of it when he writes about "a/theology," which is not, he maintains, simply atheistic, but rather "marks the *limen* that siginifies *both* proximity and distance, similarity and difference, interiority and exteriority. This strangely permeable membrane forms a border where fixed boundaries disintegrate"; see Taylor, *Erring*, 12. In similar fashion, we employ the "/" in "de/constructive" to indicate the liminal character of sacramentality. When we refer to sacramentality's "de/constructive core," then, something simply or crudely *destructive* is clearly not implied. Instead, as is the case even in a more purely Derridean sense, deconstruction (even without the "/") always refers to a never-ending process of breaking down, or exposing the brokenness of, our certainties and structures of language or thinking, precisely to break open the possibility for a constructive moment "to come." This is the basic argument Simon Critchley makes on behalf of deconstruction in *The Ethics of Deconstruction*.

At the heart of the eucharistic liturgy lies the institution narrative, which echoes Paul's instructions to the church at Corinth (1 Cor 11:23–26) as well as the Last Supper accounts in the three Synoptic Gospels. Beginning with the earliest Gospel account in Mark 14, according to both the biblical text and the words of the Church's liturgy, Jesus takes bread, offers thanks to the Father, breaks it, and gives it to his followers, addressing them with the words "Take it; this is my body" (Mark 14:22). The passage continues: "Then he took the cup, gave thanks and offered it to them, and they all drank from it. 'This is my blood of the covenant, which is poured out for many,' he said to them" (Mark 14:23–24). These two statements, taken together as one—*this bread is my body; this cup of wine is my blood*—encapsulate the twofold scandal of eucharistic theology which occupy this chapter and the following: the scandal of the Word and the scandal of the Flesh, which come together in Christ, the "Word made flesh (*Logos sarx egeneto*)" (John 1:14). In the next chapter, we will examine the scandal of corporeality, that of the body, of the flesh, of the paradox of a God incarnate within the materiality of God's own created order. But first, we shall attend to the linguistic, the verbal and the textual: word before flesh. While we do not mean to imply the significance of one over the other, the biblical creation narrative provides our template for beginning with the problem of language.

Before creation, the Word (*Logos*) of God existed: "In the beginning was the Word, and the Word was with God, and the Word was God" (John 1:1). The writer of the Fourth Gospel, playing intertextually upon the theme and poetic style of the Creation narrative in Genesis 1, observes that prior to the speech-act of Creation, which in scripture is in the first instance a *verbal* act, the Word of God always already exists in and as the eternal communion and communication of the Godhead: "Through him all things were made; without him nothing was made that has been made" (John 1:3). God's first interaction with creation, with something *other* than Godself, takes place in an act of speech: "And God said, 'Let there be light,' and there was light" (Gen 1:3). Prior to this moment, scripture tells us, all is abyss, "formless and empty, darkness" (Gen 1:2). Then, into this abyss, God speaks, and in speaking, brings about matter, bodies: celestial, terrestrial, and eventually human. But as Slavoj Žižek has observed, this act of creation is itself a scandal to Godself: "The very notion of creation implies God's self-contradiction: God had first to withdraw into Himself, constrain His omnipresence, in order first to create the Nothing out of which He then created the universe. By creating the universe, He set it free, let it go on its own, renouncing the power of intervening in it: this self-limitation is equivalent to a proper act of creation."[5] This theological conception of the impact of creation on Godself is further evinced, from the standpoint of the biblical narrative, in the inscription of God's creation as a speech-act. Language—spoken or written—is never *immediate* but always entails *mediation*, and so the distance, the gap between God and that which is *other* than God, the necessary mediation between God and creation, is established in this primal utterance. These two accounts of Creation, that of Genesis and of John's prologue, set up not a false binary between language and the body, or the priority of the word (language) *over* the body/flesh (matter), but rather capture the irreducible primordiality of language, which is also to say, of the mediation effected by all signs.

We established in chapter 1 that sacrament is both symbol and sign. In patristic literature, the Eucharist is *sacra signum* (a sacred sign) and *verbum visible* (a visible word).[6] Sacraments, as signs/symbols, are not only a part of language, but are a language unto themselves, which David Power identifies as "the language of God's giving."[7] In his pivotal second chapter, Power offers a detailed analysis of different theories and conceptions of language and how this relates to sacrament in general and liturgical language in particular. After reviewing the sacramental theories of Aquinas, Bonaventure, and the Reformers, Power discusses the work of Rahner and Schillebeeckx (considered above) as examples of contemporary sacramental theologies which cast the sacramental sign as "an act of self-communication, both divine and human, and an encounter in grace . . . [which] works through the symbolic action."[8] Observing that "all celebration in its use of words, symbols, and rites involves the interpretation of the tradition handed on," Power proposes "a theology of sacrament that brings language to the fore," electing to describe sacraments as "language events."[9] Because, as Power puts it, "humans find their dwelling place in language,"[10] if the grace of God is to come to us in and through sacrament—that is, if sacraments are, in Schillebeeckx'

5. Žižek, *Puppet*, 137.

6. See Jenson, *Visible Words*, referencing St. Augustine, *On Christian Teaching*, 31. Nathan Mitchell notes "the inherent ambiguity of this metaphor. We think of words as *acoustic* events, not visual ones. To put *verbum* ("word") and *visible* ("visible") together seems transgressive, a mistake. Augustine's decision to define "sacrament" as "visible word" embodies a metaphoric collision. It suggests that "sacrament" is a ritual experience through which we learn to "*see* with our *ears*" and "*hear* with our *eyes*." If the root of sacrament is metaphor, then a new possibility is opened up for us; we may perceive the audible as visible and the visible as audible" (Mitchell, *Meeting Mystery*, 198).

7. This phrase is the subtitle of Power's book *Sacrament*.

8. Power, *Sacrament*, 56.

9. Ibid., 51.

10. Ibid., 66.

phrase, "the properly human mode of encounter with God"[11]—then they must meet us within the language-bound world in which we live.

This conception of sacrament as language and language event is a useful point of departure at this stage of our discussion. As we have seen, sacraments are part of the created order, yet point beyond themselves. For their meaning, sacraments rely upon the decidedly pluriform linguistic structures (signs) of their liturgical celebration(s), and the somewhat more uniform material elements (also signs) used in that celebration. Thus we defend Tillich's assertion that sacraments are not the Holy, but mediate the Holy precisely by delineating the difference between themselves and that which they represent. They are this-worldly artifacts which stand in for, in the absence of, that which is beyond the mundane. As Power reminds us, "The language event of sacrament engages us at the level of the daily, the bread and the wine, the oil and the water, within the time that is the time of living day to day[;] . . . the sacramental presencing of this event interrupts, even disrupts, the flow of daily and historical time."[12] Power is right to draw attention to another characteristic of sacrament: its location within time. Like language and bodies, time also is part of the created order. Time, which conditions history, is the exact location of this-worldly actions (rituals) and artifacts (symbols) which we experience in and through language and body. However, as language events, sacraments interrupt and disrupt time, just as they erupt and rupture the simple, univocal meaning of language itself. Elsewhere Power writes, "A ritual or sacramental event relates to an event within time past through the capacities and power of language to carry it forward and to allow it to enter afresh into lives, however they may have been disrupted and broken."[13] It is precisely this sense of disruption and brokenness to which we wish to call attention and which, we argue, is bound up within the *scandal* of sacrament, the stumbling-block we encounter on our way which interrupts and disrupts our journey toward meaning.

This scandal is not something external to language but is in fact an intrinsic characteristic of language itself. In *The Trespass of the Sign*, Kevin Hart examines the problem of signification in light of the narrative of the fall of humankind in the biblical story of Adam and Eve—a dynamic that Power fails to incorporate into his conception of language. This narrative inscribes not only the fall of humankind from an original state of perfection, but also encompasses the fall of language.[14] According to Hart, Christian

11. Schillebeeckx, *Christ the Sacrament*, 6.

12. Power, *Sacrament*, 91.

13. Ibid., 75.

14. cf. Žižek, *Puppet*: "We should bear in mind here the central tension of the

theology must concern itself with signs precisely "because it regards God as a presence who, after the Fall, represents Himself and is in turn represented by signs."[15] In his lucid opening pages, he posits that

> the view that language fell with man [is an elaboration] upon a far more persistent theme—that God guarantees the possibility of determinate meaning. The Fall may establish the human need to interpret yet it simultaneously sets firm the limits to interpretation. No longer in harmony with God, this world becomes a chiaroscuro of presence and absence; everywhere one looks, there are signs of a divine presence that has withdrawn and that reveals itself only in those signs.[16]

For our purposes, as it relates to signs as well as the question of presence and absence, this specifically implicates the notion of sacrament, for the tangible signs by which this withdrawn divine presence reveals itself in this world are precisely that which we call sacraments. "By dint of Adam's sin, though," Hart reminds us, "God is for us an *absent* presence."[17] The Fall inaugurates, therefore, the brokenness and discontinuity, the fragmentation against which our desires for presence, for *im*-mediacy arise.

However, our systems of signification, our efforts to establish certitude and meaning, our sacraments and sacred symbols are in fact susceptible to the very brokenness that they themselves endeavor to overcome. And so, according to Hart, "From God's presence we pass to His absence; from immediacy to mediation; from the perfect congruence of sign and referent to the gap between word and object; from fullness of being to a lack of being; from ease and play to strain and labour; from purity to impurity; and from life to death."[18] While signs mean, point to, and participate in something beyond the sign itself, according to Hart, "what we *mean* by 'sign' is that it is

---

Christian notion of the Fall: the Fall ('regression' to the natural state, enslavement to passions) is *stricto sensu* identical with the dimension from which we fall, that is, it is the very movement of the Fall that creates, opens up, what is lost in it" (118).

15. Hart, *Trespass of the Sign*, 7.

16. Ibid., 4.

17. Ibid., 7. This notion of an "absent presence," or "the presence of the absence" of God disclosed within the sacraments that constitute God's saving activity in the word, is most fully articulated in Louis-Marie Chauvet's sacramental theology; e.g., ". . . to consent to the sacramental mediation of the Church is to consent to . . . *the presence of the absence of God*. The Church radicalizes the vacancy of this place of God. To accept its mediation is to agree that this vacancy will never be filled . . ." (*Symbol and Sacrament*, 178).

18. Hart, *Trespass*, 5.

what it is in the absence of its animating presence."[19] In other words, the distance or gap between the sign itself and its referent—its animating presence, that from which the sign derives its meaning—is the exact locus of the sign's meaning. The sign *means* by demarcating this difference, by revealing itself as *other than* that to which it points. In the absence of the real thing—the physical, historical body of Christ, which after being raised from the dead, ascended to the Father—sacraments mediate, stand in for, a real presence, which *in the sacred sign* of the Eucharist is (un)veiled as a real absence.

So we encounter the Eucharist first as a *linguistic*—both verbal and textual—*scandal*. In the poetic speech of Jesus at the Last Supper, "take, eat, this is my body . . . my blood," we are immediately enrapt in the problem of language, in the paradox of a metaphor, to be precise.[20] But before we more closely examine sacramentality as a scandal of language and the problem of Jesus' metaphoric speech, let us pause to consider the problem of linguistic mediation within the context of liturgical language. The twentieth-century liturgical movement, culminating in the Second Vatican Council's task of translating the liturgy from Latin into vernacular languages, is an embodiment of this wrestling with language, with signs and their meanings, which persistently trip us up and confound understanding. Here we witness a demonstration that liturgical and sacramental language are not exempt by any means from the brokenness, fallibility, and confounding tendency characteristic of all sign systems.

VATICAN II AND LITURGICAL LANGUAGE

The limitations of this project permit no more than an overview of the relevant features of the liturgical renewal and the Second Vatican Council. In the first chapter of *Christian Sacraments in a Postmodern World*, Catholic theologian Kenan Osborne provides a concise summary of the major contributions of the liturgical renewal, which have contributed to the shape of our sacramental theology as we attempt to figure and refigure it for the third-millennium. He concludes: "Not only was the need for liturgical reform a product of this intense activity [of the liturgical movement], but in official and unofficial ways, liturgical reforms were already taking place prior to

19. Ibid., 12. Explicating Derrida's thought, Hart continues: "No context can circum-scribe a sign's meaning; the sign's meaning will alter if repeated in a different context; but the sign is structurally open to repetition: therefore, alterity is a structural feature of the sign" (13).

20. We note the possible objections to understanding Jesus' statement "This is my body/blood," or the Eucharist as a whole, in terms of metaphor. These concerns will be addressed in due course.

Vatican II. This change in liturgy, with its call for the use of vernacular language, for more participation by the lay person, for a better understanding
of the history of liturgical practices and rituals in the Christian-Catholic
tradition was a tremendous catalyst for the revolutionary renewal of the
church's sacramental life."[21] The revolution, according to Osborne, was the
re-location of the interest in sacramental and liturgical theology away from
the isolation of the academy and into the practical life of the *ecclesia*. Also
significant to our purposes is Osborne's recognition of the influence of
twentieth-century philosophy upon many of the individual Catholic thinkers who contributed to Vatican II: "existentialism, phenomenology, process
thought, Marxism, linguistics, semiotics, and postmodern philosophy" all
feature prominently, as well as "technological advancement."[22] Osborne
summarizes that *subjectivity* (the "return to the subject"), *historicity* (the
historical contingency or relativity of truth), and *epistemology* (the limitations of human knowing) comprise the three major implications of these
philosophical trends.[23] It is on the basis of this new or renewed emphasis
on subjectivity, historicity, and epistemology that the most significant result
of Vatican II, at least for the liturgical life of the faithful, emerged: the complete overhaul of the Roman Rite and the translation of the Mass into local
vernacular languages.

Today, when one thinks of "pre-Vatican II" Catholicism, the Latin
Mass immediately comes to mind. The first official statement of the council
was "The Constitution on the Sacred Liturgy" ("*Sacrosanctum Concilium*";
hereafter *SC*), published on December 4, 1963. We are interested in this
document for several reasons, which should be outlined. First, as this statement calls for the revision and translation of the liturgy, we expect to glimpse
something in this document the council's conception of religious (broadly)
and liturgical (specifically) language. Second, the contention, which lingers
even still, that the replacement of the Latin rite with the vernacular Mass destroys the beauty and mystery of the liturgy intrigues us; for even as critics
might blame Vatican II for bringing about the "end" of liturgy,[24] the council
seems to understand the "ends" (*telos*) of liturgy quite specifically, and their
intention is to bring the liturgy back into a condition that supports those
ends. However, in stark contrast to such nostalgic objections to the liturgical
reforms of Vatican II, we shall consider in some detail Catherine Pickstock's
"radical orthodox" criticism of the replacement of the Roman Rite with ver-

---

21. Osborne, *Christian Sacraments*, 12.
22. Ibid., 15.
23. Ibid., 16.
24. E.g., Drew, "Spirit or Letter?"

nacular Masses, which on the whole we find to be a convincing and accurate proposal accounting for both the challenges of postmodernism as well as the historical tradition(s) of the Church.

In the first article of *SC*, the Council recognizes the need "to adapt more closely to the needs of our age those institutions which are subject to change"[25]—an acknowledgment that the liturgy, like all signs and sign systems, is indeed subject to change, as well an admission of the historicity ("the needs of our age") and cultural-contextuality of the liturgy. A key phrase for the council is "full and active participation"[26] of the faithful in the liturgy, evidenced by the fact that variations on this phrase are scattered throughout the text of *SC* and emerge as a kind of benchmark by which to determine whether the liturgy is achieving its goal. This "full and active participation," then, supports and reinforces the *telos* of liturgy, which is the transformation and sanctification of the people of God. In fact, the Council writes that *the liturgy itself* demands this: "all the faithful should be led to take that full, conscious, and active part in liturgical celebrations which is demanded by the very nature of the liturgy."[27] The revisions are to be carried out with the understanding that the liturgy is the "source from which the faithful are to derive the true Christian spirit."[28] In other words, as we have already come to understand from Augustine, Dix, and Zizioulas,[29] in the liturgy, the Church receives its very being; both the corporate body and individual persons *become* the Body of Christ in and through the liturgical enactment of the Eucharist. It appears thus far that the Council's vision of the liturgy is at least somewhat historically and culturally fluid, and that to a large degree the locus of liturgical meaning is the congregation.

Toward this end of full and active participation, the Council approved the translation of the Tridentine Mass from Latin into vernacular languages, with the conviction that "The rites should radiate a noble simplicity. They should be short, clear, and free from useless repetition. They should be within the people's powers of comprehension, and normally should not require much explanation."[30] The implication is, of course, that the existing liturgy is *not* short or clear, is *not* within the cognitive grasp of the people, and might even be characterized by "useless repetition," thus hindering the congregation's participation in and comprehension of the Mass. A great em-

---

25. *SC*, Art. 1, 117, in Flannery, ed. *Vatican Council II*.

26. *SC*, Art. 14, 124.

27. Ibid.

28. Ibid.

29. See chapter 1 of the present work.

30. *SC*, Art. 34, 129–30.

phasis is placed on "clarity," which we take to mean first semantic and then theological clarity. The laity's *understanding* of the liturgy is essential. The Council believed "both texts and rites should be ordered so as to express more clearly the holy things which they signify. The christian people, as far as is possible, should be able to understand them easily."[31] And so, in what Osborne calls a "watershed for the renewal of the sacraments,"[32] in Article 36(B), the translation into and use of vernacular languages is approved: "since the use of the vernacular, whether in the Mass, the administration of the sacraments, or in other parts of the liturgy, may frequently be of great advantage to the people, a wider use may be made of it, especially in readings, directives and in some prayers and chants."[33]

However convinced and convicted the Council may have been about the legitimacy of these liturgical reforms, they have not passed without critique. The conservative (for lack of a better term) arguments which simply wish to preserve the status quo are largely rooted in a nostalgia that is of no particular interest to us. However, more radical criticisms exist, perhaps the most significant of which is the one offered by Catherine Pickstock in *After Writing: On the Liturgical Consummation of Philosophy*.[34] *After Writing* is a dense work, and Pickstock's analyses are nuanced and wide-reaching, touching on Derridean postmodernism, semiotic theory, medieval Christian thought, and liturgical and eucharistic history and theology. A full-fledged engagement with her book would very nearly require its own book-length study. Additionally, hers is to date perhaps the most immediately relevant study to the present work, and as such it shall reappear continually throughout this project, so for now, we shall limit our consideration only to her critique of Vatican II.

Pickstock argues that the basic problem with the liturgical reforms of Vatican II is *precisely* the Council's effort to simplify the complex structures

31. *SC*, Art. 21, 126.

32. K. Osborne, *Christian Sacraments*, 17.

33. *SC*, Art. 36. 130–31.

34. After John Milbank's *Theology and Social Theory*, Catherine Pickstock's *After Writing* is regarded as somewhat definitive of "Radical Orthodoxy," which she describes as a "new theological imperative" offering an alternative between postmodernism's shutting down of rationalist humanism, on the one hand, and its own indisputable nihilism on the other: "Radical orthodoxy . . . has offered a third alternative: while conceding, with postmodernism, the indeterminacy of all our knowledge and experience of selfhood, it construes this shifting flux as a sign of our dependency on a transcendent source which 'gives' all reality as a mystery, rather than as adducing our suspension over the void" (*After Writing*, xii). See also the edited volume *Radical Orthodoxy*, edited by J. Milbank (et al.), which contains essays by many scholars whose work extends this theological program.

of the Roman liturgy that had served the Church since the Middle Ages. To Pickstock, this indicates a failure on the Council's part to realize that the liturgy's "theological struggle to articulate itself," is *precisely* "the crisis of articulation by which liturgical expression can be seen as a critique of secular modes of language and knowledge."[35] Vatican II contributors Jungmann, Bouyer, and others propose the unburdening of the liturgy all that hinders the understanding—again, the "full and active participation"—of the laity. She posits that "The Roman humiliation of the worshipper before God, together with the inclusion of various ceremonial accretions, confirmed [the Council's] suspicion that the Rite contained interpolation from secular court ceremonial and emperor worship, betokening a dubious politicization of the Eucharist."[36] But the problem with the Vatican II reforms, according to Pickstock, is that they "ironed-out the liturgical stammer and constant re-beginning; they simplified the narrative and generic strategy of the liturgy in conformity with recognizably secular structures, and rendered simple, constant and self-present the identity of the worshipper."[37]

Pickstock's account of the inevitable failure of the Vatican II reforms is rooted in her understanding of the Church and its liturgical practice in the Middle Ages. Of the Church's uniquely sacramental and liturgical identity, she reminds us that "it was the Eucharist, rather than any other sacrament, from which all other activities flowed, because . . . for mediaeval thought, the Eucharist gives the Church, the Body of Christ, and as such, the Church alone legitimates politics, and provides the restoration of our genuine being through salvation."[38] Furthermore, the Eucharist as such must be viewed against the backdrop of a pervasively liturgical *culture*: "[T]he liturgy of the Middle Ages was embedded in a culture which was ritual in character. This was a time when the Offertory gifts were not disconnected from the produce of every life; indeed, the category itself of 'everyday life' was perforce a thoroughly *liturgical* category. For the community was not something which existed prior to, or in separation from, the Eucharist as a *given* which simply met at regular intervals to receive the Sacrament. Rather, the community as such was seen as flowing from eternity through the sacraments."[39] The Mass, in other words, was not simply a textual or theological abstraction, offered as a beneficial or even salvific supplement to the lives of medieval folk, but rather was the basis of medieval life itself. Medieval life and medi-

---

35. Pickstock, *After Writing*, 177.
36. Ibid., 172.
37. Ibid., 176.
38. Ibid., 147.
39. Ibid., 170–71.

eval identity, both communal and individual, were premised upon participation in the sacramental and liturgical life of the *ecclesia*.

While Pickstock bypasses the accounts of medieval history which focus on the cultural "profanation" of the sacred that emerges out of this deeply liturgical worldview—such as that of Johan Huizinga, who reminds us that medieval religion was an "entirely externalized religion,"[40] characterized by a "profaning overflow" resulting from an "overabundance of devotional content"[41]—her account of medieval theological error (chiefly the nominalism of Duns Scotus), arising from within the Church itself, seeks to explain the basis for this shift toward immanentism and materialism. For this reason, Pickstock refers to "the destruction from within of the liturgical city."[42] While she admirably supports her attribution of this "destruction" to Scotist thought, she also acknowledges the role played by the "unique intensification of piety which paradoxically segregated the sacred from the secular, for by concentrating sacrality in a singular and exclusively holy event or place, any location beyond that focal intensity was effectively secularized."[43] In her account, the former leads directly to the latter. However, other viable accounts of the medieval shift from transcendence to immanence, from spirituality to materiality, might be noted as well. Johan Huizinga, for example, places more emphasis on Pickstock's secondary cause when he writes, "Life was permeated by religion to the degree that the distance between the earthly and the spiritual was in danger of being obliterated at any moment. While on the one hand all of ordinary life was raised to the sphere of the divine, on the other the divine was bound to the mundane in an indissoluble mixture with daily life."[44]

Observing this thoroughly intermingled liturgical purview of medieval society, Pickstock suggests that the liturgy cannot be simply translated, or indeed translated so as to be simplified, because the liturgy is "as much,

40. Huizinga, *Autumn*, 203.

41. Ibid., 220–21. The more carefully one follows Huizinga's reading of medieval history, the more apparent the differences between his account and Pickstock's. In fact, Pickstock all but admits this, albeit in passing, when she remarks: "None of this account is supposed to imply that a liturgical order was perfectly realized in the high Middle Ages; the claim is rather that certain social and intellectual conditions of possibility for such an order were present" (*After Writing*, 157). Huizinga's history, which unlike Pickstock's is laden with concrete/practical examples from medieval life, seems much more attuned to, and much more comfortable with, the profane and profaning tendencies that grow out of the highly ritualized and sacralized medieval *zeitgeist*. His work provides additional insight in our literary explorations in Part Two of this study.

42. Pickstock, *After Writing*, 121.

43. Ibid., 147.

44. J. Huizinga, *Autumn of the Middle Ages*, 179.

or more a cultural and ethical phenomenon, as a textual one."[45] In other words, Pickstock directs us to the truth that the struggle with language is not simply a struggle with textuality or with speech as such, but with the very social and historical contingency of language itself, which is so easily forgotten or simply passed over. She explains:

> criticisms of liturgical reform . . . are often dismissed as con-
> servative or nostalgic. But because the Vatican II reforms of the
> mediaeval Roman Rite failed to take into account the cultural
> assumptions which lay implicit within the text, their reforms
> participated in an entirely more sinister conservatism. For
> they failed to challenge those structures of the modern secular
> world which are wholly inimical to liturgical purpose: those
> structures, indeed, which perpetuate a separation of everyday
> life from liturgical enactment. So the criticisms [offered here]
> of the Vatican II revisions of the mediaeval Roman Rite . . . far
> from enlisting a conservative horror at change, issue from a
> belief that the revisions were simply *not radical enough*. A suc-
> cessful liturgical revision would have to involve a revolutionary
> re-invention of language and practice which would challenge
> the structures of our modern world, and only thereby restore
> real language and action as liturgy.[46]

In light of this illuminating summary of Pickstock's dissatisfaction with the Vatican II reforms, we realize that her critique is not based upon a reified conception of language that wishes to preserve the liturgy's se-mantic content from some bygone generation, somehow protecting it from perversion for generations to come. As Pickstock points out, the Council "failed to realize that one cannot simply 'return' to an earlier form, because the earlier liturgies only existed as part of a culture which was itself ritual (ecclesial-sacramental-historical) in character."[47] Rather, we suggest that her critique appears to be based upon an underlying belief that liturgical language, *precisely as mediate and imperfect*, is "impossible,"[48] as it is linked to the originary creative speech of God, which as we have stated above, in-troduces the very gap between God and creation upon which the necessity of mediation is based. Consistent with Kevin Hart's reading of the relation-ship between the fall of Adam and "fall of language," Pickstock asserts that "liturgical expression is made 'impossible' by the breach which occurred

---

45. Pickstock, *After Writing*, 171.

46. Ibid., 171.

47. Ibid., 176.

48. See Pickstock, *After Writing*, 169–219, esp. 176–92

at the Fall."[49] While she never puts it quite in these terms, it seems to us that undergirding Pickstock's conviction that "liturgical language is the only language that really makes sense,"[50] is the acknowledgment that language, heightened to its significatory capacity nowhere more than in sacramental celebration, comes to us as gift from a God who empties and absents God-self *for creation*. It is in this divine *kenosis*, in the linguistic act of creation, by which our capacity for language, and our irreducible mediacy, is given. In the liturgy itself the Church repeats and participates in this *kenosis* when the faithful are called to "offer themselves,"[51] the out-pouring and offering of not only the souls of the faithful but their bodies as well. They present their bodies at the altar to receive the elements into their bodies, even as they are grafted into Christ's ecclesial Body by their reception of Christ's sacramental body. All of this takes place within the linguistic structure of the liturgy, not merely as an abstracted textual artifact but, as Pickstock has shown, as a socially-bound and culturally-embedded language event that can never fully be circumscribed by language or comprehended even by the most astute participant.

We have examined the liturgy as one site of our wrestling with the problem of language. Yet, in our postmodern era, the credibility of language itself is called into question. Sign systems collapse. The relationship between the sign and its referent is revealed as not only conventional—the result of social agreement and tradition—but in fact arbitrary. This revelation has been the source of considerable theological anxiety, for as George Steiner reminds us at the outset of *Real Presences*, "any coherent understanding of what language is and how languages performs, . . . any coherent account of the capacity of human speech to communicate meaning and feeling is, in the final analysis, underwritten by the assumption of God's presence."[52] So what happens to language, then, when God is understood to be an *absent presence*, "*the presence of an absence*"? How do we make sense of language,

49. Ibid., 177.

50. Ibid., xv.

51. *SC*, Art. 48 (135); cf. oblation in the 1982 liturgy of the Scottish Episcopal Church, which puts it thus: "made one with Him, we offer you these gifts, and with them ourselves, a single, holy, living sacrifice." The congregation along with the gift(s) of the eucharistic elements together comprise the singular offering or sacrifice of the liturgy; both are offered and both are consecrated. In this way, the SEC liturgy admirably portrays the Augustinian truth about the Church receiving, in the Eucharist, that which it is. When the priest says, "the gifts of God for the people of God," he refers not only to the gifts of bread and wine, but also the gift of *personhood* which, having been consecrated/sanctified, is in the Eucharist offered back to the congregation once again as gift.

52. Steiner, *Real Presences*, 3.

religious, liturgical or otherwise, in a "postmodern" era characterized by the "death," or at the very least, the *absence* of God?

THE DEATH OF GOD

Keenly aware of the absence of God were the contributors to the "Radical Theology" of North America in the 1960s, who sought to articulate what they perceived as the "Death of God."[53] Radical Theology was less a theological program or "school" and more a general impulse arising during this tumultuous era in Western history.

Thomas J. J. Altizer and William Hamilton's publication of *Radical Theology and the Death of God* in 1966 marks the first expressly theological attempt to account for the experience of the death of God upon the horizon of contemporary life. Like Hegel, Nietzsche and others before them, Altizer and Hamilton attempt to make sense of a world without God—a world which had by that time endured the trauma of two world wars and, with America's involvement in Vietnam, found itself potentially on the cusp of another. In their introduction, the co-authors lay out ten possible interpretations of what is meant by the "event" of the death of God. We need not catalog them all; a few examples will suffice:

1. That there is no God and that there never has been.

2. That there once was a God to whom adoration, praise and trust were appropriate, possible, and even necessary, but that now there is no such God.

3. That the idea of God and the word God itself are in need of radical reformation. Perhaps totally new words are needed; perhaps a decent silence about God should be observed.

---

53. Thinkers associated with Radical Theology and/or the Death of God include theologians Thomas J. J. Altizer, William Hamilton, Gabriel Vahanian, and Harvey Cox, biblical scholar Paul Van Buren, and Jewish theologian Richard Rubenstein (see Bibliography for selected works). For a definitive collection of essays, see Thomas J. J. Altizer and William Hamilton, *Radical Theology and the Death of God*. Simplifying *ad absurdum*, Paul Tillich is a key theological forebear to the Death of God theologians; followers, who to some degree carry on the mantle of Radical Theology, include Carl Raschke, Mark C. Taylor, Robert Scharlemann, and Charles Winquist. For evidence of the lingering relevance of the kind of thinking initiated by these theologians, see Clayton Crockett, ed., *Secular Theology*. In the UK, the writings of Anglican Bishop John A. T. Robinson, especially *Honest To God*, caused a similar stir on the cultural landscape, and might be viewed as a British counterpart to the North American "death of God" impulse, albeit from a less academic and more practical and even traditionally ecclesial perspective.

4. That our traditional liturgical and theological language needs an overhaul. . . .

10. . . . that our language about God is always inadequate and imperfect.[54]

So, while the death of God may be understood variously by these thinkers,[55] ranging from a general tenor of contemporary secular culture to an actual ontic event in the life of God, of particular interest to us is the radical theology of Thomas J. J. Altizer, whose very theological poetics *inscribe* the death of God in such a way that enacts this event within language itself. For Altizer, specifically, the death of God is inextricably bound to Christ's death on the cross, making his a gospel of profoundly *Christian*, and deeply christological, atheism.

In *The Gospel of Christian Atheism*, Altizer's thesis is that a new and radical form of Christianity must be adopted which is free of the tyranny of a judicial God, an originary sacred divine which transcends all time.[56] If God is to have come in the Incarnation of Christ—the kenotic movement of God from detached divinity into self-annihilation in the crucifixion of Jesus on the cross as the definitive and supreme act of love for the redemption of the world—and if this incarnation is the basis of Christian faith, we must begin to purge faith in Christ from subjugation to the "Christian God." The atonement, therefore, is essentially the freeing of humanity from God, understood variously as the institutional Church, moral law, the sacrificial system, and so on.

54. Altizer and Hamilton, *Radical Theology*, 14–15.

55. The first book to employ the phrase in its title is Gabriel Vahanian's *The Death of God: The Culture of Our Post-Christian Era*, a title which is far more provocative than the book itself. For Vahanian, the death of God is a purely *cultural* phenomenon, marked by the extreme immanentism and secularism that arise in late-modernity. However conservative its claims, the title and subtitle flag up (almost prophetically) two very important concepts for us: that of the *death of God*, and that of a *Post-Christian* age/era/culture. See also Vahanian's *No Other God*. Interestingly, the death of God, as a movement and as theme for theological thinking, has largely passed into obscurity, having enjoyed an intense but brief day in the sun. The phrase *Post-Christian*, however, has shown more staying power, and continues to be debated and discussed. It has been employed variously to describe everything from sociological interests in declining church attendance in parts of Europe, e.g., Davie, *Religion in Britain* and Brown, *Death of Christian Britain*, to theological proposals of something like a Bonhofferian "religionless Christianity," e.g., Hampson, *After Christianity*, and Cupitt, *After All*, to the more philosophically nuanced thinking of Vattimo, e.g., *After Christianity* and Mark C. Taylor, e.g., *After God*. While we do not take up the theme explicitly here, the notion of "post-Christian sacraments/sacramentality" is a potentially fruitful avenue for further exploration.

56. Altizer, *Christian Atheism*.

Drawing much from Eastern thought, especially in his early work, Altizer points out that by default, entrenched as we are in Western thinking, we tend to place positive emphasis on "being" and resist "non-being" as something inferior or negative—an observation that will be echoed in Derrida's critique of *logocentrism* and the Western propensity to construct intellectual and moral structures comprised of binaries of oppositional terms. Ultimately, it is God's self-negation, which in radical theology becomes another reversal, the negation of negation, that is the redemptive act: the God that is Spirit becoming wholly and irreversibly flesh in Christ, and being "obedient to the point of death" (Phil 2:8). Consistent with the Christ who, according to this hymn, "emptied himself" (*ekenōsen*; Phil 2:7), Altizer's is "a fully kenotic or self-emptying theology,"[57] a theology wherein God empties Godself, and one that can only be written as the theologian empties, piece by piece, his own self as well. It is the kenosis of God, first in creation and later in the incarnation, brought to completion in the "It is finished" (John 19:30) at Calvary, which frees us from the anxiety and bondage of that satanic God who demands satisfaction and sacrifice. This kenosis makes possible the (re)union of the Word and the flesh, and our (re)union with the Word-made-flesh that Altizer has sought throughout all his work.[58]

This could simply be seen as a post-Enlightenment reinscription of Meister Eckhart's famous statement: "Man's last and highest parting occurs when, for God's sake, he takes leave of god."[59] However, the death of God, to Altizer, is more than this. Altizer is unwilling to allow theological constructs to "smooth over" the interminable problems created by the uniquely Christian conception of God. He refuses to flinch away from the truth he finds at the heart of the Christian narrative: that the God who comes in Christ in fact irreversibly dies, sacrifices Godself, on the cross of Calvary. So while for Eckhart, for God's sake, we take our leave of "God"—a name or concept that has the potential to be idolized—for Altizer, God has not only taken leave of us, but has in fact died, and has died for our sake, to liberate us from God. And while the death of God, in this sense, is understood as God's own action—God's *self*-negation—still we must say an emphatic "No" to God

---

57. Altizer, *Living the Death of God*, 12.

58. "Above all, the radical Christian seeks a total union with the Word, a union abolishing the priestly, legalistic, and dogmatic norms of the churches, so as to make possible the realization of a total redemption, a redemption actualizing the eschatological promise of Jesus"; T. Altizer, *Christian Atheism*, 25–26.

59. Eckhart, "Distinctions Are Lost in God," in *Meister Eckhart: A Modern Translation*, 204.

because God has ceased to make Godself present to us, and thus God's presence can only be known or experienced as God's absence.[60]

However, Eckhart is an appropriate figure to draw into this chapter, in fact, for as Oliver Davies points out in his "Introduction" to Eckhart's *Selected Writings*: "language itself . . . (as Eckhart knew) is a fundamental part of the problem. Language mediates the world to us with all its finiteness in space and time. And when we use it of God, it gets in the way by making an object of him, clothing him in concepts and images which are inappropriate to his uncreated nature. But if language is the obstacle, it is also paradoxically the place of our redemption. Through purifying language into its most abstract and internal forms, through using wildly metaphorical language of God . . . [Eckhart offers] a disruptive critique of language."[61] Like Eckhart, Altizer's theological works consistently push the limits of language (theological or otherwise) to a breaking-point rarely approached elsewhere. His is not a systematic theology by any means. It is a poetic theology, worked out within all the muddle and mess of the language by which we perpetually try, but always fail, to circumscribe God.[62] In *Total Presence*, one of Altizer's most potent works, he addresses the issue of language in relation to the parables of Jesus. As Altizer describes it, we detect an almost *sacramental* quality to the parabolic speech of Jesus: "Perhaps we could say that the intention of the parable is to realize an enactment of speech wherein a totality of speakable or realizable identity is wholly present and immediately at hand. . . . In this sense parable, or pure parable, is present only in its enactment, only in its telling or saying."[63] Similarly, according to Kenan Osborne, "Sacraments only exist in the *doing*, in the *celebrating*."[64] To Altizer, the language of Jesus' parables is unique in that it *is* im-mediate; and yet this "total presence," as he calls it, is at once a speech that is the antithesis of silence, and a speech which speaks about nothing at all[65]—and in this way is beyond economy and utility.

60. Altizer and Hamilton, *Radical Theology*, 137.

61. Eckhart, *Selected Writings*, xxxv.

62. Reading Altizer is more akin to the experience of reading poetry than theology; indeed, it is difficult for us to imagine the prospect of reading Altizer in translation. In a certain sense, we might say his writings are "liturgical," in that they are not meant to be understood or intellectualized so much as performed, participated in, entered into. Liturgical language is mute prior to enactment, and this enactment is communion. In this sense, such poetics as Altizer's are perhaps *sacramental*. While not a primary aim, we hope this claim will be substantiated by this book as a whole.

63. Altizer, *Total Presence*, 3–4.

64. Osborne, *Christian Sacraments*, 12.

65. Altizer, *Total Presence*, 3, 7.

To demonstrate the problem of language as it is embodied in Altizer's writing, which is at once a poetic theology and a theological *poiesis*, we must consider a longer, representative passage which wrestles with the capacity of language to express theological content:

> True parabolic speech is the speech of world itself, a speech wherein and whereby world is totally actual and immediately at hand. Then speech is world and world is speech at once. Such speech calls its hearer out of a world which is silent and apart and into a world which is embodied in the full actuality of voice. The silence of the world ends in parabolic speech, and ends because parabolic speech gives utterance to the full actuality of time and world. It is precisely the absence of metaphorical and allegorical distancing which makes possible this full and immediate presence of speech. Then the act of speech is an incarnation of world, an incarnation of world in the pure immediacy of voice.[66]

We will not, and need not, endeavor to *explain* this impossible passage,[67] for like the medieval liturgy as interpreted by Pickstock, "this impossibility does not . . . indicate a suspension over the abyss, but rather, the *occurrence* of the impossible through Christological mediation, which reveals the void as a plenitude, impossibly manifest in the very course of deferral and substitution."[68] The mediacy of language is always theologically problematic, as it tempts us both to believe we can circumscribe God within the words that we assign to God, and to look to God as a constant guarantor of meaning. However, our only access to God occurs through language, distilled most potently in the belief in Christ as the "Word (*Logos*) made flesh" (John 1:14), for as Altizer has written, "Christianity and Christianity alone knows a Word or speech which is the absolute antithesis of silence. Here, Word speaks finally or eschatologically, and Word speaks finally because Word irreversibly becomes 'flesh.'"[69] And so language, as mediation by signs, is, like

---

66. Ibid., 7–8. For a closely related passage, see ch. 4 ("Incarnation") in Alitzer, *Self-Embodiment*, beginning on 63, passim.

67. The "postmodern a/theology" of Mark C. Taylor, which is in many ways the intellectual heir of Altizer's death of God and Derrida's deconstruction, exhibits a similar theological poetics: "a/theology cannot merely write *about* this impossibility but must write this impossibility itself. The writing of this impossibility is never complete but always fragmentary. The fragment inevitably disappoints, for it inscribes the failure of language"; Taylor, "Unending Strokes," 144.

68. Pickstock, *After Writing*, 178.

69. Altizer, *Total Presence*, 2–3.

the cross itself, the stumbling-block that is also the locus of our experience of salvation.

By considering the thinking and writing of Altizer, we encounter the possibilities of the death of God understood variously as a humanistic or cultural rejection of the concept of God; as an event of self-sacrifice or *kenosis* in the life of God; and, in his writing, his poetics, as the linguistic impossibility of im-mediate encounter with the divine. So, if our language fails to make God present to us, or is only capable of re-presenting God in the mediacy and void of language itself; and if linguistic meaning is no longer underwritten by the assumption of God's presence, how do we "make sense" of anything at all? Upon what is the meaning of any sign based? How can we be certain a semantic message will hit its mark, will be understood by the recipient (reader or hearer) of the message? Can we trust language to provide the medium in which communication may take place? And if not *communication*, upon what basis could any *communion* possibly occur? If we cannot *trust* language, can it possibly contain truth?[70]

THE CRISIS OF SIGNIFICATION

These characterize some of the preoccupying questions asked by the thinkers and theorists associated with *poststructuralism*, an intellectual trend that came of age in the 1960s primarily within continental philosophy, closely linked with and somewhat characteristic of postmodernism.[71] At the

---

70. These questions should have clear implications for the Word-made-Flesh whose silent testimony, when confronted with the question "What is Truth?" (John 18:38), bore witness to that Truth which does not come as a word or statement, but as a Person.

71. Some clarification is in order here about our use of *postmodern* in its various forms. For us, *postmodernity* refers to the contemporary cultural condition of the technologized West, acknowledging that this description is irrelevant to those segments of the global community that never experienced Western modernity as such. We take *postmodernism* to describe the loose matrix of intellectual trends, especially in philosophy, sociology and literary/critical theory, that follow and supersede modernism and maintain a critical posture toward the Enlightenment (e.g., poststructuralism, postcolonialism, much gender theory, etc). We agree with Gavin Hyman's assessment in *The Predicament of Postmodern Theology* that *postmodernism* is "a negative and parasitic term that depends on the negation of something else for its self–definition. This negation and parasitism empty the term of any weight or substance. It is the *post*-script to something else and has no content or definition of its own"; furthermore, "there [are] at least as many postmodernisms as there were modernisms" (11). Any discussion of the postmodern should acknowledge the first use of the term "postmodern" in architectural theory and criticism in Charles Jencks' *The Language of Post-Modern Architecture*. Some of the defining works on the postmodern include Lyotard's *The Postmodern Condition*, Jameson's *Postmodernism, or the Cultural Logic of Late Capitalism*, and the work

forefront of poststructuralism is the late French philosopher and literary theorist Jacques Derrida, whose notion of deconstruction typifies the postmodern struggle with language and meaning. But to understand Derrida, we must first review the semiotic theory of Ferdinand de Saussure.[72] In his *Course in General Linguistics*, Saussure distinguishes between fundamental elements of the system of signification, determining that words essentially have an arbitrary relationship to their objects. However, lest we regard this as a uniquely modern critique, Nathan Mitchell points out,

> The Saussurian denial of any real or essential relation between "sign" and "signified"—between what scholastic theology called *signum et significatum*—was not itself new. Such a rupture was already well under way in the West during the late medieval and early modern periods, and it would result in a severe challenge to traditional Catholic understandings of the *real* relation between "signs" and "things signified" in sacramental rites (the basis for the assertion that signs "really contain and impart" what they signify).[73]

Likewise, this consists with the Augustinian understanding of signs which we examined in the previous chapter. Recall that already present in Augustine's semiotic theory is the essential *difference* between the sign and its referent, and the *distance* at which the sign places the interpreter of the sign from the reality to which it refers. In Saussurian semiotics, this *difference* and *distance* is taken a step further. Saussure identifies that the sign itself can be broken down into two components: the *signifier,* which describes the sign's material component—how the word sounds when verbally articulated and processed aurally, or how the word appears when printed on the page and processed visually—and the *signified,* which refers to the conceptual component of the sign—not the thing itself but the mental concept of the thing to which the sign refers. These two components, the signifier and the signified, only when taken together make up the linguistic *sign.*

Saussure identifies that it is not the thing to which the sign refers that gives it its meaning, but rather all of the things which it is not—that is, the difference between a given signifier and every other signifier in the system of signification. In other words, the sign "hat"—the signifier, comprised of the letters "h-a-t" in written (*grapheme*) or spoken (*phoneme*) sequential

---

of Bauman, e.g., *Imitations of Postmodernity.*

72. Saussure's *Course in General Linguistics* survives only as a composite of lecture notes. As a starting point, see the excerpt in Mark C. Taylor, ed., *Deconstruction in Context,* 141–68. Taylor's introductory comments on 13–14 are also helpful.

73. Mitchell, *Meeting Mystery,* 14–15, fn. 27.

combination, and the signified, or the mental concept of a covering for the head—is only meaningful because of the *difference* or *dissimilarity* "hat" bears to the sign "bat," "pat," and so on, both phonetically/graphically and conceptually (i.e., the concept of a hat is distinct from a scarf or a shoe). In a language system that relies purely on differences—definition by negation—only negative, and no positive, terms exist. This breakdown of the linguistic system reveals the unraveling of all structures of signification. Hence meaning is exposed as arbitrary, fluid, duplicitous, pluralistic. For Saussure, thought and language are coextensive, and so there can be no pre-linguistic thought. Therefore, since language contains within itself its own negation, all thought, spoken or written, is subject to this fundamental flaw.

Derrida's reading of Saussure[74] leads him to identify a characteristic of Western thought he calls *logocentrism*,[75] or the deference to and reliance upon the intrinsic truth of the Word as the arbiter of presence. "Logocentrism," Derrida has stated, "is *also*, fundamentally, an idealism. It is the matrix of idealism."[76] The result of the idealistic delusion that words and language contain some concrete, univocal meaning is a binary, oppositional system of hierarchies in which one term is always privileged over another, such as light to darkness, transcendence to immanence, presence to absence. This is evident also in the elevation of the perceived immediacy of speech over the mediate nature of writing, which is cut off from its author and requires interpretation.[77] Derrida traces the primacy of speech back to Plato's *Phaedrus*, which he reads deconstructively to show how speech is susceptible to the same critique Plato ascribes to writing; in the end, Derrida elevates the written word over the spoken. Taking this argument to its logical conclusion, Derrida suggests that this problematic nature applies to all structures of language and, by extension, all structures of thought.

74. For a concise but helpful description of Derrida's application of Saussure, see Stephen D. Moore's *Post-structuralism and the New Testament*, 14–16. It is noteworthy that Saussure's *Course in General Linguistics* is only preserved in textual form as a collection of the lecture notes of his students; in other words, it did not begin its life as a proper "book" but rather as speech, as oral presentations transcribed and later compiled by his students. This might be borne in mind when considering Derrida's reading of Plato's *Phaedrus* as a text which seeks but ultimately fails to demonstrate the primacy of speech over writing; see "Plato's Pharmacy" in *Dissemination*, 67–186.

75. See Derrida, *Of Grammatology*.

76. Derrida, *Positions*, 51.

77. According to Roland Barthes, all writing entails the "death of the author," which gives rise to the "birth of the reader." This understanding of textuality is crucial to post-structuralism, as the author is no longer the final arbiter of the meaning of his text; rather, the reader creates a plurivocity of interpretations. See Barthes' essay, "The Death of the Author," in *Image Music Text*, 142–48.

To sufficiently outline the development and implications of post-structuralism and deconstruction would require a separate study.[78] However, a basic knowledge of deconstruction is crucial to the remainder of this chapter. With Derrida's work, the possibility of absolute truth seems to disintegrate, giving rise to the duplicity and plurality of meaning—this is what Pickstock is reacting to when she criticizes the nihilism and "necrophilia" of postmodernism, or Derrida's conception of language as resulting in a situation where "meaning is indeterminate and abyssal."[79] As a result, the innate power structures and hierarchies within Western thought are exposed as ultimately biased and oppressive. The epistemological yardstick is turned on its head. The philosophical contribution of deconstruction is often thought of as the overturning of *logocentrism*, but this description is overly simplistic. Rather than a simple reversal or inversion, deconstruction produces the *rupture* of meaning, which is not purely destructive but is also constructive, generative, for what deconstruction finally discloses is that meaning is always unavoidably the product of the construction of meaning—meaning requires that we "make sense" of signs and symbols that populate our world.[80] However, in the absence of the transcendental signified—that is, some originary *essence* or source of meaning—all meaning is understood in terms of *difference*. Derrida employs the term *différance*, coined from the French for "to differ" and "to defer," thereby bringing together the ideas that meaning is not only based on an unstable relationship of *differences* but that meaning is also, as a consequence, indefinitely *deferred*.[81] It is, in what John Caputo has recognized as a sort of messianism,[82] always "to come" (*a venir*).

Différance, for Derrida, is actually no-thing in and of itself, but always already exists within the matrix of signification, a description of the absence of an origin or an originary presence. While Derrida attempts to maintain that his project is non-theological, *not* the same as negative theology, and even famously claiming that *différance* "blocks every relationship

---

78. For a thorough analysis, see Culler, *On Deconstruction*.

79. Pickstock, *After Writing*, xv; see also chapter 3, "Signs of Death" (101–18).

80. Mark C. Taylor puts it well: "Meaning is relative or relational. It arises from the play, the interplay of identity and difference, presence and absence, light and darkness, voice and silence"; *Deconstructing Theology*, 116.

81. Derrida, *Positions*, 27.

82. Caputo, "After Jacques Derrida Comes the Future"; see para. 14. Prof. Caputo was a Robertson Lecturer at the University of Glasgow in 2005 and delivered an address entitled "Circumfession: The Jewish Augustinianism of Jacques Derrida" (which as far as we are aware remains unpublished in that particular form). We cite this public lecture as our first exposure to this messianic quality in Derrida's thought.

to theology,"[83] the implications and the application of his work nonetheless have a profound impact on theological thinking.[84] "Turned toward the lost or impossible presence of the absent origin, this structuralist thematic of broken immediacy is therefore the saddened, *negative . . .* side of the thinking of play whose other side would be the Nietzschean *affirmation*, that is the joyous affirmation of the play of the world of signs without fault, without truth, and without origin which is offered to an active interpretation. *This affirmation then determines the non-center otherwise than as loss of the center.*"[85]

Throughout his *oeuvre*, Derrida's work outlines[86]—or, perhaps more accurately, *performs*—what he calls *deconstruction*, which is not so much a literary critical approach as a recognition of the inherent movement within texts, and by extension all of language, to undermine the very system(s) of signification upon which they rely for meaning to be conveyed and communication to occur. Derrida writes: "The movements of deconstruction do not destroy structures from the outside. They are not possible and effective, nor can they take accurate aim, except by inhabiting those structures. Inhabiting them *in a certain way*, because one always inhabits, and all the more when one does not suspect it. Operating necessarily from the inside,

83. Derrida, *Positions*, 40.

84. For a concise overview, see Raschke, "Á-*Dieu* to Jacques Derrida"; and Hart, "Jacques Derrida: The God Effect." Derrida's impact on theology and religious thought is best seen in the work of Taylor, cf. esp. *Erring*, passim, and of Caputo, esp. *The Prayers and Tears of Jacques Derrida*, passim. This is to say nothing of the profound influence of Derrida and deconstruction upon biblical criticism.

85. Derrida, *Writing and Difference*, 369–70. From our perspective, the Derridean notion of "the lost or impossible presence of the absent origin," which "determines the non-center otherwise than as loss of the center," does not seem too far removed from what Pickstock names when she writes: "the liturgical stammer bespeaks its admission of distance between itself and the transcendent 'real.' It is this very admission of distance which permits a genuine proximity with God." This is the liturgical instantiation of "the impossible through Christological mediation, which *reveals the void as a plenitude*, impossibly manifest in the very course of deferral and substitution" (*After Writing*, 178, italics added). We suspect that it is resonances of this sort that leads Carl Raschke to claim that "Radical orthodoxy is far more Derridean than it can confess" (Raschke, "Á-*Dieu* to Jacques Derrida," 46.). To borrow a phrase from John Caputo, while Pickstock and Derrida come at the question from very different points of faith (and different patterns of religious thinking and praxis), they both appear to be "Apostles of the Impossible"—or perhaps better, *poets* of the Impossible; cf. Caputo, "Apostles of the Impossible: Derrida and Marion," in *God, the Gift and Postmodernism*, 185–222.

86. See Derrida, *Of Grammatology*; *Writing and Difference*; and *Margins of Philosophy*, which contains the essay "Différance" (3–27; also excerpted in Taylor, ed. *Deconstruction in Context*, 396–420). See also Derrida's essential essay, "How to Avoid Speaking: Denials," in *Languages of the Unsayable*, S. Budick and W. Iser, eds., 3–70.

borrowing all the strategic and economic resources of subversion from the old structure, borrowing them structurally, that is to say without being able to isolate their elements and atoms, the enterprise of deconstruction always in a certain way falls prey to its own work."[87] Here Derrida confesses the very characteristic for which deconstruction is most often criticized; namely, that it is subject to its own critique. So when Pickstock critiques Derrida "for his exaltation of absence and postponement" which "turns out to be but the inevitably nihilistic conclusion" of an indifferent, modernist rationalism,[88] she misses what Raschke and other heirs of Altizerian "radical" (but not "radical *orthodox*") theology have no trouble grasping; that "The shattering of every orthodoxy is not nihilism, but eschatology. In its very conception eschatology betokens the overcoming of the metaphysics of presence by the Presence alone. The presencing of Presence means the smashing of the onto-theological pattern of writing as presence, of inscription as the double sentence, of the regime of being itself. Eschatology is both 'the end of theology' and the end of all 'orthodoxies' that purport to stand in for the Father, that usurp the throne of signification."[89]

Derrida, while revered and maligned in seemingly equal measure, must be credited as an impeccable and imaginative reader of texts. His work consistently demonstrates his central insight: the ultimate failure of language to comport singular, univocal meaning. Elsewhere he refers to this failure as stemming from the death of the "transcendental signified"—some point of reference outside the sign-system, and immune to the critique of signification, which guarantees linguistic meaning. These are complex assertions put forward in nuanced writings, and such a brief outline does them no justice. However, it should be noted that according to our Tillichian framework, sacraments, as sacred signs or religious symbols, must be regarded as containing the same de/constructive tendency intrinsic to all sign-systems; this challenge must be taken seriously. Sacrament, as a theological construct and a liturgical act, must be reimagined in light of this de/constructive core. The consequences for both Christian theology and liturgy of this reimagination will be explored more fully in the discussion to come.

This is an all too brief outline of some of the major contours of the postmodern era, characterized by poststructuralism and the crisis of signification as well as by the advent of Radical Theology and the death of God. It is by no means comprehensive. Rather, we have highlighted those characteristics of postmodernity that are relevant to our understanding of sacraments

---

87. Derrida, *Of Grammatology*, 24.

88. Pickstock, *After Writing*, 47.

89. Raschke, "Á-Dieu," 44–45.

and sacramentality as signs and language events. Those features include the disintegration of language systems as a sure-fire reservoir of meaning and truth, and a preference for pluralism and paradox over univocity and simplicity. Additionally, the sense of the absence of God, especially after the Second World War,[90] emerges as a disconcerting characteristic of this cultural epoch as well. These hallmarks of postmodernity, taken together, call forth the exploration undertaken here to open new avenues for sacramental thinking and experience. It is our proposal that in a manner not dissimilar to the poststructuralist crisis of signification and Altizer's vision of the death of God, the liturgical reforms of Vatican II also enact within the arena of language a *kenosis* or emptying of meaning.

"THIS IS (NOT) MY BODY . . .": THE LIVING METAPHOR

Let us turn now to the eucharistic liturgy and consider how the language of the liturgy discloses within itself the same struggle with, and for, meaning that is an intrinsic characteristic of all language. At the center of the liturgy of the Eucharist lies the institution narrative. Indeed, in a certain sense, the most critical words of the entire narrative—indeed the entire liturgy[91]—are Jesus' metaphoric declaration *This is my body* and *This is my*

90. It is impossible to overestimate the importance of the Second World War—chiefly the Jewish holocaust and the bombings of Hiroshima and Nagasaki—to any authentic understanding of postmodernity. In *Imagologies*, his experimental collaboration with Finnish philosopher Esa Saarinen, Mark C. Taylor writes, "Modernity ended on August 6, 1945. The postmodern condition we are living is not simply the result of having been raised on television. As the children of Hiroshima, we have always known that modernity is a nightmare from which we must awake"; see §"Telepolitics," 2. In light of this, it also must not go unnoticed that many of the major contributions to the intellectual make-up of postmodernism come from thinkers of Jewish descent, e.g., Walter Benjamin, Emmauel Levinas, and Jacques Derrida.

91. We recognize the potential problem of claiming that certain words or phrases of the liturgy are more critical than others; it is best to regard the liturgy as a kind of symphony, in which every note played by every instrument is crucial to the desired effect of the music. However, it might be said that without the institution narrative, and without the statements "This is my body; this is my blood" in particular, the Eucharist has not be enacted, even according to the earliest biblical/ecclesial instruction of Paul to the Corinthians and to the most basic of liturgical formulae. Furthermore, we recall those parts of the Mass that even such a liturgical reformer as Cranmer insisted must remain in Latin so as to preserve their sacral and mystical character, e.g., in the 1548 "Order for Communion in English," the priest is instructed that the prayer of consecration/epiclesis "without the varying of any other rite or ceremony in the Mass." Further, Cranmer notes that "the Bread that shall be consecrated shall be such as heretofore hath been accustomed . . . if it doth so chance that the Wine hallowed and consecrate doth

blood. The importance of these two statements is attested in the *gravitas* with which the priest commonly delivers these words, and heightened by the fact that the Church teaches that the celebrant speaks these words not in his own "voice," as though a narrator or story-teller, but rather *in persona Christi,* in the voice of Christ himself. These two statements, taken together, are the fulcrum around which the entire liturgy moves. Without them, the drama of the liturgy grinds to a halt; the words and actions that precede these metaphoric statements and proceed from them become incoherent if this central declaration is negated. So we must undertake a consideration of metaphor and fiction.[92]

In *The Rule of Metahpor,*[93] Paul Ricoeur offers a concise definition of metaphor as "the rhetorical process by which discourse unleashes the power that certain fictions have to redescribe reality."[94] We immediately encounter a tension here; perhaps metaphor is not, after all, the way into a discussion of Jesus' "This is my body/blood" when in fact the bulk of the Christian tradition has ardently fought to maintain that the bread and cup are not mere "fictions" which have the power to "redescribe reality," but are in fact the *Corpus Verum,* the true body of Christ; the *res* (reality) itself, not simply a redescription of reality. However, we must not be so quick to denigrate "fic-

---

not suffice or be enough for them that do take the Communion, the Priest, after the first Cup or Chalice be emptied, may go again to the Altar, and reverently and devoutly prepare and consecrate another, and so the third, or more likewise, beginning at these words, *Simili modo postquam conatum est,* and ending at these words, *Qui pro vobis et pro multis effundetur in remissionem peccatorum . . ."* This is evidence that at least certain parts of the liturgy are held to be uniquely sacred, and should be preserved in the ancient language of the Church.

92. Graham Ward disagrees: "The literary nature of this demonstrative identification cannot be accurately catalogued. There is no avowed element of similitude or comparison: it is not a simile, it is not a metaphor. There is no element of substitution or proportion to indicate synecdoche or metonymy: it is not a symbol. . . . The phrase has the literary structure of allegory or irony: something which seems to be the case is so, but otherwise" (*Cities of God,* 82–83). In departing from Ward's understanding of the eucharistic "is" as non-metaphorical and outside the known grammars of identification, our goal is not to *reduce* Jesus' eucharistic statement to metaphor (*contra* Ward) but rather to show how Ricoeur's understanding of the "living metaphor" resonates with our conception of sacrament. We agree with Ward that this scandalous "is" *is not* a metaphor insofar as he means what Ricoeur would call a "dead metaphor." But we contend that Jesus' statement is an instance of *la métaphore vive,* and that by extension, the living metaphor betokens a sacramentality.

93. We appreciate Prof. David Jasper pointing out to us the questionable English rendering (*The Rule of Metaphor*) of Ricoeur's French title, *La Métaphore Vive,* which alludes more to the notion of the *living* metaphor—or perhaps even the exclamation: *The Metaphor Lives!*

94. Ricoeur, *Metaphor,* 5.

tion" to the status of "*mere* fiction," just as we must not demote "symbol" in a similar fashion. We must not strip "fiction" of its association with "truth," for as Douglas Templeton has explored at length in *The New Testament as True Fiction*, the opposite of fiction is not truth but rather fact.[95] He writes, "Fiction, while it does not state, nevertheless embodies truth. . . . Fiction, the term 'fiction,' is wider than fact, because it can include fact."[96] Templeton's broad engagement with the writings of the New Testament study is helpful in that he provides a framework within which to deal with the New Testament Scriptures, especially the Gospels, as literary texts rather than historical chronicles, and indeed that such an understanding is an *elevation* of the Scriptures, rather than a diminution of their status. He observes that "Fiction differs from history as the possible differs from the actual."[97] Furthermore, "Literature differs from history as fiction differs from fact. . . . History and literature are equally modes of dealing with, of finding language for, *reality*."[98] Or as Ricoeur states of metaphor, "Reality remains a *reference*, without ever becoming a *restriction*."[99] Following Templeton, we may conclude that the best—which is to say, most fruitful, most expansive—way to regard the Gospel accounts is as "true fictions," for they are more interested in possibility, in the possibility of the impossible, than they are in facts and actualities.[100] As *literature*, we are still firmly within the realm of truth and reality, but rather than stopping with the *actual* (which remains inaccessible to us), we move *beyond* into the realm of the possible.

Returning to metaphor, it is nevertheless important to note that this "power . . . to redescribe reality" around which Ricoeur builds his definition of metaphor is an inherent characteristic of "certain fictions"—not all fictions, perhaps, but neither does Ricoeur mention anything *other than*

95. See Templeton, *True Fiction*, 29.

96. Ibid., 29.

97. Ibid., 107.

98. Ibid., 305.

99. Ricoeur, *Metaphor*, 47 [italics added].

100. To be clear, Templeton does not focus on the idea of sacrament or the Eucharist in particular. However, near the end of the book, Templeton makes this provocative suggestion: "What if fictions can be *true* fictions? What if more or less historical fictions . . . can be *true* fictions? What if Baptism, Temptation, Transfiguration, the Entry into Jerusalem, the Institution of the Eucharist . . . are *true fictions* of this kind? What if each is, within a work of art, a work of art?" (*True Fiction*, 336) We wish to claim, following Templeton's lead, that the Eucharist is indeed a work of art, contained both within the work of literary art that is sacred Scripture, as well as within the work of ritual art that is Christian liturgy—in all its diversity and through all its development across centuries of Christian practice. The Eucharist is a true fiction that re-presents not so much a *historically verifiable* moment as a *poetic moment of possible impossibility*.

fictions which hold this power. A metaphor is a language event wherein one thing is taken for another: for example *the winter wind is a knife*, or in the Eucharist, *this bread is my Body*. According to Ricoeur, "The metaphorical 'is' at once signifies both 'is not' and 'is like.' If this is really so, we are allowed to speak of metaphorical truth."[101] We should note that this view of metaphor is by no means unique to contemporary thought. St. Augustine proposes that "Signs are either literal or metaphorical. They are called literal when used to signify the things for which they were invented. . . . They are metaphorical when the actual things which we signify by the particular words are *used to signify something else*."[102] And so an additional layer of remove or mediation is added to the metaphorical sign. If there is only one interpretive "step" between the literal sign and its referent (i.e., the word "bread" for a loaf of bread), at least two interpretive steps exist between the metaphorical sign and the "something else" to which it points (i.e., the loaf of bread, conjoined with the words "this bread is my body" to refer to Christ's physical body). "The bread retains its function as bread, and in this sense it is not the body of Jesus; but the bread also becomes the body of Jesus, and in this sense it is no longer ordinary bread. Paradoxically, for Jesus as for the believer, the eucharistic bread *is and is not* bread, it *is and is not* the body of Jesus."[103]

Catholic theologian Nathan Mitchell describes metaphor in related terms, which we also find useful: "Metaphor's first movement always appears to be a *mistake*, a *transgression* within speech."[104] Within the metaphorical "is" resides a "conflict—caused by putting two things together that don't belong—[which] cannot be resolved at the literal level. . . . We are thus compelled to imagine a new possibility—something *true* that *differs* from both . . . yet illumines the significance of both."[105] Metaphor, then, in its very irresolvable character, generates meanings without end. Not only can this metaphorical conflict not be resolved at the literal level, as Mitchell remarks, but in fact, at the *literary* level its resolution is not a closing down but rather a rupture, an opening up, of meaning. At the heart of metaphor resides this paradox, the concurrence of "is" with "is not." Like Picasso's statement about art, a metaphor is a lie that tells the truth.[106] For the metaphor to "work" it

---

101. Ricoeur, *Metaphor*, 6.

102. Augustine, *On Christian Teaching*, 37 (italics added).

103. Léon-Dufour, *Eucharistic Bread*, 128.

104. Mitchell, *Meeting Mystery*, 196.

105. Ibid., 196.

106. See "Picasso Speaks." See also, Mitchell, *Meeting Mystery*: "a metaphor can tell the truth only by lying" (195).

must be acknowledged on a certain level that the two things the metaphor compares are, in fact, *not* the same, and as Ricoeur demonstrates, when "is not" passes into nonrecognition, the metaphor becomes mundane, conventional, and ceases to be a *living* metaphor.

To consider another aspect of Mitchell's description, cited above, a metaphor is categorically a *transgression*. As Ricoeur writes: "If metaphor always involves a kind of mistake, if it involves taking one thing for another by a sort of calculated error, then metaphor is essentially a discursive phenomenon. To affect just one word, the metaphor has to disturb the whole network by means of an aberrant attribution."[107] The metaphor *requires*, according to Ricoeur, an aberration, a mistake, for "metaphor does not produce a new order except by creating rifts in an old order."[108] To mean anything at all, metaphor must paradoxically violate the entire linguistic system upon which meaning relies. Metaphor represents by redescription—to paraphrase Emily Dickinson, it "tells all the Truth but tells it slant"[109]—and so is generative of new meanings, even by means of *misdirection*. As Mark C. Taylor puts it, "Metaphors and parables are stumbling-blocks,"[110] language events which trip us up, quite deliberately, on the way to meaning. This is what we refer to as the *de/constructive core of sacramentality*: a movement within sacrament, in part the result of its basis in metaphor, which "conceals even while revealing, and reveals even while concealing,"[111] destabilizing interpretation and negating simple, univocal meaning. But always this de/construction leads to construction, to the eruption of a plurivocity of meaning and interpretation without end.[112]

THE DE/CONSTRUCTIVE CORE OF SACRAMENTALITY

It is not, then, inappropriate to speak of Jesus' statements as poetic—and indeed, Jesus' command to "This do [*poieite*] in remembrance of me" which follows the metaphoric declarations about his body and blood, places the Last Supper account clearly within the realm of poetry. Just as Jesus uses

107. Ricoeur, *Metaphor,* 23.

108. Ibid., 24.

109. Emily Dickinson, "Tell all the Truth but tell it slant" (Poem 1129), in *The Complete Poems of Emily Dickinson*, edited by Thomas H. Johnson, 506–7.

110. Taylor, *Deconstructing Theology,* 122.

111. Ibid., 119.

112. cf. "A Beginning," in Andrew Hass, *Poetics of Critique*, wherein Hass suggests that deconstruction's time has passed, and now is the time for reconstruction and recreation.

"fictions" (parables) to teach his followers about the kingdom of God,[113] Jesus uses poetic speech to redescribe or transgress reality: this bread is (not) his body, and his body is (not) this bread; this wine is (not) his blood, and his blood is (not) this wine. Furthermore the command to "*do this as often as you eat/drink it*" (1 Cor 11:24–26), implies that, to some degree, *all* bread and *all* wine should henceforth be regarded as having this paradoxical connection to his body and blood. Jesus' words startle his listeners, as they have many times before.[114] Spoken in the context of this particular meal, on the eve of his own execution, the words of the Word-made-Flesh rend asunder the "old order"—the sacrificial system of the Jewish Passover—to inaugurate a new covenant. Like all metaphoric and poetic speech, Christ's words punches a hole in the mundane (bread, wine; language), creates tears and exposes openings, reveals cracks and fault lines, through which wholly (holy?) new meaning(s) may erupt—life bursting forth from the vacant opening in a stone-hewn tomb.

And yet this eruption is also a *kenosis*, as we have seen—an out-pouring of meaning. Our language not only harbors this kenosis, but calls us toward the same end, as David Power has remarked: "The self-emptying, or *kenosis*, of Christ on the cross calls forth the self-emptying of those who are his disciples, a self-emptying which acknowledges the limits of all representation and is ready to cross out whatever representations hinder the gift of love and its testimony in the breadth and universality of God's giving."[115] God's giving begins in creation in the giving of language, speech, and the responsibility of naming. This giving is the giving of Godself, in and through the language of sacrament, which we can now say is also in and through language itself *as sacramental*.

All meaningful human experience is mediated by the language(s) and the body that we have been given and, far more than belonging to us, to

113. Templeton writes, "Why does it seem natural to think of the artist as a kind of liar? Why does the artist, why does Jesus use 'is not' to tell us what 'is.' . . . ?" (*True Fiction*, 87); cf. also Robert Scharlemann's two seminal essays, "The Being of God When God is Not Being God: Deconstructing the History of Theism" (ch. 3) and "Being 'As Not': Overturning the Ontological" (ch. 4) in *Inscriptions and Reflections*, 30–65. As David Klemm explains in his introduction to Scharlemann's "Being 'As Not'": "God shows Godself in the deep structure of language ("God is God as word"); and the essence or deep structure of language shows itself as the word *God*"; Klemm, ed., *Hermeneutical Inquiry*, 272.

114. Ricoeur observes that "Instead of comparing two things, metaphor contrives a verbal short–circuit . . . and *the more unexpected their combination, the more striking and surprising is the metaphor*" (ibid., 139, italics added). Jesus "Bread of Life" discourse in John 6, a highly eucharistic passage, creates a similar "short-circuit"; see our discussion of this passage in chapter 5.

115. Power, *Sacrament*, 82.

which we belong. We are beginning to see that the struggle with the concept of sacrament stems precisely from sacrament's this-worldliness, its material-ity, and its mediative nature. Our desire, our longing is for an *im*-mediate presence which is impossible because of the irreducible distance between the creation and Godself. All that we know and are able to experience of God comes to us through the material, which is to say, sacramentally. To again quote Schillebeeckx, "every supernatural reality which is realized historically in our lives is sacramental."[116] The two-fold scandal of sacra-mentality, as we are tracing it, is identifiable as the problem of language and the problem of the body. To be clear, when we refer in this thesis to the "problem" of language or the body, we do not wish to connote something purely negative (although negation is involved), in the sense of a problem for which a solution must be found. Rather, we are calling attention to the inescapable condition common to all humanity by which we are simultane-ously bound together and distanced by our language(s) and our bodies. This condition cannot, and need not, be "solved" or overcome.

However, in humanity's aspiration to transcend its present reality, in our desire to possess that which we can never grasp, sacraments knock us back down to earth, to our material, historical reality which is comprised of the signs and symbols without which meaning is entirely inaccessible to us. Our struggle, then, with sacrament is at least in part that sacrament points us beyond itself to a supernatural reality that is paradoxically *present* within and *as* the natural, historical, material reality to which we are bound, and which is otherwise utterly *absent*. In other words, in sacrament, we are confronted with the irreducible mediacy of our creatureliness, encompass-ing both language, as we have seen, and the body, to which we now turn.

116. Schillebeeckx, *Christ the Sacrament*, 5.

3

"... *Made Flesh*"
The Problem of the Body

... faith cannot be lived in any other way, including what is most
spiritual in it, than in the mediation of the body. . . . *What is most*
spiritual always takes place in the most corporeal.[1]

When the body appears to be endangered,
it becomes an obsession.[2]

MEDIATION AND THE BODY

We have thus far established that the central corporate act of the Christian
ecclesia, from which the Church derives its identity as the Body of Christ
and its sacramental structure, is the Eucharist, the participation in Christ's
broken body and shed blood. The Eucharist not only points toward the
cross of Christ but toward the entire narrative of the incarnation of God
in human body of Jesus of Nazareth. We glimpse the central stumbling-
block—what St. Paul calls a *skandalon*—of Christian faith and practice: "we
preach Christ crucified: a stumbling block to Jews and foolishness to Gen-
tiles" (1 Cor 1:23). Paul discloses the root of the *skandalon*: "Jews demand
miraculous signs"—they require visual or tangible evidence—"and Greeks

1. Chauvet, *Sacraments*, xii.
2. Taylor, *Hiding*, 129.

look for wisdom"—some sense of knowledge, grasping, comprehension. Yet the cross of Christ provides neither. Indeed, it leaves a double absence: a dead body, emptied of its spirit, and then a tomb absent its corpse. Even between Christ's resurrection and ascension, his is an elusive body that can be touched but not grasped, a body that will not submit to the categories of knowledge or the scrutiny of human wisdom. This is a radical reversal where life is found in death and death becomes life.

In chapter 2 we focused on the scandal of sacramentality as bound up with the problem of language itself. We established that sacrament must be understood as an event within language insofar as sacrament takes on the structure of symbol and, as we have seen following Ricoeur, the rule or "logic" (or "illogic," as Mark C. Taylor names it)[3] of the *living* metaphor in particular. Sacrament is a way of proclaiming what *is* by what *is not*. It is a poetic rupturing of language which protects the ineffability of the divine by opening up a distance between the signified and the signifier, and revealing this distance or gap to be internal to sacrament itself. In sacrament, language, as symbol and metaphor, mediates the Sacred, providing us with the means by which material elements of creation may be re-inscribed as the location of the divine. However, by pointing us toward the created order, which is irreducibly *other than* and at a distance from the divine, rather than beyond it, sacraments open the possibility of participation in divine absence, an absence symbolized as a real presence in the sacramental celebration.

The symbol also leads us back to the body as the site of sacramental encounter; as "the primordial and arch-symbolic form of mediation, as well as the basis for all subjective identification."[4] Guided chiefly by Louis-Marie Chauvet's eucharistic theology, will continue our effort to cursorily diagram the anatomy of sacrament by turning our attention now toward the irreducible *materiality* of sacrament—sacrament as a body which is given to bodies, and gives a Body. Chauvet is sensitive to the tension between the biblical injunction to worship God "in spirit and truth" (John 4:24) and the material, ritual trappings of the liturgical (which is to say "bodily") encounter with God,[5] for as Nathan Mitchell points out, "liturgies have no content other than the body itself in prayer, the body-as-prayer."[6] Chauvet reminds us "On

---

3. "Language has within it, however, an illogical element, the metaphor. Its principal force brings about an identification of the nonidentical; it is thus an operation of the imagination"; Taylor, *Deconstructing Theology*, 119; quoting Jacques Derrida, "The Supplement of Copula," 83. (Note: Derrida is quoting Nietzsche.)

4. Chauvet, *Symbol and Sacrament*, 111.

5. cf. Lacoste, *Experience*, esp. § 8 "Liturgy as Transgression," 20–22.

6. Mitchell, *Meeting Mystery*, xv.

the basis of faith in the incarnation of God in Jesus, Christians confess that they go to God not in spite of the heavy ambiguity of their humanity, but *at the very core of it*; not in spite of their bodies . . . but in their very bodies."[7] This is a pronouncement of the final and irreducible mediacy of sacramentality, which infuses the entire creation.[8] "Among the various mediations of the faith, the sacraments are the highest figure of the impossibility for faith to be lived in what is most spiritual in it—as adoration of the Father 'in spirit and truth'—outside the most 'bodily' and most 'religious.' The sacraments thus serve as a *buffer* which repels every temptation Christians might have to ignore body, history, society in order to enter without any mediation into communication with God."[9] Despite our tendency to denigrate the body and our desire for an experience that transcends our "locatedness" within space and time, sacraments remind us that such experience is inaccessible. Communication, relationship, of any sort, whether with God or fellow creatures, is impossible apart from the mediation (which can be called *sacramental*) of language and the body. So our dominant themes continue to arise: mediation and distance, presence and absence, signs and symbols, language and meaning. Our experience of the world is not only linguistic but also, and perhaps even more fundamentally, an experience of being in the body.[10] Our bodies mediate our world to us, and indeed, if Scripture and Christian teaching is to be believed, we were created as bodily creatures, to exist for eternity in the body,[11] for even as Job cryptically declared, "after my skin has been thus destroyed, then in my flesh I shall see God" (Job 19:26).[12] Even

---

7. Chauvet, *Sacraments*, 113–14.

8. On "The World as a Possible Place of Sacramentality," see Osborne, *Postmodern World*, 74–83.

9. Chauvet, *Sacraments*, 114.

10. We simply acknowledge here that even those persons who do not possess the capacity for language still live in-the-body and encounter the world as mediated by the body. Yet we wonder how, without language, a body is able to apprehend or interpret bodily experience? (Answering this question in any meaningful way would require the contribution of sciences of the mind which are beyond both our ability and the purview of this project.) Cf. Chauvet's excursus on the film *The Gods Must be Crazy*, in *Sacraments*, 9.

11. cf. 1 Cor 15; see Wright, *Surprised by Hope*. See also David Jasper's characterization in *The Sacred Body* of the "scandalous body—so blatantly displayed in the insistent 'this is my body,' and in the 'wildly counter-evidential, counter-cultural claim' that 'in my flesh, I shall see God'" (114). Jasper is referring to the final passage of Margaret Miles' *The Word Made Flesh*, 391; cf. *Sacred Body*, 33.

12. We say "cryptically" because the Hebrew meaning of this verse is ambiguous. According to the translators' footnotes in *The New Oxford Annotated Bible* (NRSV), the Hebrew could also imply "*without* my flesh." The editors' annotations state: "The meaning of v. 26 is too uncertain a one on which to base a firm conclusion, but the

in death, the Christian hope in the resurrection of the body, with which is inextricably bound up our belief in the incarnation, death and resurrection of the bodily Jesus—the "living bread who came down from heaven" (John 6:51) who may be eaten unto eternal life (John 6:58)—as well as our faith in the efficacy of the Eucharist to sanctify us unto eternal life ("the bread of life; the cup of salvation"): all of this attests to the unerasable Christian conviction that bodies matter. The God who formed bodies from dust also took on a human, fallible body, so as to redeem all bodies, as Gregory of Nazianzus understood: "That which He has not assumed He has not healed."[13] Indeed, sacraments "teach us that *the truest things in our faith occur in no other way than through the concreteness of the 'body.'*"[14]

To pursue the question of the body, of sacrament as an irreducibly corporeal or "bodily" experience, and of the sacramentality of the body itself, we shall begin by tracing the Church's struggle with the conception of and the relationship between the various "bodies" of Christ—that is, his historical, sacramental and ecclesial bodies. Henri de Lubac's unsurpassed study *Corpus Mysticum* will guide this discussion. We shall also look to the biblical text, focusing especially on the account of Jesus' encounter with the two travelers on the road to Emmaus (Luke 24) as a literary exploration of eucharistic theology which provides insight into the early Church's conception of both the body (or bodies) of Christ and the Eucharist as the sacrament of His body. We will arrive at the conclusion that sacraments are, as Chauvet has named it, "the grace of God at the mercy (*au risque*) of the body," or perhaps better, at the *risk* of the body. In sacrament, precisely because of its *corporeality*,[15] both God and we are placed at a profound risk: the risk of dispossession and death.

---

rendering of this verse in the NRSV would allow the possibility of a resurrected Job. The doctrine of the resurrection, however, appears late in Hebrew thought . . . and nowhere in the rest of the book does Job seriously consider the possibility" (646 OT). It occurs to us that, resurrection or no, whether in life or in death, Job's statement implies that the encounter with God occurs firmly in the body, and in Job's case in particular, the body *broken*.

13. Nazianzen, "To Cledonius the Priest Against Apollinarius," in *NPNF*, Series II, Vol. 7; Online http://www.ccel.org/ccel/schaff/npnf207.iv.ii.iii.html. [accessed 28 Mar 2010]

14. Chauvet, *Symbol and Sacrament*, 140–41 [ital. in original].

15. We are using *corporeality* in the sense of "bodiliness," what it means to be in-the-body. Chauvet uses the term *corporality* to talk about the same thing, e.g., "the human being does not have a body, but is body" (149), which he conceives as the "triple body"—social (within culture), ancestral (within tradition), and cosmic (within nature/the universe); cf. ibid., 149–52, passim.

David Power has guided our thinking about sacrament as language and language event, as "the language of God's giving." But this is not to say he is unaware of the corporeality of sacrament, both in the sense of the material sacramental elements and of the bodies of the recipients; indeed, "People enter into sacrament first through their bodies."[16] Word bodied forth in action; the intangible given form in tangible elements; the confusion of the material with the immaterial, the visible with the invisible—these are several ways to describe what happens in sacrament. But there is no sacramentality apart from this corporeal basis. In the broad sense, there is no sacrament without a body, just as in the narrower Christian sense, there are no sacraments without the Body—that is, the historical body of God incarnate in Jesus bodied-forth in the liturgical/sacramental action of the *ecclesia*.

Sacrament involves a poetic *making* or *doing* within language, yet in which linguistic meaning is not detached from material elements and embodied performance. In this sense, sacraments exist as concrete artifacts incorporated into physical human action. In the grammar of traditional Christian liturgy, sacraments involve tangible elements like water, bread, wine, oil, the laying on of hands, the giving and receiving of a ring or a kiss, and so on. One of the many paradoxes of sacrament is that it exists as a symbolic or linguistic event, and yet not simply so, for a symbolic/linguistic event that is not adjoined by tangible elements or embodied ritual is not rightly described as *a sacrament* in the strict sense. A linguistic utterance devoid of any physical instantiation, however gracious and grace-giving, can only be named *sacrament(al)* to the disservice and dilution of the concept of sacramentality I general. The corporeal must accompany the linguistic. "*The Word became flesh*"—flesh and word, together.

SACRAMENT AND PERFORMATIVE UTTERANCE

This observation helps to differentiate sacrament from various "speech act" theories in the philosophy of language, in particular from J. L. Austin's conception of *performative utterance*. This may at first appear to be a backtrack into the question of language. However, any linguistic utterance springs forth from the body, and *performance* implies embodied action, and so, as Austin claims, "if a person makes an utterance of this sort we should say that he is *doing something* rather than merely saying something."[17] This is

16. Power, *Sacrament*, 149.

17. Austin, "Performative Utterances," 235 [ital. added]. Austin cites such examples as saying "I do" at a wedding; saying "I apologize," "I bet you . . . ," or "I promise . . . ";

a helpful concept for thinking about sacrament, for several reasons. First, sacramental rituals are performances, the bodying-forth of prescribed words, gestures, postures, actions, movements, etc. Second, the sacramental liturgies of the Church indeed *contain* performative utterances; to use an example from the eucharistic liturgy, the priest's declaration, echoing Jesus' words at the Last Supper, "This is my body . . . this is my blood," in the institution narrative, as well as the words of consecration spoken over the elements, fits the criteria of performative utterance. Third, we find that the notion of performative utterance does not go far enough to sufficiently describe sacramental activity *in toto*, as should soon become apparent.

Interestingly, in his discussion of performative utterances Austin seems adapt one common definition of sacrament when he writes, "In the case of promising . . . it's very easy to think that the utterance is simply the outward and visible (that is, verbal) sign of the performance of some inward spiritual act of promising."[18] Despite this reference to the spiritual, Austin does not reflect substantially on examples of religious language as performative utterance, and surprisingly (at least to us), he never uses the word *sacrament* or even symbol in the essay. However, Austin does enlist as one example of performative utterance the "I do" in the ceremony of marriage, which is regarded as a sacrament by many, but not all, Christian churches, but which Austin seems to regard more from the standpoint of a secular/legal institution. For Austin the couple's "I do" is a performative utterance because in that moment, the bride and groom do not merely state or recite their vows, but *enact* that which they state, in that moment taking the other as her/his lawfully-wedded spouse. The minister's declaration "I now pronounce you husband and wife" bears a similar status. This pronouncement *is*, in a certain sense, the carrying out of the marriage itself. These words literally *wed* the couple, for without them, a marriage has not taken place, at least in the eyes of any legal or ecclesiastical authority. And yet, per Austin's conception, it is the "I do" itself, devoid of any material element or physical gesture, which qualifies as performative utterance.[19]

A clear relationship exists, however, between even Austin's "secular" examples, which might be played out in the social or legal sphere (promising, betting, apologizing), and similarly performative utterances within the

and the christening/naming of a ship.

18. Ibid., 236.

19. We are thankful to Troy Carter for reminding us that the sexual union of the couple is in fact the physical instantiation of the marriage, from both a legal and religious standpoint, insofar as consummation may be held up as evidence as to whether a marriage actually exists. This is significant to the sacramentality of marriage, but does not factor into Austin's conception of performative utterance.

Church's sacramental life. Examples might include the priest's absolution in the sacrament of reconciliation ("God almighty forgive you and free you from your sins . . ."), the words spoken at one's ordination into Christian ministry, accompanied by the laying on of hands, as well as various moments of the baptismal liturgy ("I baptize you . . . ," or accompanying the oil of chrism: "you are sealed with the Holy Spirit and marked as Christ's own forever") or the reaffirmation of baptismal vows. Differences do exist even between these examples of performative, sacramental words or phrases. The "I do" in a wedding is a chiefly linguistic pronouncement with no necessary material accompaniment, although we would point out, and Austin would doubtless admit, that the phrase "I do" outwith the wedding ceremony is decidedly not the enactment of marital vows, but rather, its meaning relies upon and must be taken as part and parcel of the wedding ceremony as a whole, which includes such material elements and embodied actions as the exchanging of rings and the kiss, as well as the secular/legal acts of the signing of the registry or marriage license. Confession and absolution also take place primarily within language, although it is common to kneel to confess (bodily posture) and make the sign of the cross (physical gesture) along with the priest as the absolution is pronounced. In the latter example, the body of the priest, which speaks and touches, might be regarded as the "elemental" synonym to the bread and wine of the Eucharist or the water of baptism, deriving this sacramental status via the sacrament of holy orders (ordination), which is a chiefly eucharistic vocation in the first instance.

However, the other examples we have outlined from sacramental rites all *require* not only a verbal or linguistic but also some kind of material instantiation: the laying on of hands (ordination), the immersion in or application of water (baptism) or the oil of chrism (baptism, unction), the paten and chalice containing the bread and the wine which are given to the congregation to see and touch and taste (Eucharist). Here Austin's example of a ship's *christening* (a word which itself hints at the buried religiosity of this action) is helpful: words must indeed be uttered, but tradition holds that a bottle of champagne is to be broken over the ship's bow *as* the naming is carried out. In this way, while the performative utterance (the words spoken) is carried out within language, it is reinforced and given material, visible form as well: it is embodied. Like Ricoeur's living metaphor, which contains the power to redescribe reality, the words—again, not a mere *saying* but a *doing*—are not only inextricably intertwined with action, but quite literally *are* actions.

However useful it is to note these commonalities, sacrament exceeds Austin's concept of performative utterance by failing to fully incorporate embodiment (materiality and physicality) into his concept. From the standpoint of Christian sacraments, the entire ritual comprises the sacrament; there is no sacrament apart from the liturgy as a whole (which admittedly may contain certain essential and nonessential elements). The liturgy, in its most essential form, may contain several moments of performative utterance. So for example, the sacrament of marriage has not occurred without the entire wedding liturgy, and all that it entails. Of course, a wedding ceremony may involve additional, non-essential elements (contemporary rituals, musical selections, etc.), but without certain prescribed and easily identifiable ceremonial elements (e.g., declaration of intent, vows, pronouncement of the couple, etc), the sacrament of marriage has not occurred. The wedding ceremony, as it might be printed in a liturgical manual, is the textual repository of those essential elements that ensure the officiant and participants, and generations to come, that the sacrament has legitimately come to pass. But the printed wedding liturgy is not the sacrament of marriage, for as Kenan Osborne reminds us, "Sacraments only exist in the *doing*, in the *celebrating*."[20] So we may conclude that while sacraments bear resemblances to performative utterances, and will *de facto* contain liturgical moments which fit Austin's description of performative utterance, they are not synonymous terms. The difference, primarily, is the essential corporeality of sacrament, the materiality of its element(s) and the physicality of its celebration. However, while not of necessity constituting a sacrament, we can permit the possibility that every performative utterance has a *sacramental* quality, which derives from its incorporation of both word and action, language and embodied performance.

CORPUS MYSTICUM, CORPUS VERUM

This excursus on the relationship between sacrament and performative utterance is intended to further clarify the distinctiveness of sacramentality. A sacrament imparts grace (however that might be conceived), and so not just anything can be construed as sacramental or as a sacrament. But it is also unique in the difficulty that arises in our attempt to understand what sacramentality is and does. The confusion that surrounds the notion of sacrament, as language event and embodied action, is not simply a recent development arising from the postmodern critiques of language and fixations on the body. As we shall see, it permeates the entire history of Christian

---

20. Osborne, *Postmodern World*: "Indeed, the only time that one can speak of baptism or eucharist is in an actual baptismal ritual or in an actual eucharistic celebration. These actual, localized, existential events of liturgy are the only moments when baptism, eucharist, confirmation, and so on exist" (12).

thought. What we are tracing here is the detachment in the Middle Ages of the notion of Christ's "mystical body" (*corpus mysticum*) from the Eucharist, and its gradual transposition to the Church as its referent, which results in the demystification of the sacrament and what Pickstock calls the "decline of the liturgical order"[21] or the "destruction from within of the liturgical city."[22] It is important to see both sides of this transposition as well, for as the sacrament is de-mystified, regarded increasingly as the "real" or true body (*corpus verum*), and as it becomes a focal point of analysis for medieval scholasticism, so also the Church begins to be conceived less as a concrete, social entity and more as a mystical (spiritual, cosmic, etc.) body. The social and political consequences of this shift are too vast to examine thoroughly here, but amongst other things, this movement is intrinsically linked to the privatization of religion; to the belief (which will survive the Reformation and the Enlightenment) that religious practice is an inward act of devotion or piety, and not the performance of a public, corporate action; and to an increasing concern in Christianity over the souls of the faithful to the neglect of their bodies.[23] Indeed, as Regina Schwartz points out, by the early years of the Reformation this culminates in the *mystification* or *mysticalization* of the political body of the State.[24] William Cavanaugh has observed that "the increased localization of the sacred in the Eucharistic host in effect secularized all that lay beyond it."[25] As such, this is one episode in the immanentizing or secularizing movement of sacrament as it becomes distanced from its original sense of mystery.

Let us pause momentarily and clarify our position on this "secularizing movement" we have been tracing since chapter 1. We are on the one hand ambivalent about the value (positive or negative) of this movement, as it appears to us to be, to a greater or lesser extent, the natural progression of what was a co-opted secular concept in the first place. This distancing from the sense of mystery that accompanied the shift from *mystērion* to *sacramentum* seems to lead naturally to the conception of sacraments as signs/symbols (and ultimately "mere" signs/symbols, in the wake of the

21. Pickstock, *After Writing*, 135 *passim*.

22. Ibid., xii, 121.

23. cf. Cavanaugh, *Torture and Eucharist*, especially 151–252.

24. See Schwartz, *Sacramental Poetics*, 20–22, 30–35. Schwartz cites Ernst Kantorowicz's *The King's Two Bodies*, which while not examined here, also informs the theo-political narrative as articulated in Cavanaugh's *Torture and Eucharist* (see 207–21). Pickstock's *After Writing* traces this narrative as well, focusing more on the influence of Scotist thought not only on the political realm, but also economy, law, social and civic bonds of kinship, etc (see 135–58).

25. Cavanaugh, *Torture and Eucharist*, 214.

Protestant Reformation), requiring for their meaning and comprehension the hermeneutical and theological task of interpretation, leading to the incisive theological analysis of the medieval scholastic thinkers, reaching a boiling point in the Reformation-era debates about the Eucharist (and by extension ecclesiology), and so on to the extreme plurivocity of Christian sacramental praxis and theology such as may be observed across Christian traditions today. In short, our intention is not necessarily to read this narrative as inherently negative, a loss to correct (á la Pickstock or Schwartz), nor as a liberating positive in the progression of human thinking (á la Hans Gumbrecht),[26] but rather as the historical outworking of the implications inherent to the concept itself. In this sense, what sacrament *is* is the culmination of the struggle with and stumbling-up-against the concept of sacrament throughout history. Miri Rubin's conclusion to her study of the late-medieval Eucharist expresses a conviction and impulse behind her narrative that resonates considerably with our own: "It may be sometimes exasperating in allowing for no causal drive—no narrative of the Rise of the Individual, no Secularisation, no Decline of the Church. . . . And yet a process is suggested by the material, not a story of causation and directed growth, but one of unfolding capabilities, a story about *the filling unto density of a symbol through the testing of its possible meanings and uses.*"[27] We do concede unreservedly, on the other hand, that there are consequences of this progression that can be read as positive or negative depending on the vantage point of the reader (e.g., the destruction of the liturgical city is calamitous from the perspective of high-church ecclesiasticism, although it might be regarded as something to be celebrated by secular humanism). The conviction underlying this entire thesis is that for sacramentality to be meaningful at all the present day—whether as a literary and/or artistic motif, as a purely ecclesial concept and action, or as a desire or aspiration within post-ecclesial culture for an experience that transcends the mundane—such a sacramentality must be radically (re)imagined as a part of the communicative and significatory fabric of our common life and as deeply grafted into the materiality of the body.

26. We have not said much thus far about the work of Hans Ulrich Gumbrecht, who in *Production of Presence* wrestles with the task of thinking "presence" from a nonreligious standpoint (i.e., beyond metaphysics and meaning); cf. esp. his discussions of the Eucharist on 28–30 and 85–86. Near the end of the book, Gumbrecht considers his own thinking in relation to Radical Orthodoxy and Catherine Pickstock in particular, concluding that his affinities are more of the ilk that Radical Orthodoxy critiques and ultimately rejects; see 146–49.

27. cf. Rubin, *Corpus Christi*, 361 [italics added]. We relate this also to Ricoeur's famous observation that "the symbol gives rise to thought"; cf. the conclusion of *The Symbolism of Evil*, 347–57.

Whatever our interpretation of the historical out-working of the (il)logic of sacramentality, or the present state of affairs, the Church's wrestling with the Body of Christ, both conceptually and concretely, has been a preoccupation down through the ages, as Henri de Lubac has shown in great detail. Looking specifically to the medieval period, in "an inversion that only came about by degrees,"[28] the traditional "three-fold" conception of the body of Christ—his historical body born of the Virgin which hung on the cross; his sacramental body in the Eucharist; and his ecclesial body, the Church—is reduced to a dichotomous, two-fold conception (a binary) wherein the historical and sacramental bodies are undifferentiated and both regarded as the "true body" (*corpus verum*) of Christ. This shift begins in the ninth century in the writings of Ratramnus and St. Paschasius Radbertus, at which time "mystical body" (*corpus mysticum*) still refers, as it did originally, to the Eucharist. But gradually this terminology is transferred over exclusively to the Church, a trend that has persisted even through the twentieth century.[29] As we showed in chapter 1, the implied belief here is that the Church *is the Church* in its celebration of and participation in the Eucharist; the true body is the means by which the Church may be legitimately called the mystical body.[30] But words mean things and shape realities, and as we shall see, this semantic shift is not without consequence for both ecclesiology and sacramental theology. Further, this is not merely a semantic debate, once again setting us back into the linguistic realm (although, indeed, we find it difficult to move past the problem of language, which arises perpetually even in our discussion of body), but rather a theological struggle, played out in language (writing), with the distinctions between the different modalities of Christ's body, or rather, the three planes on which the one body of Christ seems to operate.

At any point in the history of Christian thought, a distance must be recognized between the historical body of Christ, which was born, died, rose again, and ascended, and the presence of Christ in the Church and in the Eucharist by which each is ascribed with the name *corpus Christi*, body of Christ. The original theological unity in the conception of the sacramental and ecclesial bodies, as distinct from Christ's historical body, is lucidly expressed in de Lubac's analysis. As such, Christ's ecclesial body the Church,

28. De Lubac, *Corpus Mysticum*, 9.

29. The conception of the Church as the *corpus mysticum* is present in the twentieth-century Catholic theologians we have considered above (Rahner, Schillebeeckx), as well as in the documents of Vatican II. Contemporary Catholic theologians have begun to critique this conception, notably, Cavanaugh in *Torture and Eucharist*; see 123–281.

30. See Cavanaugh's helpful synopsis of this narrative in *Torture and Eucharist*, 212–13; cf. also C. Pickstock, *After Writing*, 158–66.

and his sacramental body in the Eucharist, "are not so much used to describe two successive objects as two simultaneous things that make one whole. For the body of Christ that is the Church is in no way *other* than the body and the blood of the mystery. And properly speaking, this is not a piece of word-play. Through the Eucharist each person is truly placed within the one body. It unites all the members of it among themselves, as it unites them to their one head,"[31] that is, Christ. But eventually, according to de Lubac, "the very foundation of the distinction that was once made between the '*body which hung on the wood*' and the '*Body which is immolated in the mystery*' for the large part disappeared."[32] Thus Christ's true body (*corpus verum*) comes to refer to both his historical and sacramental bodies. As increased priority was given to the belief that the bread and wine of the Eucharist actually transform into the body and blood of Christ, "the invasion of *true* caused *mystical* to give way."[33] This maneuver is not difficult to grasp, given the ardent belief of the medieval Church that the Eucharist made present the actual, historical body and blood of Christ, concealed under the accidents of the bread and the wine. And lest we are tempted to downplay this literalist understanding of the Eucharist which dominates the period, or pass over it quickly as a novelty of a bygone era, Caroline Walker Bynum testifies to the late-medieval belief that "What we eat in the Eucharist is so truly the flesh born of Mary," the historical body in the three-fold schema, "that we might indeed see it bleed and be then 'horrified to touch it with our lips.'"[34] (However, this eucharistic realism is a striking contrast to the conception, which is present quite early, of the Eucharist as a "bloodless" or "unbloody" sacrifice.[35])

Over time, however, the gap between the Church as Christ's mystical body, on the one hand, and Christ's true body—a conflation of the historical

31. De Lubac, *Corpus Mysticum*, 23.

32. Ibid., 164.

33. Ibid., 221. De Lubac claims, in defense of the Christian tradition, that "This evolution should not be imagined as a rupture or a sudden deviation" (256). Instead, he proposes that this is simply a result of the ebb and flow of time, of different viewpoints disclosing different aspects and truths but maintaining "a real doctrinal continuity" (257); and while we do not deny a continuity, we would point out that de Lubac never makes the point we wish to make: that this struggle with the conception(s) of the bodies of Christ is as much a struggle with the problem of the body and of language *writ large* as it is of parsing nuanced theological concepts.

34. Bynum, *Resurrection of the Body*, 149, citing Honorious' *L'Elucidarium et les lucidaires,* and pointing out that "the idea is found in Paschasius Radbertus" (see fn. 106).

35. E.g., throughout The Divine Liturgy of James the sacrifice of the Mass is referred to as a "bloodless sacrifice," as well as a "sacrifice of praise," a "spiritual and bloodless sacrifice," etc; see *ANF*, vol. 7, 537–50.

body born of the Virgin and the body made present in the sacrament—on the other, becomes an interminable distance. According to de Lubac, "*sacramental* and *mystical*, which until recently had still been considered synonymous, and are basically the same word, were now separated and placed in opposition to one another."[36] And so de Lubac concludes: "Of the three terms: historical body, sacramental body and ecclesial body, that were in use, and that it was a case of putting into order amongst each other, that is to say, simultaneously to oppose and unite them to one another, the caesura that was originally placed between the first and the second, whereas it subsequently came to be placed between the second and the third. Such, in brief, is the fact that dominates the whole evolution of Eucharistic theories."[37] The implication here is that the Church's tendency throughout her history to *stumble over sacrament*, and by extension stumble over her own very identity *as a corporate body* (Church), may be reduced, *ad absurdum*, to the difficulty of the body to be circumscribed by language, and the difficulty of language to convey the relationship between these three distinct conceptions or "incarnations" of the body of Christ. Instead of making the unity or the continuity of the three-fold body clearer, language problematizes this relationship by inserting into the analysis a necessary and irreducible layer of mediation between the descriptor (*signifier*; e.g., "historical body," "true body," "mystical body," etc.) and thing itself (*res*) the reality of its referent (*signified*; e.g., the body born of the Virgin and crucified on Calvary; the eucharistic host; the Church as a local and/or cosmic entity).[38] The only way to analyze these concepts and their unity and/or difference is within the realm of signification; and yet, it is precisely the mediacy of the body and of language which scandalizes our theological thinking by revealing the very distance and difference we endeavor to overcome.

36. De Lubac, *Corpus Mysticum*, 103.

37. Ibid., 256. This idea of *caesura* is helpful to illustrate this movement. Basically the conception of Christ's bodies shifts from "*historical (corpus Christi verum)—sacramental/ecclesial (corpus mysticum)*" to "*historical/sacramental (corpus verum)—ecclesial (corpus mysticum)*." Chauvet also provides a helpful review in *Sacraments*, 139–40.

38. De Lubac writes: "Through the stages that have been described, the expression *mystical body* passed from the Eucharist to the Church: and once again there was, in an analogous sense, a *mystery of the body*. The *mystical body* was the mystery that described this ecclesial body by means of the sacrament, and, in its radical meaning, it could strictly speaking be described as being 'contained' in the Eucharist. Then, from the *mystery of the body* it developed into being a *body in [the] mystery*; from the signification itself to the thing signified. Thus the Church is the mystical body of Christ: that is to say, quite simply, that it is the Body of Christ signified by means of the sacrament" (*Corpus Mysticum*, 250).

And yet, in highlighting what at first appears to be simply a semantic struggle, we also uncover at its core the problem of the body, of materiality or corporeality. Indeed, these theological ideas, and the language by which they are expressed, would never present a problem if it were not for God's coming in the historical body of Jesus of Nazareth:[39] born of a Virgin, hung on a cross, raised from the dead, ascended to the Father, perpetually given as the sacramental body, the tangible eucharistic elements of bread and wine, giving birth to a visible, ecclesial body, the local-yet-universal body of Christ called Church. The Word became flesh; the body became word, the word of Scripture *and* the word of sacrament.

THE PRESENT ABSENCE OF THE RESURRECTION BODY

We turn now to the corpus of Scripture, the body of the text(s) about Jesus. From the epistles of St. Paul to the Gospels, the authors of the New Testament Scriptures are already plagued with the problem of the body of Jesus, present in both life *and even in death*, but profoundly *absent* both in resurrection and ascension. Nowhere in the Gospels is this paradox more apparent than in Luke's account of the encounter between the Risen Christ and the two travelers along the road to Emmaus. This narrative has been developed theologically most fully by Chauvet,[40] but has also been read by Marion, and our reflections here draw upon their considerable insights. Our primary focus is on the Emmaus story (Luke 24:13–35), culminating in a meal that takes the form of a Eucharist. We will relate this intertextually with John's Gospel, beginning with Jesus' encounter with Mary near the empty tomb, and climaxing with Thomas's declaration of belief (John 20). Attention will be given to the ways in which both the text(s), and the characters therein, struggle to apprehend the *present absence* of Jesus' body subsequent to his death, entombment and resurrection. We are also interested in how these post-resurrection encounters with Jesus' body relate intertextually to the

---

39. It appears to us that de Lubac somewhat makes this point, if in passing, when he writes: "between the Father and the Son there is a personal distinction, which, in any event, is the foundation of this ambiguity in the language" (ibid., 317). This resonates with what Žižek calls the "gap" that is internal to God: "It is the very radical separation of man from God that unites us with God, since, in the figure of Christ, God is thoroughly separated from himself—thus the point is not to 'overcome' the gap that separates us from God, but to take note of how *this gap is internal to God Himself*" (*The Puppet and the Dwarf*, 78).

40. See Chauvet, *Symbol and Sacrament*, 161–70, and *Sacraments*, 20–28.

Gospels' narration of Christ's pre-resurrection body (and bodily actions) as "eucharistic," as well as to the Church's liturgical enactment of the Eucharist.

Perhaps we should begin with a clarifying comment about our terminology. We regard the difference between *absent presence* (or *absence of the presence*) and *present absence* (or in Chauvet's usage, *the presence of the absence*[41]) to be an important one. Like Aristotle's distinction in *The Poetics* between "probable impossibilities," which are preferable to "implausible possibilities,"[42] we consider *present absence* to be the more profoundly paradoxical and thus preferable way to talk especially about bodies in general, and Christ's historical, sacramental, and ecclesial bodies in particular. To illustrate the importance of using these terms carefully, especially when applied to the body of Jesus, consider this passage by Stephen Moore: "Jesus' living presence among his disciples precipitated confusion; the absence of his dead body at the tomb precipitates confusion. The climactic scene of comprehension in Mark—the centurion's confession (15:39)—follows Jesus' desolate cry of abandonment at the apparent absence of God (15:34). At the moment in which Jesus departs his body, becoming absent, the centurion realizes in whose presence he has been, recognizes Jesus as an absent presence."[43] In this passage, the terms *presence* and *absence/absent* are tossed around rather loosely. Jesus as an *absent presence* is neither profound nor paradoxical: what was once present as a living body is now simply absent (dead). First, Moore contrasts Jesus' living *presence* to the *absence* of Jesus' corpse in the tomb—a tangible, physical body in life and in death. But then Moore seems to miss the point when he declares Jesus *absent*—"Jesus departs his body," by which we assume he implies a dichotomy, i.e., Jesus "spirit" vacates his "flesh"—when in fact his lifeless body is still profoundly present. This seems to violate the concepts of presence and absence by reducing them to spiritual rather than material (bodily) categories. However, as we shall see, the Gospel accounts of the post-resurrection encounters with Jesus, which bear an intertextual relationship to the sacramental *praxis* of the Church, wrestle with a body that is present *as an absence*, and this absence is narrated or interpreted to be a present presence: a new form of bodily presence which is manifest as and *contains* absence.

The Emmaus narrative, as both Chauvet and Marion observe, has embedded within it the structural features of the liturgy itself.[44] First, we

41. Cf. Chauvet, *Symbol and Sacrament*, 62–63, 404–5, passim.

42. Aristotle, *Poetics*, 41.

43. Moore, *Mark and Luke in Poststructuralist Perspective*, 39.

44. See Marion, "They Recognized Him; and He Became Invisible To Them"; Chauvet, *Symbol and Sacrament*, 161–70; Chauvet, *Sacraments*, 20–28.

have, by inference, an *ecclesia*; there are two disciples, Clopas and another, allowing Jesus to fulfill the promise that "where two or three are gathered in my name, I am there among them" (Matt 18:20). Second, they tell the story of Jesus; though he is present, to their perception he is absent, and yet he is the focal point of their discourse. Third, there is a clear opening and interpretation of the Scriptures, a hermeneutical moment, as evidenced by 24:27: "Then beginning with Moses and all the prophets, he interpreted (*di-ermeneuen*) to them the things about himself in all the Scriptures." Fourth, the liturgical connection which eventually formed between the Word and the Sacrament is embedded within the narrative: first, Jesus "breaks" open the Scriptures to the two travelers; *then,* he sits down with them to "break bread," which turns out to be their moment of recognition, of *anagnoresis*, the same moment in which his physical body disappears from their sight. Fifth, the meal itself resembles the shape of the Eucharist: Jesus "took bread, blessed and broke it, and gave it to them" (Luke 24:30).[45] Sixth, this eucharistic meal indeed becomes an encounter with the Risen Christ who is "made known to them in the breaking of the bread" (24:35). The correspondence between the Word and the Bread of life manifests itself in the notion of both the Scriptures and the sacrament—as de Lubac attests, "the *breaking of the host* and the *opening of the Scriptures*"[46]—as a locus where *revelation* or understanding occurs. Finally, there is a dismissal, a "sending out," as "they got up and returned to Jerusalem" (Luke 24:33) to share the good news with the rest of the disciples. As the word "gets out," meaning(s) break forth in the signs, the linguistic signs of Scripture and the sacred signs of the sacrament, simultaneously veil and unveil the divine mystery they represent.

Let us unpack this further. Christ's body is first present via remembrance, then via interpretation, and finally he is fully disclosed to them "in the breaking of the bread." In this way, as these verses unfold, Christ's risen body seems to gradually come into focus for the two disciples; yet we only know this when we reach the end of the narrative, after Jesus has vanished from sight, when the disciples exclaim to each other, "Were not our hearts burning within us while he was talking to us on the road, while he was

45. Chauvet, *Symbol and Sacrament*: "to speak of a 'breaking of bread' at Emmaus is a 'revealing anachronism; it is a phrase taken from the Christian liturgy,' showing that 'the story is intended to be understood in the time of the Church'" (164). Edward Yarnold also draws the connection between the Emmaus narrative and the Eucharist, asserting that "Whatever the intention of St Luke, the Church came to read a eucharistic meaning into the disciples' recognition of our Lord at Emmaus in the breaking of bread"; see Yarnold, *Rites of Initiation*, 51–52. However, Paul Bradshaw cautions against a hermeneutic that reads later, more established practice back into the biblical text; see *Origins*, 47–56.

46. De Lubac, *Corpus Mysticum*, 68.

opening the Scriptures to us?" (v. 32). The irony of course is that he is absent to their perception, even though he is physically present. By the end of the narrative, this conception is reversed—Jesus moves from being absent, even in his corporeal presence (he is there; they do not perceive him), to being a presence, even in his corporeal absence (in their moment of recognition, he vanishes). Put otherwise, "Jesus the Christ is absent as 'the same'; he is no longer present except as 'the Other.'"[47]

In *Deconstructing Theology*, Mark C. Taylor also reflects on this narrative. Taylor connects the problem of the present-absence/absent-presence of Jesus' body to language: "When Jesus was present, he was absent, when absent, present. Why? Because he is Word." The disciples "see, but do not see; they hear only the silence of an empty tomb."[48] Marion notes that for the two disciples, like the eleven to whom they take the news (Luke 24:33) and to whom Jesus subsequently appears (Luke 24:36), the problem is not any physical impairment of their vision, but rather their lack of hermeneutical categories by which to comprehend the physical presence of the risen Christ: "The obstacle . . . [is] the deficiency of concepts and significations: they do not have the rational means to think that of which they have sensible intuition."[49] What they see runs up against everything they know and believe. "They do not recognize him because they cannot even imagine that this is really him, Him, who has rejoined them, so far do their poor, cobbled-together, honest-to-goodness concepts find themselves outstripped by 'events' that leave them petrified within a matrix of irrefutable prejudices. Not that they would not want to believe: they simply do not even imagine the other hypothesis, it never crosses their minds, even for an instant. The dead man is dead, period."[50] In that subsequent encounter with the eleven, what Jesus presents as evidence is not the hermeneutical categories or concepts of signification that they lack, but rather his body: " 'Look at my hands and my feet. . . . Touch me and see; for a ghost does not have flesh and bones as you see that I have.' And when he had said this, he showed them his hands and his feet" (Luke 24:39–40).

The *skandalon* runs deeper still, as Chauvet has made clear in a lengthy passage that deserves to be quoted fully,

> the stumbling block for a Jew was not that God could resuscitate someone, for a majority of Jews at the time of Jesus did in fact believe in a final resurrection of the dead; nor was it that

47. Chauvet, *Symbol and Sacrament*, 170.
48. Taylor, *Deconstructing Theology*, 124.
49. Marion, "They Recognized Him," 151.
50. Ibid., 147.

God could resuscitate someone before the day of general resurrection. . . . Rather, it centered on a more radical point: Could
God still be God, our God, the God of our ancestors, if he raised
up *someone who had been justly condemned* to death for having blasphemed against the Law of God given to Moses, that is,
against God himself? Could God contradict himself? Could it
be, as Paul puts it, that someone who had died cursed by God
. . . would later be recognized as in fact God's blessing on all the
nations? What kind of God would allows his own Christ to die,
and then, in raising him up, vindicate him against his own Law?
Could it be, finally, that God himself rolled such a rock of scandal away from the mouth of Jesus' tomb? One gets an inkling of
the depth of the necessary conversion: for the two disciples it
is a question of accepting the possibility that the word of God,
according to the Scriptures, *has come to "deconstruct" their best
established evidence* concerning the "reality" of God.[51]

This rich passage deserves more attention than space permits here, but
Chauvet calls attention to the way the entire resurrection event scandalizes God himself. And yet this risk was taken first in the incarnation, in
which God took on human flesh, becoming irreversibly "body" for us, so
as to redeem all bodies. The entire Christ event is a means of grace, from
incarnation to ascension, and extending even to the continual sacramental
mediation of God through the materiality of creation. This is what Chauvet
means, at least in part, when he conceives of sacrament as "the grace of God
at the mercy (*au risque*) of the body."[52]

At the end of the narrative, the two travelers and Jesus arrive at the
house at Emmaus. Jesus seems ready to continue on, while the two disciples
intend to stay and rest. They invite Jesus to come in and eat with them, and
he accepts their invitation. Another reversal takes place wherein the guest
becomes the host: *Jesus, who is the stranger*, is the one who takes, blesses,
breaks and gives the bread. The text tells us "their eyes were opened, and
they recognized him; and he vanished from their sight" (Luke 24:31). "*Hoc
est corpus meum* [This is my body]," Taylor writes. "Hocus-pocus: a vanishing act that really opened their eyes!"[53] In Chauvet's reading, "Their eyes
open on an *emptiness*—'he vanished from their sight'—but an emptiness
full of a presence"—a plenitudinous void.[54] All attempts to pin (or pen)

51. Chauvet, *Symbol and Sacrament*, 168.

52. Chauvet, *Sacraments: The Word of God at the Mercy of the Body* (the French
subtitle reads *parole de Dieu au Risque du corps*).

53. Taylor, *Deconstructing Theology*, 124.

54. Chauvet, *Symbol and Sacrament*, 170. Recall from the previous chapter what

Jesus down to a metaphysic of presence will only result in the grasp of a dead body—the only encounter we can have with a Living Lord/Risen Christ is an encounter with the presence of his absence. As Taylor writes, "They see his presence in absence. But to do so, they must likewise see absence in their presence."[55]

John's Gospel takes this a step further by depicting Jesus' body materializing inside a locked room (John 20:19). The climax of the account, and in many ways of the entire book, is the moment Thomas's doubt turns to belief when he not only sees but is invited to interpenetrate Jesus' body. The invitation is striking especially in light of Jesus' command to Mary outside the empty tomb: "Do not hold on to me" (John 20:17). But Jesus does not invite Thomas to grab hold of his body—to *grasp* him (the cognitive parallel should not go unnoticed). Instead he is instructed to reach out his hand and place it in the wound in Jesus' side, into the gaping void which is the *symbolon* of his having passed through death.[56] This body, which cannot be grasped or even touched,[57] is the same Jesus, but different. These two bodies—the one that was placed in the tomb, and the one encountered after the tomb was found empty—bear a (dis)continuity that is neither similitude or identity. *"This is (not) my body."*

The disciples still struggle to accept the veracity of this in-credible body, which does not operate according to any of their expectations and confounds their comprehension. Jesus' statement to Thomas is "Do not doubt but believe" (John 20:27). It is important to note that nothing in the text, not even Thomas's declaration of faith ("My Lord and my God!" John 20:28), implies that his doubt was replaced with knowledge or certitude, but rather that it was converted into *believing*.[58] So finally, to prove once and for all, Jesus requests *food*, and in an act that defines his entire ministry, in ways more often scandalous than not, he eats with them.[59] Spirits and ghosts do

Pickstock refers to as "the *occurrence* of the impossible through Christological mediation, which reveals the void as a plenitude"; *After Writing*, 178.

55. Taylor, *Deconstructing Theology*, 124.

56. Recall that fracture, brokenness, is inherent to the original meaning of *symbolon*, and to its conceptual structure as we have framed it *vis-a-vis* Tillich and Chauvet (see ch. 1).

57. Marion, "They Recognized Him," 151.

58. Michel de Certeau has called attention to the weakness of believing in *La Faiblesse de Croire*; a portion of this work has been translated by Saskia Brown as "The Weakness of Believing," in *The Certeau Reader*, edited by Graham Ward, 214–43.

59. The preceding observations are also indebted to Marion's essay. He points out that the fish Jesus consumes in their presence connects this encounter to Jesus' multiplication of the loaves and fishes in the feeding of the multitude (cf. Luke 9:10–17; Matt 14:13–21; Mark 6:30–44; John 6:1–14).

not eat; bodies do. The body that will become sacramental food partakes of their food to demonstrate his corporeality. And so Jesus offers (again) his body as the sign and symbol of the grace—gracious and gratuitous—of God in and through the body.

(TRANS)CORPOREALITY

In light of the preceding discussion, it appears it is a mistake to regard Jesus' body as subject to the limits of bodies as we generally understand them. This is a body which incorporates both presence and absence. It is tangible without being graspable, visible without being circumscribed by what is seen. In *Cities*, Graham Ward uses the term *transcorporeality* to describe the "displacement" of Christ's body and its "intratextuality" to all other bodies.[60] For Ward, the "displaced" body of Christ is endlessly disseminated in and through other bodies, "physical bodies, social bodies[,] institutional bodies, ecclesial bodies, sacramental bodies."[61] The transcorporeal body "is fractured endlessly, by the Spirit, and yet also, simultaneously, gathered into the unity of the Word and the unity of the Word with the triune God. The eucharistic 'This is my body' performs that first act of dissemination, that first transcorporealism."[62] And so we see that transcorporeality is also, for Ward, a way of talking specifically about the eucharistic body, which "does not dissolve or ab-solve, it expands *en Christo*."[63] This is a useful concept to the present discussion as we attempt to understand the difficulty—what Ward calls the "ontological scandal"—of the body of God in the incarnate Christ. We will continue to use *corporeality* as a synonym for "bodily-ness," but will begin to employ Ward's term transcorporeality to indicate certain characteristics of the body of Christ—its brokenness, its displacement, its textuality and sexuality, and its operation as nourishing food and drink.

We have seen in the Gospels of Luke and John that Jesus' resurrection body, in the way it inhabits space and interacts with other bodies, does not operate according to our expectations of bodies. But is this characteristic also of Jesus' body *prior to* his crucifixion and resurrection? To answer this, we must return to the text of John's Gospel, which is also a jumping ahead as

60. cf. Ward, *Cities*, 81–116; cf. esp. 92–96 and ch. 4, passim. While space limits us from engaging Ward's conception as fully as it deserves, his writings have significantly informed the present work as it engages the question of body, and will continually illuminate the discussion that follows, not only in this chapter, but in Part Two as well.

61. Ibid., 93.

62. Ibid., 92.

63. Ibid., 95.

this text that will be considered more fully in chapter 5. In John 6, the "bread of life" discourse that creates such consternation for Jesus' listeners ("This teaching is difficult; who can accept it?" John 6:60), John has Jesus narrate his own body according to the figure of the manna of the Old Testament. We will not at this time explore all of the details or intertextual connections of this passage. However, illuminated by Chauvet's theological reading of this (inter)text, we find that it makes a significant contribution to our thinking about bodies and about Jesus' body at this stage in the discussion, in particular about the way Jesus' resurrection body, and by extension his sacramental body, is located outside all coercive economies of value and possession.

After Jesus feeds the multitude in John 6:1–15, the crowds return, expecting him to provide more bread to fulfill their bodily needs (6:26). Jesus tries to redirect their focus from "food that perishes," to "food that endures for eternal life" (6:27), but they demand a sign, which is yet another demand for bread: "What sign are you going to give us then, so that we may see it and believe in you? What work are you performing? Our ancestors ate the manna in the wilderness; as it is written, 'He gave them bread for heaven to eat'" (6:31). Jesus gently corrects their interpretation in vs. 32–33, saying that it was God and not Moses who gave the bread, "'For the bread of God is that which comes down from heaven and gives life to the world.'"[64] They said to him, 'Sir, give us this bread always.' Jesus said to them, 'I am the bread of life'" (John 6:34–35). Thus the symbolic connection is made between Jesus' body-as-bread and the manna upon which Israelites fed in the wilderness.

Chauvet highlights the characteristics of manna which place it outside the realm of market-value and exchange. If we read Chauvet's commentary against the backdrop of John chapter 2, Jesus' cleansing of the temple, we see that each text illuminates the other. Jesus drives the money changers out of the temple and chastises them for making His "Father's house a market-place!" (2:16).[65] This might at first seem disconnected to "the bread of life" discourse, but Jesus' body is implicated here as well in at least two ways. First, when the Jews demand some explanation or authority upon which Jesus has created this commotion, he remarks, "Destroy this temple, and in three days I will raise it up" (2:19). In an aside, John immediately interprets this for his reader: "he was speaking of the temple of his body" (2:21). Hence the crucified and resurrected body is of interest here, as throughout the

64. Jesus finally becomes exasperated with them and *destroys* the symbolic connection previously drawn between his body and the manna of old: "This is not like that which your ancestors ate, and they died" (John 6:58).

65. Interestingly, the parallel texts in the Synoptic Gospels (Matt. 21:12–17, Mark 11:15–19, Luke 19:45–48) fall much later in the timeline than John's chronology.

text. Second, Jesus' connection of his own body as the "bread of life" with the manna of the Old Testament places his "bread-body" precisely outside the economy of the marketplace, and so it is perhaps revealing that Jesus drives a wedge between the market and the house of prayer, the place of worship, which in John's explanation, is also being given a symbolic link to his body—*destroy this temple . . . the temple of his body.* So as zeal consumes him, he not only purges the temple (and/of his body) of the marketplace, but also by inference purges the market of the bread (and/of his body).

The economy of the marketplace has no place in Jesus' temple-body, and his bread-body has no place in the market economy. This is the nature of grace, of gratuitous gift, which cannot be bought or sold, possessed or hoarded. "Like the *manna* in the desert, which is perhaps its most beautiful biblical expression," writes Chauvet, "grace is of an entirely different order from that of value or empirical verifiability."[66] As it cannot be "known"—it is irrational—neither can it be "possessed"; it has no lasting *value*. "It appears literally as given free of charge, always free of charge, since it defies the laws of calculation. . . . It also defies the laws of capitalization and stockpiling: those who, disobeying Moses' order, tried to store some for the morrow saw that 'it bred worms and became foul.'"[67] In fact, similar to what we have been arguing about the structure of sacramentality, this uncircumscribability of the manna is not just a feature of its operation, but according to Chauvet it intrinsic to the structure of the manna itself: "Its very name is a question: *Man hu?* Its name is 'What is it?' Its consistency seems to be that of a 'something' which has all the traits of 'nothing.'"[68] As a prototype of Jesus' sacramental body in the Eucharist, this is fitting, for it manifests the present absence of the one who "*emptied himself*"—*became nothing*—"taking the form of a servant," which John also shows us in chapter 13 when at the Last Supper Jesus humbles himself and washes his disciples' feet.

In Christ, God becomes man in an act of ultimate *kenosis*—a movement consistent with the God who is the gratuitous, ever-given gift of love.[69] God, being continually self-emptying, taking on the form of a servant in the person of Jesus Christ, whose body, even in life, is ever out of reach. Even Christ's followers struggle to grasp and grapple with him—he speaks to them, teaching them, telling them stories, telling them that his flesh and blood are the food and drink that lead to eternal, interpenetrative life. Yet

---

66. Chauvet, *Symbol and Sacrament*, 44–45.

67. Chauvet, *Sacraments*, 88.

68. Chauvet, *Symbol and Sacrament*, 45.

69. Cf. Marion, *God without Being*, 45–49.

his teaching offends them (John 6:61), offends their desires for certainty, for possession, for bodies that are fixed and whole.

It is in the Eucharist, as the host is taken that it might be blessed, and fractured that it might be distributed, that we, too, are taken, blessed, broken, and given. To be *taken* requires dispossession of self. It must always be that we are Christ's *broken* body, for without this celebratory fracture, we cannot participate in God as the ever-given gift by also be(com)ing given, be(com)ing like God in God's givenness. These fragments constitute a community that is by its very nature elusive, illusory. The Church is visible as a community despite fragmentation. We are caught in a double-mediation. God, ever elusive, ineffable, invisible, offers to humanity communion with Godself by be(com)ing man in the person of Jesus Christ—this is the first mediation—and then, in Christ's death, resurrection, and ascension offers to humanity through sacramentality the real presence of the Divine, which is actually an absence—this is the second mediation. In both cases, the mediation is Christ: in the first instance, Jesus' singular, physical person, embodied historically, and in the second instance, the universal Body of Christ, the community of faith that is the Church, gathered to partake of this communion. "In Christ's ascension," Graham Ward writes, "his body is expanded to become a space in which the Church will grow."[70]

READING AND WRITING THE BODY

I am a body, yet my body is not all there is of me. I am bodily, yet my body is not my "possession"; I have no, or little, mastery over it. I am not my own (1 Cor 6:19). My body narrates my story even as my story is inscribed onto its skin, its scroll. The body is a text that cannot avoid communication, that demands to be read.[71] Ward reminds us that "Communication is embodied giving, and what I give is consumed by the others to whom I give. I touch upon their bodies by the presence of my own body heard and seen, smelt and sometimes tasted by them. The fluidity of time itself is the fluidity of identity. 'This is my body. Take eat. This is my blood. Drink.' The body is always in transit, it is always being transferred. It is never there, as a commodity I can lay claim to or possess as mine. This is the ontological scandal announced by the eucharistic phrase—bodies are never simply there (or

---

70. Ward, *Cities*, 94.

71. Writing these last two sentence, we are reminded of Peter Greenaway's provocative film *The Pillow Book* (1996), which is obsessed with the body as text/writing, and writing (on) the body.

here)."[72] Like language, the body places us at a distance from others, from every other, including God, and even including my self. But we have begun to understand this distance as contained within Godself. "It is the very radical separation of man from God that unites us with God, since, in the figure of Christ, God is thoroughly separated from himself—thus the point is not to 'overcome' the gap that separates us from God, but to take note of how *this gap is internal to God Himself*."[73] Žižek reminds us here that this gap is the irreducible condition not only of human experience, which we posit as a consequence of language and body, but is a characteristic of the God in whose image we are created and by whose Word, all that is came into being. (Comm)union with God, which is the purpose of sacrament, is only possible by learning to dwell within this gap, this wilderness. In the liturgy, we offer ourselves up to be consecrated, along with our material gifts of bread and wine: "made one with Him, we offer you these gifts, and with them, ourselves—a single holy living sacrifice." And it is by our participation in the Eucharist that "our life and yours [God's] are brought together in a wonderful exchange. He made his home among us that we might for ever dwell in you."[74] This concept of *liturgical dwelling* David Jasper has shown to be precisely and universally "the life of struggle with and in the body."[75] Liturgical dwelling *waits*. It keeps vigil. It is outside the sphere of work, of production. Yet liturgical dwelling begins with a profound sense of being in-the-body, being a body in-the-world; this as the condition of possibility for any encounter with the Absolute.[76]

Throughout the biblical text, Jesus' body is ever moving, ever slipping through people's ever-grasping hands. Only occasionally is Jesus "caught," as when the woman with the issue of blood touches the hem of his garment and is healed; Jesus is aware that "power has gone out" of him in this instance (Luke 8:43–48). To grasp Christ is to receive his power, to enter into a parasitic relationship with this unusual body. Even in his capture, trial, torture, and execution, Jesus' body cannot be handled in the usual way. This body defies all convention. It sweats blood in the agonies of deepest prayer.[77]

72. Ward, *Cities*, 91.

73. S. Žižek, *Puppet*, 78.

74. "Scottish Liturgy (1982) with Alternative Eucharistic Prayers," 6.

75. Jasper, *Sacred Body*, 175 (see 175–185). This thematic originates with Martin Heidegger's essay "Poetically Man Dwells," in *Poetry, Language, Thought*, and is developed considerably by Lacoste in *Experience and the Absolute*.

76. Cf. Lacoste, *Experience and the Absolute*.

77. Oliver Davies, "The Sign Redeemed," 221: "We can already see this [radically dislocated subjectivity] prefigured in the accounts of Jesus' *Todesfurcht* in Gethsemane where, according to the vivid language of a Lukan variant, 'his sweat became like great

It requires a kiss to even be apprehended by the authorities, the kiss of betrayal masquerading as brotherhood, or perhaps *vice versa*. During his trial, Jesus' body remains equally illusory, seeming to waver in and out of focus, to flare and fade before the very eyes of his accusers; his dispossession of his very self, represented in his silence, keeps his body just out of reach. It seems the only way his enemies can be sure that Jesus is even bodily at all—for remember, it has been said that this man is God's Son, which would certainly call the physicality of his body into question—is to enact violence upon his body. In all the drama of the Passion, Jesus' corporeality is perhaps only realized as a sure thing, but only for a moment, in his torture, as whip-straps meet with flesh, thorns sink into head, nails impale hands and feet, and as an unwieldy piece of wood, the instrument of his impending death, is dragged by this ghost of a man up the hill toward the site which will simultaneously be his execution and his exaltation. In his execution, Jesus' body once again slips from within reach as it is taken from the cross and caringly placed in a borrowed tomb. The more Jesus' body is broken, the more fractured and fragmented it becomes, the more elusive it becomes—*he is not here* (Luke 24:5). These fragments are too minuscule and yet simultaneously too vast, larger-than-life, to be held by human hands. And yet the more fractured and elusive this body becomes, the more *real* it becomes, for as the crumbs of Christ's bread-body and the wine of his blood run through grasping human fingers, a stain is left behind that will not wash away.

As we conclude Part One of this study, it should be apparent that the initiative of God to meet us in and through the material mediation of sacrament entails an interminable risk. This passage from Don Saliers puts it well:

> That is, if the practice of Jesus' memory and the calling upon God to make real the signs of bread and wine is to constitute our primary theology as Christians, is this not a most fragile foundation? . . . There is no need to deny the fragility of sacramental actions of the Christian assembly seen from a human point of view. Nietzsche, Freud, Marx, and others rightly see the weakness and human vulnerability in these practices. For them such practices are, amidst a world such as ours, an illusion. But the Eucharist and Baptism are precisely the divine vulnerability. For at the heart of the Eucharist are the broken symbols of suffering and death—God's humanity made visible and palpable. The risk is both divine and human. At the center of this limit, the self-emptying (*kenosis*) of God in human form and death.[78]

---

drops of blood falling down on the ground' (NRSV). I think it is important, however else we see these life-giving words, that we do not lose sight of their disturbing quality."

78. Saliers, *Worship As Theology*, 61.

PART TWO

Literary and Theological Perspectives

4

Fracturing
Brokenness and Sacrament

*Continually called to move beyond itself, the transcorporeal body
itself becomes eucharistic, because endlessly fractured and fed to
others. It becomes the body of Christ, broken, given resurrected and
ascended. . . . The transcorporeal body extends in its fracturing, it
pluralises as it opens itself toward an eternal growth. Only as such,
can the wounding, can the differences, be redemptive.*[1]

FRACTURE: "THIS IS MY BODY, BROKEN"

In Part One, the *skandalon* of sacramentality was established as a two-fold
scandal of language and the body. Beginning with language, this raises a
hermeneutical problem: how to determine meaning, significance, from
speech or text. But the *skandalon* of the body is also a hermeneutical problem: how to "read" the body, especially the present absence of Christ's "displaced" body, which overextends its bounds and incorporates all bodies.
In both cases, we encounter a plurisignificance that is unsettling. It seems
there is no possibility of singular or univocal meaning. However, it is here
that the eruptive truth of sacramentality arises, which is necessarily plural.
The texts and practices that take on a sacramental character in postmodern
life are means of grace *precisely* because their meaning cannot be nailed or

1. Ward, *Cities*, 95

91

narrowed down to a unity. When the body is broken, torn, rent asunder, so as to be given as nourishment, as food to be eaten, ingested, received into one's own flesh, the body can no longer be regarded as a pure or unadulterated unity, but only as a plurality. The body—Christ's human body, and ours, as well as the mystical body of the eucharistic host—is itself a text, presenting and representing itself to be read, consumed, digested. This thematic—the eucharistic body as a body fractured, consumed, and eroticized—will occupy us in Part Two of this study. The Eucharist demonstrates the body at the point of utter abasement, abjection, abandonment, and absence, and renarrates this body as *most really* present precisely in this absence, this moment of extreme kenosis—*"he made himself nothing"* (Phil 2:7).

By now, we have seen that, just as the body can be read as text, so also the text *is* a body: the *corpus* is a *corps* (in the sense this word has in French). However, though incorporating death (in) itself, it is not a dead letter (corpse) but a living story (corpus), a growing Body of work, as well as a community, a corporate body—a corps of writers and readers of the Body of the Word, and of the text of the Body. The story that gives content to the form of the Eucharist is bodied forth in and as text: biblical and liturgical, certainly, but also the text of body-language, of ritual action and collective performance, the body-at-prayer and in communion. And so we must attend to the body itself, its ineradicable materiality, endlessly and irreparably fractured, as a site from which the Eucharist derives its meaning, its plurisigificance.

For the remainder of this opening section, we shall engage the 1982 Liturgy of the Scottish Episcopal Church, which textually inscribes and liturgically performs a most unique moment of fraction.[2] We will progress from there to an excursus on the degradation of the eucharistic body of Christ, which incorporates the historical body which "hangs as one accursed," as well as the resurrection body that we touched on in chapter 3. This will set the stage for three literary explorations of the sacramentality of the body broken in contemporary fictions: Graham Greene's *Monsignor Quixote*, Ron Hansen's *Mariette in Ecstasy*, and Chuck Palahniuk's *Fight Club*.

In the Christological Prayer of the 1982 Scottish Liturgy, emphasis is placed on not simply the historical reality of the incarnate Christ, but echoing Jesus' "bread of life" discourse in John 6 (which we will consider more fully in the next chapter), the emphasis is on *flesh*: "the gift of your Son, born in human flesh."[3] This phrase is only included in Eucharistic

2. We are using *fraction* to indicate the liturgical moment of the breaking of the host in the Eucharist, and *fracture* more generally as a synonym for "breaking" or "brokenness."

3. *SL* 1982, 7

Prayer I, which is non-occasional and the most commonly used. Not only is the language of flesh used, in contrast to other less visceral language (form, likeness, body), but immediately the connection is made to the Word, as in the prologue to John's Gospel: "He is the Word existing beyond time, both source and final purpose, bring to wholeness all that is made."[4] The liturgy, then, inscribes this paradox, that the eternal *Logos*, which is both beginning and end, "source and final purpose," is also the baby born at Bethlehem, taking on helpless, infant flesh in a supreme act of *kenosis*. As St. Athanasius famously stated, "He was made man so that we might be made God."[5] This basic christological dictum is often taken to mean that he took on our humanity so that we could put on his divinity—and it is fairly certain that this is precisely what the author meant. However, Christ is not only divine, but both fully human and fully divine. And though created in God's image, and siblings with Christ by adoption through baptism and new birth into his Body the Church, we are not divine, but fully and irreducibly human. Which leaves us to ask, what did it really mean for Christ to become like us, in our humanity? And what does it really mean for us to be *like him in his humanity*? How do *we* "incarnate" the kenotic, all-too-human flesh of Christ in our own bodies?

The Scottish Liturgy provides one clue in the prayer of Oblation: "Made one with Him, we offer you these gifts, and with them ourselves, a single, holy, living sacrifice."[6] The moment of fraction, which we will soon consider, must be viewed against the backdrop of these words. The implication here is that because the Word became flesh—because the Son became incarnate in the baby, who went on to suffer, die, and was raised—what is being offered in the gifts of bread and wine, the symbols of Christ's broken body and shed blood, is both Jesus' life, which is intertwined with Godhead in the *perichoresis* of the Trinity, but our lives as well, "brought together in a wonderful exchange" because of the incarnation. So this offering of bread and wine—not mere grain and grape—is, in the words of the Alternative Offertory Prayer, both that which "earth has given and human hands have made . . . fruit of the vine, and work of human hands."[7] We offer what

4. *SL 1982*, 7

5. St. Athanasius, "On the Incarnation of the Word (*De Incarnatione Verbi Dei*)" 54.3, *NPNF*, 2:4. Online: http://www.newadvent.org/fathers/2802.htm [accessed 31 March 2010].

6. *SL 1982*, 8. The prayer of oblation is identical in Eucharistic Prayers I–IV. Eucharistic Prayer V is an anomaly. The same idea is present, but without the language of *sacrifice*: "together with him we offer you these gifts: in them we give you ourselves." Oddly in form V, these words are spoken only by the priest and not the congregation.

7. *SL 1982*, 27.

we have made, the product of our own *poiesis*, our making or doing, our "work." And yet our work is premised upon the original work of God in creation. Just as the creator is part of the creation and the artist is part of the art, so the offerers are part of the offering. When we give, we give of ourselves, and we give ourselves. This is true of the God who was in Christ as well. And yet, in each case, there remains a distance, an *other*-ness. When the congregation offers up their gift to be consecrated, blessed, broken and given, offered back to them as food that is both spiritual and yet very much real (what they eat is still wholly bread and wholly wine, whatever else it might be), what they offer is part of the created order, of which they are a part, all of which is the *poiesis* of the creative *Word* of God—in the words of the Nicene Creed, "Through him all things were made."[8] The material-ity of this bread and this wine, "the gifts of God for the people of God" as other liturgies state, is bound up with our corporeality, initially insofar as human labors produce bread and wine from grain and grape, and then as we receive it back and incorporate into our bodies the food upon which we feast. As the ancient fathers understood, we are being consumed in this act of consumption, "metabolized" into the body of Christ, individual members "made one with him," even as the elements are metabolized into our physi-cal flesh and blood.[9]

All of this hinges on what we suggest is the pivotal moment in the 1982 Scottish Liturgy: the fraction. After the celebrant breaks the host into two (or more) pieces with the words, "The living bread is broken for the life of the world," the congregation responds, "Lord, unite us in this sign."[10] In our survey of eucharistic liturgies, past and present, across a myriad of tradi-tions, we found little precedent for these words spoken at the fraction. The only reference points we uncovered were in some Eastern (Byzantine) litur-gies, wherein the priest is instructed to say ("in a low voice") at the fraction: "The Lamb of God is broken and distributed; broken but not divided. He is forever eaten yet is never consumed, but He sanctifies those who partake of Him."[11] Whether the *SEC* commission that produced the 1982 liturgy was

8. *SL 1982*, 4.

9. Cf. Louis–Marie Chauvet, "The Broken Bread as Theological Figure of Eucha-ristic Presence," in Boeve and Leijssen, eds., *Sacramental Presence in a Postmodern Context*, 248.

10. *SL 1982*, 20.

11. Cf. the Byzantine Liturgy of St. Basil and its successor, the Liturgy St. John Chrysostom, both of which date to ca. 800 and remain in use in Orthodox churches today (see R. C. D. Jasper and G. J. Cuming, eds. *Prayers of The Eucharist: Early and Reformed*, 114–15, 129–30). Both liturgies contain similar instructions at the fraction. However, in contrast to the *SEC* liturgy, there is no congregational response, and scant implication in the language that it is this brokenness—paradoxically "broken but not

drawing upon another source is uncertain,[12] but even here we encounter words of profound paradox, for how can something be "broken but not divided"? "eaten yet never consumed"? This is impossible insofar as we understand what bread *is* and *means* and what the body *is* and *means*; and yet, in the sacramentality of the liturgy, it becomes im/possible. Returning to the Scottish Liturgy, for all the flexibilities and alternative forms included by the commission, there is no alternative to these words at the fraction, and no indication (as there is elsewhere in the liturgy) that this moment, this enactment may be omitted. It is in the sign of profound brokenness, of fractured humanity—ours becoming Christ's and Christ's becoming ours—that the Church is given her true identity as the Body of Christ, an identity that is not a foundation but a gift, freely given, one of brokenness, of kenotic outpouring for the life of the world. The *ecclesia* misunderstands both the nature of its identity and the *gravitas* (in the sense not only of weight but of immanence, corporeality, this-worldliness) of its calling and mission when it neglects or seeks to domesticate this symbol of fracture, instantiated in every eucharistic liturgy even apart from the words of the Scottish Liturgy that interpret the symbol so explicitly. We are *united* as a Body—bodies given a Body—in a sign that is irreducibly and irreparably a sign of *brokenness*.[13]

---

divided . . . forever eaten yet never consumed" in these Eastern rites—which is the sign of the unity in and of the ecclesial Body of Christ. The profound christological paradox is present, but absent is the sense that, in this sacramental act, the Church receives its (comm)union with and as the Body of Christ in a symbol of brokenness. See also, C. Jones, et al., eds. *The Study of Liturgy (Revised Edition)*, 252–63.

12. In the Eucharist of the 1929 Scottish Prayer Book, ceremonial instructions seem to be given for two fractions. The first takes place during the institution narrative, the celebrant "acting out" with the elements the words "he took bread; and when he had given thanks, he brake it . . ."; then after the Lord's Prayer, the Presbyter is instructed to break the consecrated bread, saying: "The peace of the Lord be with you all; (Answer) And with thy spirit. (Presbyter) Brethren, let us love one another, for love is of God." Precedent for the 1982 words is absent in the 1970 liturgy as well, which more or less follows the 1929 form:

(celebrant) The peace of the Lord be always with you.
(people) And with thy spirit.
(celebrant) Beloved, let us love one another, for love is of God.

The implied basis for these words is the understanding of the Eucharist as an agape meal, a love feast. The 1982 commission betokens a radically different reading of this moment of the liturgy.

13. We recognize that the general interpretation of liturgical scholars is to view the fraction as mostly if not purely practical to the distribution/communion which follows, rather than symbolic. However, Geoffrey Wainwright admits some validity to a symbolic interpretation of the fraction: "In Churches in the BCP tradition, recent revision have removed the Fraction at the Prayer of consecration . . . and have restored it as a distinct 'action' between thanksgiving and communion . . . the tendency is *not* (as it long was in the Reformed tradition) to associate the Fraction with the 'breaking' of

We have observed some celebrants in the SEC interpret this moment through gesture and body-language as well. With the words "The living bread is broken," the host is snapped equally in two, and the priest spreads her arms widely apart, placing as much distance between the two halves as her body will allow. Less commonly, but occasionally, the celebrant will bring the two halves back together with the congregational response, the host appearing momentarily to once again be a unified whole. Yet the faultline cannot be repaired. The paradox of brokenness that is wholeness, wholeness that is brokenness, is interminable. *The living bread is broken.* The paradox reaches out and incorporates us. *Lord, unite us in this sign*, this symbol of fracture, this broken symbol, which all symbols (*symbolon*) are.[14] Our wholeness, as liturgical subjects, is fractured. Our unity, as a Body, is fragmentary. We are one, and we are many. Our (w)holiness is ripped through, our holes are exposed. The openings, the gaps, the distance not only between each individual and every other, but even within our divided Selves,[15] is acknowledged and *enacted* in the breaking of the bread. It is no longer a loss to be mourned or overcome, but a celebration of our true humanity, broken yet redeemed, in Christ's fractured Body.

THE DEGRADATION OF THE BODY OF CHRIST

Christianity, in its theological, liturgical, and artistic imaginations, cannot but be haunted by the image of Christ's broken body. Friedrich Herlin's painting *Schmerzensmann* (Man of Sorrows) (1469)[16] (see the front cover), depicts a grotesque body, exposing its gaps and fissures *precisely* as the location of the Eucharist. The body of Christ in this painting is the abject, emaciated body of the crucified Jesus, skin stretched taut over the ribcage, arms and legs disproportionately slender. The crown of thorns is on his head, and blood trickles down from his brow to his breast. The wound in his side is visible and flows the blood and (we assume) water to which Scripture and tradition attest. Almost imperceptibly, this trail of blood from the wound in

---

Christ's body on the cross (see John. 19.36! 'Broken' at 1 Cor 11.24 is secondary), but rather to see the Fraction, in so far as it is at all symbolic, in terms of the many and the one (1 Cor 10.16–17)"; Jones, et al., eds. *Study of Liturgy*, 332; see also Yarnold, *Awe-Inspiring Rites*, 51–52.

14. See chapter 1 of the present study.

15. Cf. Ricoeur, *Oneself as Another*.

16. This painting is reproduced in Caroline Walker Bynum's *Holy Feast, Holy Fast*, (plate 4) and *Fragmentation and Redemption* (fig. 3.9, 107). We discuss this painting further in the following chapter in relation to the body of Christ as food. See the cover of this book for a copy of the image.

Christ's side also flows down and then out from underneath his loincloth, and almost halfway down the inside of his right leg. According to Bynum, who draws upon Leo Steinberg's *The Sexuality of Christ in Renaissance Art and Modern Oblivion*, the link is made here between Christ's first wounding, his circumcision as an infant Jewish male, and his final wounding in the spear-pierced side on the cross.[17] From this wounded side, as has been interpreted by the early Fathers and modern readers alike, flows the waters of Baptism, the sacrament of initiation or identity, and the blood of the Eucharist, the sacrament of sanctification.[18]

Paradoxically, these openings in Jesus' body are simultaneously negative—the marks of his crucifixion are wounds, *aporias*, negations—and positive, generative, life-giving. Jesus eyes are open, penetrating the viewer—*see what you've done to me?*—even as they indicate a certain serenity—perhaps rather than the former, the gaze says to us, *this is what it means to "bear in the body the marks* (stigma) *of the Lord Jesus"* (Gal 6:17). This is what incorporation into Christ's body *looks like—I am the vine, you are the branches* (John 15:5). This decimated body, full of holes, is the holy body of Christ that gives life to the world. It is a dying but not-yet-dead body, yet one from which life springs forth, the Tree of Life growing past the limits of the crucified body, abandoned and nailed to the tree.

Herlin's visual representation of Christ's eucharistic body is consistent with Russian literary theorist Mikhail Bakhtin's characterization of the body's degradation in what he calls the "grotesque realism" of the literature of Rabelais:

> Degradation here means coming down to earth, the contact with the earth as an element that swallows up and gives birth at the same time. To degrade is to bury, to sow, and to kill simultaneously, in order to bring forth something more and better. To degrade also means to concern oneself with the lower stratum of the body, the life of the belly and the reproductive organs; it

17. Bynum, *Fragmentation*, 84, 89; Steinberg, *Sexuality of Christ*, 58–61, 160–62. In brief, Steinberg's thesis is that much medieval painting is fixated on the genital sexuality of Christ—his "male-ness"—as an indication of his true humanity in the incarnation. Bynum's response is that medieval theology, expressed in the art of the period, is also interested in Jesus' body as (allegorically) female: as a mother who nourishes the Church at her lactating breast, and the wound in Christ's side as the womb from which the Church is birthed in the sacramental symbols which spill forth; cf. Bynum, *Fragmentation*, 79–117.

18. cf. Ward, *Cities*, 97–116; e.g., "The medieval Church bears witness to this ambivalence in finding it appropriate to gender Jesus as a mother at this point, with the wounded side as both a lactating breast and a womb from which the Church is removed" (105; Ward cites Bynum here).

therefore relates to acts of defecation and copulation, conception, pregnancy, and birth. Degradation digs a bodily grave for a
new birth; it has not only a destructive, negative aspect, but also
a regenerating one. To degrade an object does not imply merely
hurling it into a void of non-existence, into absolute destruction, but to hurl it down to the reproductive lower stratum, the
zone in which conception and new birth take place. Grotesque
realism knows no other level; it is the fruitful earth and the
womb. It is always conceiving.[19]

Christ's degraded body, as depicted in the Herlin painting, is grotesque, characterized by its "protuberances and offshoots."[20] But in the crucifixion and resurrection, it is a reproductive body—*the seed must fall to the
ground and die.* Christ is almost always shown wounded, bleeding—his is
an "unfinished and open body . . . not separated from the world by clearly
defined boundaries; it is blended with the world. . . . It is an incarnation of
this world at the absolute lower stratum, as the swallowing up and generat-
ing principle, as the bodily grave and bosom, as a field which has been sown
and in which new shoots are preparing to sprout."[21] These transgressions
of bodily integrity and closed unity characterize the crucified, eucharistic
body as a grotesque body, and, we wish to claim, *vice versa*: the grotesque
body as a eucharistic body. Therein lies the truth of the cross and of the
liturgy, but in such a way as is unrecognizable from within the (theo)logic
of the liturgy itself—it can only be recognized from the outside, by revelers
and blasphemers, by the unruly Masses outside the Mass—from within the
profane framework of festival and carnival.[22] Indeed, as both Bakhtin and
Huizinga make explicit, "Nearly all the rituals of the feast of fools are a grotesque degradation of various church rituals and symbols and their transfer
to the material bodily level: gluttony and drunken orgies on the altar table,
indecent gestures, disrobing."[23]

And yet, what Bahktin indicates in his study, which Huizinga is sensitive to as well in his reading of the period—and, it stands to be said, which
the theologians of Radical Orthodoxy, who elevate the eucharistic practice
of this period as the pinnacle of the transcendent sacramentality of the

19. Bakhtin, *Rabelais*, 21. "The essential principle of grotesque realism," Bakhtin
writes, "is degradation, that is, the lowering of all that is high, spiritual, ideal, abstract;
it is a transfer to the material level, to the sphere of the earth and body in their indis-
soluable unity" (19–20).

20. Ibid., 29.

21. Ibid., 26–7.

22. cf. Ibid., 74–85, passim; see also Cox, *Feast of Fools*.

23. Bakhtin, *Rabelais*, 74–75.

liturgical city, completely overlook—is that provinces of literature and the arts are capable of exploring these themes in a way that the "sanctioned" discourses of Christian theology and liturgy seem unable to sustain. For example, Catherine Pickstock follows her teacher, John Milbank, who characterizes this as the period prior to which the *secular* did not exist in binary opposition to the *sacred*. If we follow this school of thought, we come to the conclusion that some "purity" of liturgical and sacramental doctrine and practice that characterized the Middle Ages was somehow destroyed by the Enlightenment and the solipsism that accompanies modernism; at best, this lost purity may be retrieved in postmodernity through a kind of second naiveté. Of course, as Jean-Francois Lyotard has explained, the postmodern and the premodern mirror one another in a kind of *anamnetic* remembrance,[24] which itself bears a liturgical resonance. Recognizing the pronounced re-emergence of the body, the theologians of Radical Orthodoxy accept a qualified postmodernism as a way of retrieving a harmonious rather than dichotomous understanding of immanence and transcendence, materiality and spirituality.[25] In this effort, their project is both successful and useful. However, Radical Orthodoxy fails to fully account for the fundamental paradox of the Middle Ages, the historical era they idealize for the high emphasis placed upon liturgy and the Eucharist as central features of civic life. For as Huizinga suggests, it is medieval culture that seems to most fully comprehend the fusion of the sacred and the profane. While perhaps not immediately apparent, Huizinga's conclusion stands in stark contrast to John Milbank's assertion that "Once, there was no 'secular.'" Milbank explains further: "And the secular was not latent, waiting to fill more space with the steam of the 'purely human,' when the pressure of the sacred was relaxed. Instead there was the single community of Christendom, with its dual aspects of *sacerdotium* and *regnum*. The *saeculum*, in the medieval era, was not a space, a domain, but a time—the interval between fall and *eschaton* where coercive justice, private property and impaired natural reason must make shift to cope with the unredeemed effects of sinful humanity."[26] In Milbank's vision (which lays the groundwork for most subsequent Radical Orthodox thinking), there was no sacred/secular dichotomy in the Middle

---

24. In "Answering the Question: *What is Postmodernism?*," Lyotard writes: "*Post modern* would have to be understood according to the paradox of the future (*post*) anterior (*modo*)"; *Postmodern Condition*, 81.

25. Here we limit our characterization of "Radical Orthodoxy" as a whole to the three editors of the defining volume *Radical Orthodoxy*, John Milbank, Graham Ward and Catherine Pickstock: cf. for Milbank, *Theology and Social Theory*; for Ward, *Cities of God*; and for Pickstock, *After Writing*.

26. Milbank, *Theology and Social Theory*, 9.

Ages because life was defined by and derived all meaning from Christian liturgy, the Eucharist in particular.[27] Milbank's thesis is that the modern conception of the sacred and the secular as opposing "spaces" or "domains" had to be constructed (falsely) or imagined, as the two in fact existed in harmony during Christendom (*Christendom* being a positive designation to Milbank and most all Radical Orthodoxy theologians). The secular, as a "between-time," was the *historical* location of the sacred, in other words, the sacred *in time*. Similarly, transcendence and immanence did not exist in binary opposition from one another, for in the Eucharist, heaven and earth, our lives and the Divine life, meet in the "wonderful exchange."[28] However appealing this might sound from the theological or liturgical viewpoint of Christianity (a somewhat conservative, Anglo-catholic Christianity at that), Huizinga casts this dynamic in a less beatific light when he characterizes the Middle Ages thus: "Life was permeated by religion to the degree that the distance between the earthly and the spiritual was in danger of being obliterated at any moment. While on the one hand all of ordinary life was raised to the sphere of the divine, on the other the divine was bound to the mundane in an indissoluble mixture with daily life."[29] In fact, as we have been trying to argue, the "profanation" of the Eucharist as a symbol is inevitable, as it is built into the structure of language itself, and as Huizinga observes, "the most tender of all mysteries, the Eucharist, is threatened in this way," through profane customary language itself.[30]

It occurs to us, however, that this "profane" and "profaning" tendency within the Eucharist is not only built into the structure of language (recall that the Eucharist is on one level a linguistic event, the work of the Divine *logos*), but is indeed inherent to the symbolism of the Eucharist, for in the complex metaphor Christ has given us, sacred and profane, presence and absence, divinity and humanity, life and death, abjection and glorification, are inextricably intertwined in a coincidence of opposites—this is the fundamental mystery of the incarnation of God in Christ, represented most profoundly and paradoxically at Golgotha, where hangs the ruined, lifeless divine body which invites us to feast upon it, not just with our eyes but actually consume it, flesh and blood. In this sense, that which "threatens" the Eucharist is derived from within the Eucharist itself: what we have called the

---

27. Catherine Pickstock has articulated this conviction even more fully than Milbank in her book *After Writing*. See ch. 2 of the present work for a fuller engagement with her work.

28. *SL 1982*, 6.

29. Huizinga, *Autumn*, 179.

30. Ibid., 178.

de/constructive core, or what Mark C. Taylor might call the a/theological core, of sacramentality.

The tendency of sacramentality to exceed its ecclesially defined strictures issues in the appearance of sacramental traces within the practices of everyday life. "The mind was filled with Christ to such a degree that the Christological note immediately began to sound whenever any act or thought showed even the slightest congruence with the life or suffering of the Lord," writes Huizinga. For example, "A poor nun who carries firewood to the kitchen imagines that she is carrying the cross. The notion of carrying wood by itself is enough to bathe the activity in the bright glow of the highest act of love"—Huizinga calls this a "profaning overflow" which "was equally the result of that overabundance of devotional content" characteristic of the period.[31] The distinction between the sacred and the mundane, the heavenly and the earthly, becomes so blurred that it was not uncommon for folk to refer generally to the eucharistic host *as "God."* In fact, Huizinga gives an account that if a priest were to pass by on a donkey, transporting the eucharistic host, a common person might exclaim the passing of "*un Dieu sur un asne*" ("a God on an ass/donkey"),[32] exemplifying this "profanation." Elsewhere he makes reference to satirical literature of the period which might include word-play on *saint/seins* (bosoms) and make sexual innuendos out of *devotion* (submission, piety), *confessor, bless/blessed* ("bénir," pregnant). These "obscene meanings" are indeed a parody of religious and liturgical speech, but in fact they are less a rejection or subversion of the religious as a de/constructive outworking of religious language itself.[33] In Huizinga's words, "Here is well demonstrated something of the dangerous contact between the religious and the erotic that the church, with good reason, so feared. . . . The profanation of daily religious practice was almost without bounds."[34]

We will return to the relationship between the religious and the erotic in due course (chapter 6). However, here we simply wish to note the confluence—in the medieval as well as the postmodern imagination—of the sacred with the secular, the mundane, and even the profane. This confluence is dependent in no small measure upon the liturgy as a defining medieval cultural form; indeed, it makes no sense apart from the rhythms of life as shaped by the liturgical assembly and ecclesial feasts, festivals and fasts. As Huizinga writes, "In all these *sacrileges* of the holy through the

31. Ibid., 220–21.
32. Ibid., 178.
33. Ibid., 182.
34. Ibid., 182.

unabashed intermingling with sinful life there is more naive familiarity with liturgy than open godlessness. Only a culture that is thoroughly permeated with religiosity and that takes faith for granted knows these excesses and degenerations."[35] In other words, Milbank's "once there was no secular" is precisely equivalent to saying "once there was no sacred"—because if at the height of the "liturgical city," the two were indistinguishable, then neither sacrality or secularity has any real meaning.[36] Huizinga speaks of an "entirely externalized religion," which at first resonates with the emphasis Radical Orthodoxy places on materiality. However, superstition and supernaturalism abound in the Middle Ages. He reads the veneration of the Eucharist not as a exaltation of materiality (as Pickstock or Milbank might want to see it), but a profound *materialism*. As Huizinga explains about this period, "the urge to worship the Lord in a visible sign soon found a different and sanctioned form: the monstrance, which displaced the Host itself as an object of veneration."[37] Throughout his narrative of the period, which differs considerably from Pickstock's idealized (though perhaps not theologically spurious) reading, Huizinga observes: "The process is one of ongoing reduction of the infinite to the finite; the miracle is reduced to atoms. To every holy mystery, there attaches itself like a barnacle to a ship, a growth of external elements of faith that desecrate it. The miracle of the Eucharist is permeated with the most sober and material superstitions: that one cannot go blind or suffer a stroke on the day one hears a Mass or that one does not age during the time one spends at a service. The church has to be constantly on guard so that God is not brought too close to earth."[38] We believe Huizinga, along with capturing the spirit of the Middle Ages through a myriad of concrete examples from folk culture, has *almost* captured what we are calling the de/constructive core of sacramentality as well. What he, too, fails to make explicit is that which we have been arguing all along: that this tendency of sacrament is not the product of "a growth of external elements of faith that desecrate" the "holy mystery," but rather, that this movement, this de/constructive core resident is *within* sacramentality itself. Indeed the outworking of the implications of the Eucharist's profound immanence reaches a certain height in the Middle Ages, before it is demolished by the Cartesian shift toward the disembodied thinking subject.

And so the sacred is profaned. The profane is sacralized. The degraded, fractured body of Christ, which is present as an absence in the sacramental

35. Ibid., 186 (italics added).
36. cf. Ibid., 199–202.
37. Ibid., 234. We suspect that Pickstock would disapprove of this displacement.
38. Ibid., 177.

body of the Eucharist, and in the ecclesial body of the Church gathered to celebrate the sacrament, cannot be circumscribed to these rituals.[39] It is a body which pours itself out into even the most mundane tasks of everyday life. Every meal becomes a Eucharist. Every bath becomes a baptism. Is not this spill-over of the sacramental into the mundane both inevitable, inasmuch as it is the outworking of the inner logic of sacramentality itself, and thereby even desirable? It is precisely this tendency towards excess and "spillage" or "slippage" that indicates the sacramentality of the Sacraments, and this is *precisely* the scandal at the heart of the Eucharist: the scandalous risk of mediation which necessarily entails a process of seemingly endless secularization, insofar as the "sacred/secular" distinction is maintained at all.

We now turn to three contemporary literary explorations of the sacramentality of the body broken. Our aim is to demonstrate how these novels are attuned to this dynamic, this sacramental imagination, in ways that Christian theology and liturgy dare not think.

IMAGINING THE EUCHARISTIC BODY IN *MONSIGNOR QUIXOTE*

We begin at an ending. An old priest staggers into the chapel of a monastery. He is under sedation, having previously suffered an automobile crash. He approaches the altar as his caretakers rush in after him, rightfully concerned about his condition. They watch as he begins to mumble from his broken memory the remaining fragments of the Mass, the performance of which has so profoundly shaped his clerical life. When the time comes for the Eucharist, his delirium prevents him from realizing that the communion elements are absent. He consecrates an imagined wafer and chalice, and then extends this imaginary sacrament to a single communicant. The unlikely recipient has been the priest's faithful companion throughout the narrative, the Marxist ex-mayor of their village, an avowed atheist who yet in this moment kneels and partakes in an act not of faith but of friendship, in the hope that it may provide comfort to his *compañero* in these final moments. The priest's fingers press against his tongue, the felt presence of the really absent Host. The monsignor's final act: this errant Eucharist. His dying words, "By this hopping . . ."—this leap of faith—a phrase he never completes, as he had

---

39. "The rite of the breaking of the bread is of primary importance in this respect, in that it manifests that if the presence of Christ is indeed inscribed in the bread and the wine, it is not circumscribed there"; Chauvet, "The Broken Bread," 259.

previously in the story: "by this hopping . . . you can recognize love."[40] The priest collapses into the arms of his friend, his body broken, his heartbeat now as absent as the literal bread and the wine.

Where is the "real presence" in this imaginary Eucharist, shared between a defrocked, delirious priest and an ardent atheist? Professor Pilbeam, a character brought in near the end of the novel to play the role of skeptic, claims there is none: "There was no consecration. . . . There was no Host and no wine." But Father Leopold, the man of faith, challenges him: "are you sure? . . . [we] *saw* no bread or wine. . . . But Monsignor Quixote quite obviously believed in the presence of the bread and wine. . . . Do you think it's more difficult to turn empty air into wine than wine into blood? Can our limited senses decide a thing like that?"[41] It is not a question of *reality*—"Fact or fiction—in the end you can't distinguish between them—you have just to choose"[42]—but rather of *truth*, as are all questions of theology, a question of truth and fiction, framed within a fiction, a doubly-fictional Eucharist that somehow becomes a "true fiction."[43] At the heart of this event is *love*, the greatest of the three Christian virtues according to St. Paul (1 Cor 13:13). The "infinite mystery"[44] of this imaginative (which is perhaps not to say *imaginary* after all) Eucharist becomes for the unbeliever a true sacrament in his communion with and remembrance of his friend, the good priest, and an inkling of openness to the possibility of salvation extended not *in spite of* but *by virtue of* his fractured body and broken imagination.

Monsignor Quixote presents a narrative which challenges our understanding of communion and extends, if not obliterates, the boundaries of community. Graham Greene's novel, which arises from a profoundly Catholic imagination, raises significant questions about the nature of the Eucharist, about friendship and "communion," and in a subtle way posits that the *real presence* found in this Christian practice is, in truth, the presence of the "other"—an emphasis on the connection between persons, and the sacrality of human relationships. The novel, which on one level is a delightful intertextual conversation with Cervantes' *Don Quixote*, recounts the journey of these two companions, the Priest and the Mayor: both misfits of sorts, both men whose identifying roles—for one religious, for the other political—have been stripped from them. Yet these two men, both of whom

---

40. Greene, *Monsignor Quixote*, 246–51.

41. Ibid., 253–54.

42. Ibid., 238.

43. "Doubly-fictive" because it is a "fiction" (work of imagination) in the novel's narrative, which is itself also a fiction. Again, however, we would make much of Douglas Templeton's conception of "true fiction." (Cf. Templeton, *True Fiction*).

44. Greene, *Monsignor Quixote*, 254.

in their own way have spent their lives in the service of the people, find in communion with one another the identification of which they otherwise have been robbed.

Early in the novel, the Priest states that "Habits can be comforting, even rather boring habits"[45]; indeed, almost as if to prove this, after we have witnessed Father Quixote's unmaking (a de/construction of sorts), his final comfort lies in the performance of his oldest and most identifying habit—the celebration of Eucharist. Near the novel's conclusion, when as Father Quixote staggers toward the altar to begin his fragmentary liturgy, it occurs to us that, even in this most broken condition, the Priest remains in possession of *only* his identity as eucharistic celebrant, a vocation which is of course performed *in persona Christi* and is therefore not his possession at all—rather *he* is the one possessed. Hence, even in his delirium, Father Quixote's words to his friend, the Mayor, are both poignant and prophetic, perhaps spoken *in persona Christi* as well: "I don't offer you a governorship . . . I offer you a kingdom."[46] *Today you will be with me in paradise.*

Monsignor Quixote is also a work of social, political, and religious commentary, written by a novelist who maintained rather tenuous relationships with each of those three spheres. Similarly, the titular character functions on multiple levels. He is a simple parish priest who nevertheless poses a threat to the ecclesial authorities. He is a faithful follower of Christ who becomes an unwitting radical—like Christ, by association. He is a saint who regards himself a sinner, and who treats sinners as though they were saints. The good priest is suspended between two realms, the here-and-now and the kingdom-coming ("here, not yet here . . . now-and-not-yet," to borrow a phrase[47]), between the material and the mystical (*hoc est enim corpus meum,* which appears as hocus pocus[48]). Wittingly or not, he draws those around him into another world, one which is sacramental, shaped according to the shape of the liturgy. Likewise the novel which tells his story, a work of fiction, draws the reader outside the ordinary and into the extra-ordinary, a fictional realm made no less "real" by its existence within imagination. This is precisely what poetic language does: it takes the mundane—common words, ordinary materials—and imbues it with wholly new significance. Jesus does this at the Last Supper,[49] at the institution of the Eucharist, when

---

45. Ibid, 33.
46. Ibid, 213.
47. Willimon and Hauerwas, *Lord, Teach Us,* 57.
48. Taylor, *Erring,* 103.
49. For the Synoptic accounts, see Matt 26:26–29; Mark 14:22–25; Luke 22:14–20; see also 1 Cor 11:23–29 for St. Paul's instructions to the church in Corinth.

he took bread and wine, common elements at any meal, the most basic elements of human subsistence, and radically transformed their meaning, altering his followers' perception immediately and for centuries to come. We, like they, submit to the power of the poetic through the willing suspension of our disbelief, which constitutes poetic faith.[50] By this leap of faith, "this hopping," we enter a narrative world where we are transformed. There is always an element of risk involved, but "when one has to jump, it's so much safer to jump into deep water."[51]

In his dying action, Monsignor Quixote's very body becomes sacramental, the present absence of his life standing in for the absent bread and wine. It is his body which, throughout the narrative, has been taken, even as it has been forsaken; blessed, even as it has been cursed; broken, even as in death it is restored to eternal life; and finally *given*. His suffering body is a visible challenge to the Powers of the World, which have sought to strip him of his ecclesial identity, the essence of his persona. In this final act, their failure is exposed. Even in his delirium, he breaks their rules and recites the Mass—re-sites the liturgy in his very body—extending communion to a professing atheist, an ex-communicant, one who for decades has avoided confessing his manifold sins. In his death, however, the lingering trace of his body becomes a sacrament, to the discomfort of his unbelieving communicant, who would prefer to discount the efficacy of this strange communion: "once when I was young I partly believed in God, and a little of that superstition still remains. I'm rather afraid of mystery . . ."[52] And so, at the end of the novel, the Monsignor's lifeless body is taken away, but his atheist companion is haunted, not by the real presence of the risen Christ in whom he does not believe, and not by the fear that he has eaten and drank of his own condemnation (1 Cor 11:29), unworthy recipient though he is, but by "the love which he had begun to feel for Father Quixote, [which] seemed now to live and grow in spite of the final separation and the final silence—for how long, he wondered with a kind of fear, was it possible for that love of his to continue? And to what end?"[53] Of this imaginative, doubly-fictive Eucharist that concludes the novel, David Jasper asks: "Can we ever do more than this even with the fragments of bread and the drop of wine, touching for a

---

50. Coleridge, *Biographia Literaria*, 179. See also Holman, ed., *Handbook to Literature*, which describes "suspension of disbelief" as "The willingness to withhold questions about the truth, accuracy, or probability of characters or actions in a literary work. This willingness to suspend doubt makes possible the reader's temporary acceptance of the vicarious participation in an author's imaginative world" (435).

51. Greene, *Monsignor Quixote*, 238.

52. Ibid., 254.

53. Ibid., 256.

moment the deepest interiority of the body—our bodies—with the divine absent presence in an act of pure remembrance?"[54]

MARIETTE IN ECSTASY: STIGMATA AS SACRAMENT

We turn now to another novel that is the product of a Catholic imagination, profoundly shaped by the Eucharist. Ron Hansen's *Mariette in Ecstasy* is the story of a young, beautiful postulant who shortly after taking her vows and entering the priory receives the *stigmata*, the marks of Christ's wounds on her flesh (cf. Gal 6:17). Her body, as we shall see, becomes a sacrament to some, and a horror to others, upsetting the liturgical life of the community. The novel is part mystery, part romance, and part what we would like to call a "theo-poetic" excursus on faith, in particular faith in-the-body—that is, faith as realized and practiced in-the-body, and the body as the object of faith.

Mariette is seventeen years old when she enters the priory as a postulant. Just before the High Mass in which she will be received into the convent, we find her in her room, preparing to go away forever, to be wedded to Christ. She is a commixture of brimming sexuality and fervent spirituality. Her body, precisely in its sexual potential and appeal (even to her!), is the locus of her spiritual devotion. "She stands and unties the strings at her neck so that the pink satin seeps onto a green Chinese carpet that is as plush as grass. And she is held inside an upright floor mirror, pretty and naked and seventeen. She skeins her chocolate-brown hair. She pouts her mouth. She esteems her full breasts as she has seen men esteem them. She haunts her milk-white skin with her hands. *Even this I give You.*"[55] She gladly offers herself as a living sacrifice, a consecration of the erotic to God by denying herself and others of her body's potential for sexual fulfillment. Her body is her offering, her sacrifice. All the while her father, Dr. Claude Baptiste, broods in the kitchen below her, "looking outside as if his hate were there."[56] Like Graham Greene's Professor Pilbeam, he a man of science and reason, serving the narrative as a foil to faith. He does not—cannot—understand Mariette's religious vocation. He has already "lost" one daughter to the convent, Mariette's sister Annie, twenty years her elder, known at the priory as Mother Céline, the Prioress of the Sisters of the Crucifixion. In the end, he does not attend Mariette's reception.

54. Jasper, *Sacred Body*, 111.
55. Hansen, *Mariette*, 8–9.
56. Ibid., 9.

According to author Ron Hansen, Mariette Baptiste is a fictional composite of several late nineteenth- and early twentieth-century female stigmatics: Saint Thérèse de Lisieux, Anne Catherine Emmerich, Louise Lateau, Theresa Neumann, and Gemma Galgani.[57] Hansen, a devout Catholic, explains in his essay "Stigmata" that "Mariette Baptiste was, for me, the real thing, a stigmatic; but I inserted an element of questionableness because in my research that seemed standard even in those instances in which the anomalies seemed authentic and all medical science could do was scratch its head in puzzlement."[58] In this essay, Hansen betrays the very ambiguity his fiction maintains; and yet, if we are to avoid the intentional fallacy, we must consider Hansen's statement alongside the beliefs and conclusions drawn by every other reader of the text. For, even granting that he is the author of the text, the character of Mariette, and the events he describes, are not *his own possession* in any ultimate sense; as inhabitants of the narrative, they take on a life of their own. Even the author must stand outside this text and interpret, just as every reader must decide (or decide to remain agnostic) whether Mariette is "the real thing," as Hansen chooses to believe, or simply an attention-seeking, hyper-sexed hysteric; whether she is the "holy girl," the "cause" of the showers of blessing Sister Catherine describes,[59] or a clever and manipulative "flirt."[60] In the end, Père Marriott, who is called in to assess the disruption caused by Mariette's situation, is convinced of her authenticity; Mariette's father, Dr. Claude Baptiste, maintains his skepticism: "You all have been duped," he tells them. "Christ talks to her. . . . The Devil strikes her when she tries to pray. She is always saying preposterous things; that's why we don't get along."[61] The clash between the spiritual/mystical perspective and the scientific/medical mind is evident here—again, reminiscent of the final pages of *Monsignor Quixote*, the discussion between the priest (believer), the professor (skeptic) and the Mayor (atheist), who

57. Hansen, *Stay Against Confusion*, 8–9. Hansen's first essay in the collection, "Writing as Sacrament" (1–13) briefly discusses the novel; herein he explains about the historical figures which comprised his character Mariette. He discusses the phenomenon of the stigmata, and his novel, in more depth in the essay "Stigmata" (177–191).

58. Ibid., 177–78.

59. Hansen, *Mariette*, 73. Sister Saint-Denis describes Mariette thus: "Christ shines from her. She is Christian perfection. She is lovely in every way" (68).

60. This accusation comes later in the narrative; even after Mariette receives the stigmata and therefore takes on a more serious and even revered personae within the community, Sister Marguerite accuses "dear sweet child" Mariette of being a "flirt" (69–70). On the other hand, in her interview for Father Marriott's investigation, Novice Sister Philomène states simply: "I think she is a saint" (*Mariette*, 62).

61. Ibid., 173.

in the end opens himself up to a kind of *mysterium tremendum et fascinans* toward which he had previously remained closed.

Mariette's religious devotion is fully embodied, even prior to her receiving the stigmata. The day she enters the convent as a postulant, she is directed to the haustus room and instructed to remove all her worldly clothing, which she now exchanges for her habit: "She uneasily gets out of her dress and underthings and she is a girl again, four years old and staring at the Christ in her mother's room. She touched his pink mouth, the pink rent in his side, and then she touched her own mouth. She touched underneath her skirt."[62] In this passage, Mariette's childhood memory floods onto her present in an anamnēsis of bodily intertextuality, her early impression of the symmetry between Christ's transcorporeal body and her own. We recall this chapter's earlier discussion about the femininity of Christ's body, as characterized by Bynum: his lips, her lips . . . the labial opening in his side, the one between her legs. The Christic body informs her own, transgressing the boundaries of time, place and even gender. Immediately following this recollection, she kneels and is soon thereafter found in a state of religious ecstasy, "unclothed and seemingly unconscious as she yields up one hand and then the other just as if she were being nailed like Christ to a tree."[63] Her body, blessed and cursed, as the recipient of the wounds of Christ.

However, early in the novel, Mariette demonstrates that she can also coyly play the role of *provocateur*. Upon joining the religious community, many of the other sisters are instantly taken with her beauty and kindness. An interesting scene occurs when a few of the sisters are, by their own admission, "being bad," which consists of stealing away to a secret location and talking about old boyfriends from their past lives before entering the convent. One sister recounts an occasion when, from the window of their secret place, they watched a young woman and a man in soldier's uniform having a picnic in a nearby field and, after the meal, kissing on a green plaid blanket. To the bemusement and intrigue of the other sisters, "Mariette smiles tauntingly and says, 'You don't suppose it was me, do you? . . . Are you sure it was a *green* picnic blanket?'"[64]

Hansen deliberately leaves to the imagination the question of Mariette's sexual experience prior to entering the convent, and likewise any surviving traces of carnal desires may or may not be genuine to her character; indeed they may only appear as such to those less holy than she. Even the significant question of her virginity is addressed with brilliant ambiguity

62. Ibid., 16.
63. Ibid., 16.
64. Ibid., 36.

in Hansen's prose when Mariette is being examined by Sister Aimée, the Infirmarian.

> "Weren't you going to ask if I'm a virgin?"
>
> Sister Aimée assesses Mariette. "I assume you are."
>
> Mariette says nothing and then she says, "Yes."
>
> "Isn't that interesting," says Sister Aimée, and she simpers as she puts towels away.[65]

Mariette's seeming eagerness for this question to arise—followed by her hesitation—and finally the knowing "simper" with which Hansen colors Sister Aimée's response all heighten the sense of inconclusiveness contained within the scene. Is she proud of herself for remaining chaste? Is she even telling the truth? Hansen's third-person narrator is decidedly *not* omniscient, and avoids any temptation to psychoanalyze or speculate. The narrator reports events with an almost journalistic prejudice toward the observable facts. It is the *characters themselves* who disclose emotions, question motivations, and subjectively approach the psyche. The narrator simply tells us what happens: Mariette is discovered in states of religious ecstasy; she develops bleeding wounds in the palms of her hands, which later inexplicably vanish. What this *means*—how to interpret these happenings—remains inconclusive. Her body becomes a mysterious text to be read, studied, interpreted, and even consumed.

Part One of the novel concludes with an excerpt of Mariette's writing. In response to her ecstatic "experiences," she is given pen and paper and instructed by Père Marriott to write truthfully about her experiences. But her description is one not of God's overwhelming presence, but of the absence and even abandonment of the Divine. She writes of Christ's promise to her of trials and suffering to come. Christ speaks to her, and his words are anything but comfortable: "*You will be punished and humbled and greatly confused, and Heaven will seem closed to you, God will seem dead and indifferent . . . you will seek me fruitlessly and without avail for I shall hide in noise and shadows and I shall seem to withdraw when you need me most. . . . And yet you will believe, Mariette, but as if you did not believe; you will always hope, but as if you did not hope; you will love your Savior, but as if you did not love him . . .*"[66] This confluence of presence and absence, of belief and disbelief—this reversal and coincidence of opposites—resonates with the story of the meal at Emmaus, and of course with the very

---

65. Ibid., 22.

66. Ibid., 43–44 [italics in original].

heart of the Eucharist. At Emmaus, Christ is no more than a stranger—the crucified Christ is utterly absent to the two travelers—until that moment of *anagnoresis*, recognition in the breaking of the bread. Then they know him, realize and experience his unmistakable presence, but at the very moment when he vanishes from their sight. In this sense, as Chauvet has argued, what the two travelers experience is the *presence of the absence* of Christ; or, put otherwise, they experience his absence *as a presence*, and renarrate their experience of this absence as presence in yet another reversal. They rush to tell the other disciples that they have been with Jesus, when in fact, when they were with him, they knew him not. This confluence of presence and absence, this "as if" quality is characteristic of how Christ is experienced in the sacrament—as absent (bodily), but an absence which is peculiarly experienced and (re)narrated *as presence* in symbols received, consumed *as if* they are Christ's body and blood. ✝

Sister Hermance, the first to show Mariette around her new home, becomes particularly devoted to the new postulant. She is unflatteringly described as "a sweet, fat, toad-eyed novice" who "trundles" down the corridors of the convent.[67] The non-linear structure Hansen's prose inter-cuts the narrative of Mariette's entry into and life within the convent with snatches from a future conversation—we later regard it as a kind of debrief or exit interview upon Mariette's dismissal from the convent—describing and analyzing the events that have taken place, reminiscent, again, of the epilogue to *Monsignor Quixote*. In a snippet of the later dialogue, Mariette's interviewer tells her that Sister Hermance was in love with her, news which Mariette receives with nonchalance.[68] Against this backdrop, we are taken through several events involving both Mariette and Sister Hermance which deliberately blur the already ambiguous lines between the sexual and the spiritual. The most potent occurs in a scene where we find Sister Hermance nursing Mariette, whose degraded body has been ravaged by the effects of the stigmata. Like Monsignor Quixote during his strange final Mass, Mari-ette is delirious, drifting in and out of consciousness, her capacity for speech obliterated. Sister Hermance

> lifts up the postulant's hand and presses it into her habit as she considers Mariette. "We aren't amazed. We thought you were different from the first."
>
> She pets Mariette's wrist and kisses a knuckle. She whispers, "We are so privileged." She holds the palm open and kisses it. "You have turned your face from me too often. You have been

67. Ibid., 19.
68. Ibid., 22.

✱ Is it that Christ's Body and Blood are not present as we expect reality to be present (and thus as if absent) only in essence?

frightened by my affection." With reverence Sister Hermance licks the blood inside the hand wound. "I have tasted you. See?" Tears streak shining paths down her cheeks as she says, "Ever since I first met you, I have loved you more than myself."

Half a minute later she says, "You know this is true."

"She stares at Mariette's sleep and whispers, 'You have been a sacrament to me.'"[69]

Mariette is an object of sexual desire, a mysterious body/language to be interpreted, a sacramental presence and a horrible and horrifying curse to the community. She is all of these things. However, the locus of her body's sacramentality hinges primarily upon the manifestation of the stigmata, which, like the wounds of Christ which they mediate, are present *absences*— holes, aporias in the flesh, tears in the fabric of embodied humanity. We turn now to examine one more example of contemporary fiction which, un- like our two previous examples, does *not* arise from a Catholic imagination, and incorporates no explicitly sacramental or even Christian content, and yet is fixated on the sacramentality of the body broken.

SACRAMENTAL SELF-ANNIHILATION: *FIGHT CLUB* AS EUCHARISTIC COMMUNITY

Chuck Palahniuk's novel *Fight Club*[70] expresses a particular theologi- cal, perhaps more appropriately a/theological, vision: in a God-forsaken world, where identity is based on jobs, cars, and clothes, the only way out of this mind-numbing cycle of acquisition is destruction, beginning with the societally-conditioned, acquiescent self. This powerful novel offers a disturbing and challenging indictment of contemporary society, includ- ing aspects of religion, gender, sexuality, corporatization, and materialism. In conversation with Palahniuk's novel and the postmodern a/theology of Mark C. Taylor, this section will explore the a/theological visions of these two writers. What emerges is an ontology based on human brokenness, incarnation, mortality, and sacrifice. As these themes are embedded in the theology of the Eucharist, the Church, as a eucharistic community, should realize the universality of these themes—brokenness leading to wholeness, death giving way to life—which are personified in the life and message of Jesus Christ. Identity *will* be found in *communitas* based on common belief

69. Ibid., 121.

70. Palahniuk, *Fight Club*; cf. the excellent film adaptation, directed by David Finch- er, starring Brad Pitt as "Tyler Durden" and Edward Norton as the nameless narrator.

and practice, whether in the sanctuary or, as in *Fight Club*, after-hours in the basement of a bar. If the Church purports to offer true "being" found in a community gathered around the image of the broken, crucified Christ, she must reach out and touch the body's brokenness within contemporary society.

In Mark C. Taylor's postmodern a/theology, the concept of *erring* stands within a subversive tradition that includes the person of Jesus Christ and his followers. *Erring* is a "praxis" of sorts; it must be actively practiced. This is for Taylor not simply theory but something that we must *do*, in which we must *participate*: "The a/theologian asks errant questions and suggests responses that often seem erratic or even erroneous. Since his reflection wanders, roams, and strays from the 'proper' course, it tends to deviate from well-established ways. To traditional eyes, a/theology doubtless appears to be irregular, eccentric, and vagrant. At best it seems aimless, at worst devious."[71] It is not for *idle* wanderers, but *aimless* wanderers engaged in "ceaseless wandering."[72] We become the James Dean, the "rebel without a cause," as we know that "such erring is purposeless, [although] it does not necessarily represent desperate exile."[73]

Taylor continues to draw upon the figurative image of the *carnival* as the celebration of our incarnation, mortality, and death. We celebrate our incarnation in the same way we celebrate the incarnation of the W/word. Just like Jesus, we are incarnate; we are carnal, fleshly, made of meat. And as we wander "along the margins of the carnival, the body appears to be *grotesque* . . ."[74] While others might be ashamed of this, errers relish their incarnation, even the bodily functions that demonstrate their mortality— sustenance, defecation, procreation. Like John and Jesus, we will be called deviant, perverse, or worse—crucified perhaps (but "blessed are you . . ."). Walter Brueggemann describes the "church as an alternative community in the world[,] . . . as a home for the odd ones."[75] In a sense, Christianity should never be able to escape the wilderness, for its very instantiation is as a community of outsiders, rebels, wanderers, "(ab)errant" ones, whose lives model the life their founder. His was a life that never escaped the margins: birth

71. Ibid., 13.

72. Ibid., 71.

73. Ibid., 15.

74. Ibid., 162.

75. Brueggemann, *Postmodern Imagination*, 36. Granted, Brueggemann remains committed to a concept of God as an "originary" source, which places him within a much more conservative theological framework. But in this instance his critique of the role and function of the church is not far removed from Altizer's and is conducive to our purposes.

in a barn, quarantine in the desert, life on the move, death on a cross, and a disappeared body that, in the end, vanishes like a phantasm. And the death of the Word that became flesh, this *particular* death, contains the marks of the errer, the piercings, the markings, the brokenness and degradation of the body, and the mutilation of the flesh. It is a spectacle on display for a voyeuristic mob—seeming to be simply "aberrant entertainment provided by aliens and freaks."[76] Recall the grotesque body of *Fight Club*'s anti-hero Tyler Durden, hitting rock-bottom at the novels end (and its beginning), face bruised, the corners of the mouth split into "a jagged smile from ear to ear."[77] We are both protagonist and antagonist in this drama. "Maybe self-improvement isn't the answer," he posits; "Maybe self-destruction is the answer."[78]

Palahniuk's narrative begins where it actually ends—with the final act of self-destruction. But the story begins with an insomniac, to whom "everything is so far away, a copy of a copy of a copy."[79] Our main character should be happy with his perfect life: he is single, has a well-paying (if ethically questionable) job as a risk assessment manager for a "major" auto manufacturer, and a 1700-square-foot condo equipped with all of the trendiest accoutrements, "full of condiments but no real food."[80] On the sarcastic recommendation of his doctor, he begins attending support groups for people with various diseases and maladies, hoping this will cure his inexplicable insomnia. He discovers that if he can succumb to the emotion of these meetings—the crying, the hugging, the guided meditation—he is suddenly able to sleep like a baby. Our "hero" finds temporary comfort in these "communities," these decaying groups holed up in church basements sharing their deaths with other dying strangers. While he attends many such

---

76. Taylor, *Hiding*, 95.

77. Palahniuk, *Fight Club*, 207.

78. Ibid., 49.

79. Ibid., 21. Taylor also discusses this notion of abysmal mimesis: "Since the human subject's full realization of the *imago dei* necessarily entails the *imitatio christi*, the self is actually an image of an image, an imitation of an imitation, a representation of a representation, and a sign of a sign. By becoming a copy of a copy, the self paradoxically becomes itself. In struggling to relate itself to itself, the human subject attempts to enact the complex movement of repetition that would fulfill the divine mandate: 'Become what you are!' The aim of this imitative repetition is self-appropriation. By means of the activity of self–relation, the subject attempts to take possession of itself and to secure its identity. The interplay of image, imitation, and identity reveals that the stages on life's way that comprise the believer's journey to selfhood repeat the stations of the cross marked by Christ" (*Erring*, 40).

80. Ibid. 45. This description of the contents of the narrator's refrigerator is, in a way, a metaphor for his entire life.

meetings, his primary group is "Remaining Men Together" for men with testicular cancer—many of whom have had their testicle(s) removed. This seems to be the solution to his problem, for he discovers in these groups, with his little healthy life surrounded by so much death, that "losing all hope was freedom . . . every evening, I died, and every evening I was reborn. Resurrected."[81] But this quasi-religious "fix" does not last long, especially when, upon returning home from a business trip, he discovers that his condo has been destroyed in a mysterious explosion. This is when he becomes acquainted with Tyler Durden, who up until the end of the novel is written as a distinct character, but who turns out to be an insane, risk-taking, totally repressed facet of our narrator's fragmented persona.

Tyler helps the narrator along a journey toward enlightened self-discovery via self-annihilation. They seek to cultivate their repressed, primal nature as both animal and man through their creation of "fight club." This support group does not meet in the stale basement of a church but rather after-hours in an obscure bar. This support group has not been emasculated but is rather is being re-masculated (testicles remain intact). This support group does not hug and say prayers and submit to guided meditation but rather beats the shit out of each other just for the sake of doing it—nothing personal: "You aren't alive anywhere like you're alive at fight club. When it's you and one other guy under that one light in the middle of all those watching. Fight club isn't about winning or losing fights. Fight club isn't about words . . . There's grunting and noise at fight club like at the gym, but fight club isn't about looking good. There's hysterical shouting in tongues like at church, and when you wake up Sunday afternoon you feel saved."[82] Fight club is the anti-church, or it is the church for the anti-hero. They evangelize by keeping it all a secret—"The first rule about fight club is you don't talk about fight club."[83] (This is also the second rule.) "You don't say anything because fight club exists only in the hours between when fight club starts and when fight club ends."[84] These men who congregate in their bar-basement sanctuaries in the wee-hours of Sunday mornings, searching for something deeper, something meaningful, even in pain and destruction, breaking the rules of the outside world and making their own rules; these men find access to another world, another kingdom, where everything is upside-down. They increase in numbers because they find others like them: "You have a

81. Ibid., 22.

82. Ibid., 51.

83. Cf. the "Messianic Secret" in Scripture—Jesus' instructions that his followers "tell no one" of his identity as the Messiah. This appears most notably in Mark 8:27–30; cf. Mark 1:43–45.

84. Ibid., 48.

class of young strong men and women, and they want to give their lives to something. Advertising has these people chasing cars and clothes they don't need. Generations have been working in jobs they hate, just so they can buy what they don't really need. We don't have a great war in our generation, or a great depression, but we do, we have a great war of the spirit. We have a great revolution against the culture. The great depression is our lives. We have a spiritual depression."[85] Their "counter-evangelism" is effective. Fight clubs are set up first all over the city, then in most major cities throughout the country. Their "little acts of rebellion" organize and develop until fight club becomes "Project Mayhem," the goal of which is "the complete and right-away destruction of civilization."[86] A community in the purest sense emerges; Tyler knows that "everything is more fun as a shared activity."[87] To be a part of Project Mayhem means first the complete relinquishment of personal identity and property. To become "disciples" the members shave their heads and burn their fingerprints off with lye.[88] Have they read the Gospel of St. Matthew? "If any want to become my followers, let them deny themselves and take up their cross and follow me, for those who want to save their life will lose it, and those who lose their life for my sake will find it" (Matt 16:24–25). The Apostles' Creed of fight club goes something this:

> You're not how much money you've got in the bank. You're not your job. You're not your family, and you're not who you tell yourself . . .
>
> You're not your name . . .
>
> You're not your problems . . .
>
> You're not your age . . .
>
> You are not your hopes . . .
>
> You will not be saved . . .[89]

The outcome of the novel is not necessarily the point here. Our aim in bringing this fictive work into dialogue with Taylor's a/theology is to construe Chuck Palahniuk's "community" *Fight Club* as one that errs, and one that deliberately transgresses, commits *errors,* and most significantly celebrates the sacramentality of the body broken. The fight club community embraces death and destruction; they reveal and revel in their bodies, their

85. Ibid., 149.

86. Ibid., 76, 125.

87. Ibid., 84.

88. Ibid., 160.

89. Ibid., 143.

carnality—even, by necessity if not intention, their criminality. Fight club is out to destroy civilization, to turn the *status quo* into *status perversum*. The members know they will never be content with the world as they know it; they must establish an alternative, a world in which death is life, in which the goal is not getting ahead but "hitting rock bottom," in which bodies are beaten and broken and blood is spilled. This is their ritual. This is their celebration, their Eucharist. That which is incarnate cannot be perfected. This community is formed in the shape of a cross, this symbol of death— Golgotha, marked by the X of the skull and bones, is the location where everything is turned on its head.[90] Death is life. Up is down. Sacred is profaned and the profane is sacralized.[91] The words of the tempting serpent are, "You will not surely die" (Gen 3.4). Contrarily, the words of *Fight Club*'s prophet are, "Believe in me and you shall die, forever."[92] "I *die daily*" are St. Paul's words (1 Cor 15:31 NASB), in the steps of the one who gives the invitation, "Take up the cross."[93]

Can any direct interface exist between these visions of eucharistic brokenness and our understanding of the Christian Church as a "eucharistic community"?[94] The Christian ecclesial community is defined by, and in a sense created by, the practice of and participation in the sacrament of the Eucharist, celebrating the death of Christ for the salvation of the world. In the Eucharist, Christians do not merely *recall* but enact and embody Christ's redemptive crucifixion. The Eucharistic meal is a celebration of Christ's broken body and shed blood, poured out freely, willingly, sacrificially. "This is my body, which is given for you. *Do this* in remembrance of me" (Luke 22:19, italics mine). We are called upon to act; this is praxis. We can speak or write, for these are certainly actions as well, but in the Eucharist, "what happens . . . doesn't happen in words."[95] It is the performance of this sacrament which instantiates and gives life to the community. It is the breath of life that is also the dying breath, the death-rattle, (re)creating the community as the *imago dei* which is only realized in the *imitatio Christi*.

---

90. Taylor, *Erring*, 62.

91. Ibid., 160–61.

92. Palahniuk, *Fight Club*, 145.

93. Matt 10:38; 16:24–26; Mark 8:34–36; Luke 9:23–24; 14:27; 17:33.

94. William Cavanaugh uses this phrase throughout *Torture and Eucharist*. While *Torture and Eucharist* deals primarily with the Eucharist as a response to the destruction of physical bodies via state-sanctioned torture in Chile under Pinochet, Cavanaugh's text resonates with our purposes in its description of the Eucharist as subversion, as an act of resistance to the this-worldly "powers-that-be."

95. Palahniuk, *Fight Club*, 51.

The word *eucharist* means literally "a giving of thanks," but the Greek root *charis* ("favor, grace, thanks") is also akin to *chairein* ("to rejoice"). In this celebration, body and blood are bread and wine. Taylor's carnival is the venue for this celebration in which "the blood of the incarnate word appears to be intoxicating wine, the bringer of riotous revel."[96] As solemn an event as it is in most places of Christian worship, the repressed logic of the Eucharist calls out to be a Dionysian celebration not of life but of death. (Would we commemorate Christ in such a way if it were *not* for his death?) This death in all its senselessness is the only passage into life, into meaningful existence. Meaninglessness yields meaning *ad infinitum*. Only infinite death produces authentic life and true salvation. This is the rationale, which is of course completely unreasonable, for our festivity, for our feast of fools.

The Eucharist seems to be transignificant with much of what we have discussed so far. That is, in remembering Christ's sacrifice through this sacrament, in this communal longing after a "real presence," the Eucharistic community is faced with the reality of *absence*. For Taylor, these two are brought together in an a/theology in which there is only absence, in which everything is dispossessed of its identity; similarly, the characters of *Fight Club* are a generation of men longing for a God *and* father, a God who is truly *Father*.[97] In this subversive celebration, we acknowledge that these mere symbols are all we have. Divinity is lost and God, our father, is dead. "When God is dead," writes Taylor, "it becomes clear that 'not only is the only true paradise the paradise that we have lost, but the only regained paradise is in the final loss of paradise itself.' This loss is grace."[98] Like the members of fight club accessing their "alternative kingdom" (but only during the hours of fight club), the Eucharist is but a brief foray into another world (but only in that mystical moment), a world that is very different from the one we now know. "[In] the Eucharist," Cavanaugh writes, "the church deconstructs the world and is caught up in to the Kingdom . . . the church anticipates the Kingdom . . ."[99] The kingdom is not of this world. Nor is this a simple reversal or inversion of the structures and powers of this world; rather, it is the *rupture* of this world, a deconstruction that gives way to (re)construction. "The result is a 'confusion' of the spiritual and the temporal, and invasion of worldly time and space by the heavenly, and thus

96. Taylor, *Erring*, 160.

97. Palahniuk, *Fight Club*. "If you're male and you're Christian and living in America, your father is your model for God. And if you never know your father, if your father bails out or dies or is never at home, what do you believe about God?" (141).

98. Taylor, *Erring*, 169. Taylor is quoting Altizer in *Total Presence*, 94.

99. Cavanaugh, *Torture and Eucharist*, 250.

the possibility of a different kind of social practice."[100] This is not merely a glimpse of what is to come, but a momentary window of access to it. It is the kingdom coming, here but not yet. This practice constructs its broken, fragmented practitioners into a community that, in the absence of Christ on earth, literally becomes the body of Christ, the Church—beaten until near death, yet still a sanctuary for the "odd ones."[101] "They all know what to do. . . . No one guy understands the whole plan, but each guy is trained to do one simple task perfectly."[102] Only our combined efforts can effect change or work toward a common goal. The goal is the upheaval of the world; this is what it means to "Eucharitize" the world.[103]

This is subversive; this goes against the grain. "[Our] culture has made death something wrong."[104] Death is to be avoided by all means possible, sparing no effort or expense. But this is the way of the world, the way of humanism; this is not the way of Christ or his followers. On the contrary, salvation is only achieved through death. "The first step to eternal life is you have to die."[105] We wander the margins, live life on the edge, far from safety. "[If] I don't fall all the way, I can't be saved. Jesus did it with his crucifixion thing. I shouldn't just abandon money and property and knowledge[,] . . . I should be running toward disaster. I can't just play it safe anymore."[106] We must join in celebrating the deaths of the martyrs, of Jesus and the saints, of Tyler Durden and Robert Paulson.[107] "As such, martyrdom recalls into being a people . . . and makes their life visible to themselves and to the world. They remember Christ and become Christ's members in the Eucharist, reenacting the body of Christ, its passion and its conflict with the forces of (dis) order."[108] The Eucharistic meal, partaken by the Eucharistic community, is coordinate to Tyler Durden's "little acts of rebellion." "Opposition to the powers and principalities of the world is written into the very narrative of

---

100. Ibid., 251.

101. Brueggemann, *Postmodern Imagination*, 36.

102. Palahniuk, *Fight Club*. 130. See also Paul's account of the Body of Christ in 1 Cor 12:12–27.

103. Cavanaugh, *Torture and Eucharist*, 14.

104. Palahniuk, *Fight Club*, 103.

105. Ibid., 11.

106. Ibid., 70.

107. Ibid., 176–80. This chapter describes the death of Robert Paulson, a casualty of Project Mayhem. "Only in death will we have our own names since only in death are we no longer part of the effort. In death we become heroes."

108. Cavanaugh, *Torture and Eucharist*, 64–65.

the death and resurrection of Jesus Christ which is commemorated in the Eucharist."[109]

Like Taylor in both theory and practice, we play freely with the words, the concepts, of the liturgical embodiment of Christ, the Word of God made flesh: "When freely enacted, the drama of the word proves to be self-consuming. While the incarnation of the divine is the death of God, the dissemination of the word is the crucifixion of the individual self. This dismemberment inflicts an incurable wound, which gives birth to erratic marks and errant traces."[110] In this celebration, we relinquish our own identity; we are brought face to face with death. We are made radically aware of our own mortality, our own carnality and "incarnationality." "To drink the word that has become wine is to suffer death. . . . The word is spread through the crucifixion of the self."[111] St. Paul's words indicate an acceptance of this: "For to me, living is Christ and dying is gain" (Phil 1:21). We must take after our founding member, our Tyler Durden, our Jesus Christ. Indeed, living as Christ lived necessitates death; it requires a self-sacrifice that must be total, nothing held back. "From now on, let no one make trouble for me; for I carry the marks of Jesus branded on my body" (Gal 6:17). Arriving finally at the *end*, which is not finality but fulfillment, beginning,[112] we may discover that "it's only after you've lost everything . . . that you're free to do anything."[113]

The literary explorations on the theme of bodily brokenness as sacrament contained in this chapter are legitimated by the conception of sacramentality set forth in Part One. We have drawn upon the understanding of the (trans)corporeality of the body in chapter 3, the indeterminacy and fragmentary nature of language considered in chapter 2, and the inherent brokenness of the symbol itself in chapter 1. We turn now to a theme that scandalized the eucharistic practice of the earliest Christians, and which continues to echo down through the ages as a reminder of the scandal of sacramentality even in recent fictions: the universal taboo of cannibalism.

---

109. Ibid., 273.

110. Taylor, *Erring*, 120.

111. Ibid., 142.

112. We are reminded of what David Jasper calls "a fraction of language" that takes place in the reading of James Joyce's *Finnegans Wake*, in which the final words of the book are not the end, but circle back around to the opening line only to begin again; cf. *The Sacred Body*, 148–56. "Language . . . truly begins only when conversation and speech are truly impossible, an end that is the true beginning, as in Jesus' final word from the cross . . . 'It is finished'" (149).

113. Palahniuk, *Fight Club*, 70.

5

Consuming
Cannibalism and Sacrament

*Eating the things of the world, including the practices of anthro-
pophagy and theophagy . . . or eating the body and drinking the
blood of Christ, all belong to one obvious and crucial mode of
world-appropriation . . . eating the world as the most direct way of
becoming one with the things of the world in their tangible presence.
. . . Eating the world, then, will always trigger the fear, for humans as
bodily parts of the world, that they might themselves be eaten. And
this is precisely why most human societies make the eating of human
flesh taboo . . .*[1]

CANNIBALISM: THE BODY AS FOOD

In the previous chapter, we examined the traces of sacramentality in the broken, fractured body of Christ and the bodies of characters in contemporary
literature. In this chapter, we will focus on the *skandalon* of the Eucharist
as it relates to bodily consumption. We deliberately employ the ambiguous phrase *bodily consumption* precisely because it implies both eating—the
physical, digestive processes associated with bodily consumption—as well
as the more cannibalistic connotation of the phrase: the consumption of
the body (as food) as well as the body's consumption (of food). To grapple

1. Gumbrecht, *Production of Presence*, 86–87.

with the Eucharist as *necessarily* scandalous and scandalizing to Christian doctrine and ritual, the importance of this node in the referential network from which the Eucharist derives its significance must not be underestimated. For if the scandal of sacramentality is bound up with the materiality and corporeality of the body, we eventually arrive at the necessity of food as nourishment for the body.

Indeed, eating plays a significant role in the narrative of Jesus in Scripture, reflecting both the importance of food and dietary practices to the Jewish tradition as well as the centrality of the ritual meals of the early Christian movement. Anthropologist Gillian Feeley-Harnik makes clear that food was "one of the most important languages in which Jews expressed the relationship among human beings and God. . . . Food was identified with God's word as the foundation of the covenant relationship in Scripture and in sectarianism. During the inter-Testamental period, as God's word become increasingly identified with the law, food law came to represent the whole law. Sectarianism was expressed above all through differing interpretations of the dietary rules. Violation of the dietary rules became equivalent to apostasy."[2] This passage indicates a symbolic continuity between food and word, which implies the relationship between body and language: food symbolizes law, which symbolizes covenant, which symbolizes the very word of God itself. Food, as a language, is without doubt a body/language, as it communicates only by being consumed. Similarly, "Christians of the first century C.E., as observant Jews, used the language of food to establish both the legitimacy of Jesus and the novelty of his interpretation of the law."[3] That the earliest Christians elected to eat a meal together as an encapsulation of their fundamental belief in the incarnation of God in Christ and their faith in his bodily resurrection was not unusual in itself, for as practitioners (with Christ) of the Jewish faith, they were accustomed to dietary practices that were internally coherent to adherents of the faith, but nonsensical to the surrounding culture.[4] So with Feely-Harnik we may establish that food is a language, a system of signification. Like circumcision (a Jewish practice equally absurd to those outside the faith), it was a symbol of the covenant relationship between God and Israel.

Doubtless what made this a scandalous practice in the eyes of those outside the Christian communities was that this meal was imbued with overtly cannibalistic symbolism. The early Church was by no means unaware of this interpretation of their liturgical practice, which created a stumbling

2. Feeley–Harnik, *Lord's Table*, 165.

3. Ibid., 166.

4. Chadwick, *Early Church*, 19.

block from the outset. Early Christians were accused of cannibalism, incest, and infanticide, mostly on the basis of misapprehended liturgical and sacramental practices, an issue addressed by both Justin Martyr and Tertullian. While Justin Martyr attempts to explain away the confusion (and with it the scandal), defending Christians as "good citizens and keepers of the commandments," and describing Christian liturgical and sacramental praxis in a way that is credible and defensible to the civic and political powers of the day,[5] Tertullian's more sarcastic response maintains the scandal, in a way. Addressing the accusations, he writes: "Monsters of wickedness, we are accused of observing a holy rite in which we kill a little child and then eat it; in which, after the feast, we practise incest, the dogs—our pimps, forsooth, overturning the lights and getting us the shamelessness of darkness for our impious lusts."[6] Tertullian continues his extended farce: "Come, plunge your knife into the babe, enemy of none, accused of none, child of all; or if that is another's work, simply take your place beside a human being dying before he has really lived, await the departure of the lately given soul, receive the fresh young blood, saturate your bread with it, freely partake."[7] The "reward for these enormities," Tertullian tells his imaginary initiate, is "the promise of eternal life. . . . Initiated and sealed into things like these, you have life everlasting. Tell me, I pray you, is eternity worth it? If it is not, then these things are not to be credited. Even although you had the belief, I deny the will; and even if you had the will, I deny the possibility."[8] In his attempt to expose the absurdity of this pagan misunderstanding of the Christians' sacred rites, he subtly concedes the validity of the basis of the misunderstanding by pointing to the murderous and cannibalistic rites already prevalent in the culture. Detailing the bloody practices of various tribes and even the Roman arena, Tertullian argues: "If you partake of food like this, how do your repasts differ from those you accuse us Christians of?"[9] In a helpful passage from *Beyond Belief,* Elaine Pagels engages Tertullian's response to the scandal of early Christian eucharistic practice, observing that

> early followers of Jesus, like the majority ever since, saw the sacred meal in a much stranger—even macabre—way: as eating human flesh and drinking human blood. . . . Tertullian satarizes the reaction of outsiders to this peculiar practice. . . . Despite his sarcasm, Tertullian cannot dispel the shocking fact that the

5. Justin Martyr, *First Apology,* ch. LXV–LXVI. *ANF* vol. I.

6. Tertullian, *Apology,* ch. VII. *ANF* vol. III.

7. Tertullian, *Apology.* Quoted in Pagels, *Beyond Belief,* 18.

8. Tertullian, *Apology,* ch. VIII. *ANF* vol. III.

9. Tertullian, *Apology,* ch. IX. *ANF* vol. III.

Christian "mystery" invites initiates to eat human flesh—even if only symbolically. Pagans might be repelled by the practice of instructing newcomers to drink wine as human blood, but devout Jews, whose very definition of *kosher* (pure) food requires that it be drained of all blood, would be especially disgusted.[10]

It is evident, then, that a tension is present in the sacramental symbol from the earliest stages of Christian worship. With his biting sarcasm, Tertullian may endeavor to dismiss the accusations of cannibalism as ridiculous, but as Pagels points out, his attempt to unmask the absurdity of these allegations *simultaneously* reveals the inescapable association of the Christian Eucharist with not simply bodily consumption (eating) but with the consumption *of the body* (cannibalism). In fact, in a footnote Pagels suggests the possibility "that Paul and his followers adopted this ritual to repel traditionally minded Jews and so to set themselves apart from Jewish communities."[11] Whether or not this is the case, one thing is certain: "By placing the drama of Jesus' death at the center of their sacred meal, his followers transformed what others would see as total catastrophe—what Paul calls 'scandal'—into religious paradox: in the depths of human defeat they claimed to find the victory of God."[12] As we have continuously endeavored to articulate, Pagels attests that "the sacred meal took on not a single meaning but clusters of meanings that became increasingly rich and complex."[13] It is the outworking of this symbolic matrix that we are calling the de/constructive core of the Eucharist, which is but one instantiation of the scandal of sacramentality. The cannibalistic images are not glossed over, and yet this explicit association with cannibalism eventually fades into obscurity after the legalization of Christianity and its eventual establishment as the state religion in the early fourth century, with the unveiling of the mystery of the heretofore secret ritual to which only baptized Christians were admitted. And yet, as Pagels points out, "despite the weirdness of such images—and perhaps because of it—every version of this last supper in the New Testament, whether by Paul, Mark, Matthew, or Luke, interprets it as a kind of death-feast," but paradoxically "one that looks forward in hope."[14]

When Jesus gave his body and blood for the life of the world, the sacrificial system of old was annihilated as well. No more must flesh be destroyed

10. Pagels, *Beyond Belief*, 18–19.
11. Ibid., 194, fn. 36.
12. Ibid., 20.
13. Ibid., 22.
14. Ibid., 25.

or blood spilled as payment to God for sin.[15] Jesus' identification of his own physical body as the bread of life, which must be eaten to obtain eternal life, as well as his association of himself with the manna that nourished the children of Israel during their wilderness wanderings, extracts his given body and blood from the economies of value, exchange and productivity that characterize other religious sacrificial rituals by which the gods receive payment and are thus appeased. The Eucharist, then, celebrated in remembrance of Christ, while never a "bloody" sacrifice, cannot be understood apart from sacrifice (as attested by most Catholic sacramental theology[16]), if even in the negative, for it is a radical refiguring of the meaning of sacrifice. However, drawing upon René Girard,[17] Chauvet proposes a radical alternative to traditional interpretations by introducing the notion of "anti-sacrifice," which he calls "an obligatory third term" to mitigate the untenable dichotomy between sacrifice and non-sacrifice. Chauvet does not dispute Girard's thesis in that Jesus unmasks the hidden sacrificial processes and reveals a God who no longer demands sacrifice, but yet he stops short of an unconditional acceptance of the thesis. For Chauvet, "'anti-sacrifice' is not the denial of the sacrificial pattern that dwells in all of us. . . . The anti-sacrificial regimen to which the gospel calls us *rests* upon the sacrificial, but it does so to *turn it around* and thereby to redirect ritual practice, the symbolic point of passage that structures Christian identity, back toward ethical practice."[18] The challenge, in Chauvet's figuration, is that anti-sacrifice is "not the negation of the sacrificial . . . but *the task to convert all the sacrificial to the gospel in order to live it, not in a servile, but in a filial (and hence in a brotherly and sisterly) manner. . . .* [which] constitutes the premier place of *our* 'sacrifice.' That is what the anti-sacrifice of the Eucharist shows us and enjoins us to do."[19] However, "the Church, which is under the anti-sacrificial law of the Spirit, is always in danger of sliding back toward the sacrificial."[20]

Even keeping this sacrificial system intact, or redescribing it as an (anti)sacrificial structure of ethical relations, as Chauvet does, the Eucharist fundamentally cannot be understood apart from its symbolic association with cannibalism—that primordial cultural taboo—and the ritual *participation* in the *life* of the body, now dead, that is consumed. This belief is not as primitive as might first be assumed, for it was never far from the mind of

15. Cf. Chauvet, *Symbol and Sacrament*, 290–316.

16. E.g., McGuckian, *Holy Sacrifice*.

17. See Girard, *The Scapegoat* and *Violence and the Sacred*.

18. Chauvet, *Symbol and Sacrament*, 307.

19. Ibid., 311.

20. Ibid., 308.

medieval Christendom, when eucharistic realism was at its height. Caroline
Walker Bynum states that one of the most often cited late-medieval miracles
is the bleeding host, "in which consecrated eucharistic wafers turned into
bleeding flesh."[21] She also recounts an episode in the *Legenda aurea* of James
of Voragine wherein "a woman who doubts the Eucharist sees it as the
body of Christ. But what she sees lying on the altar at the consecration is a
finger!"[22] And in *Corpus Christi*, her historical survey of the Eucharist in the
late-medieval period, Miri Rubin observes:

> The body is always a complex image, and eating the body is a
> particularly disturbing one. . . . The juxtaposition of simplest
> natural act, of eating, with the holiest and most taboo-ridden
> of nourishments, the human body, associates acts and symbols
> which in any other contexts would be abhorrent and unutter-
> able. Cannibalism is never absent from any society. . . . But in the
> eucharist God's body was said to be eaten, blood, flesh and all,
> as a matter of course. Heretics homed in on the horror of it, just
> as Christians had once accused pagans of cannibalistic excesses.
> . . . [B]y combining the most holy with the most aberrant/abhor-
> rent, the routine workings of sacramental power—and image of
> the fulness of life-giving, which dwells in the image of utmost
> transgression—a very powerful symbol was created, as awesome
> as it was promising.[23]

As we discovered in the previous chapter, in light of the medieval studies of Huizinga and Bakhtin, it is not uncommon in the middle ages for this
coincidence of opposites to appear as "the most holy with the most aber-
rant/abhorrent." In the centuries that have passed since that time, we have
ceased to see what was so apparent at that time of most intense liturgical
imagination: that the profane, the aberrant/abhorrent, the disturbing and
unutterable and universally taboo, is in fact the transgression of the symbol
of the Eucharist *from within*. It is endemic to sacramentality.

The writings of French novelist and theorist Georges Bataille, to whose
literary reimagining of the Eucharist as a sadomasochistic erotic ritual we
attend in the following chapter, has also contributed to our understanding
of cannibalism and sacrifice in religious ritual in his theoretical writings.
Bataille observes:

> Man is never looked upon as butchers' meat, but he is frequently
> eaten ritually. The man who eats human flesh knows full well

21. Bynum, *Fragmentation and Redemption*, 102
22. Bynum, *Resurrection*, 316.
23. Rubin, *Corpus Christi*, 359–60.

that this is a forbidden act; knowing this taboo to be fundamental he will religiously violate it nevertheless. There is a significant
example in the communion feast following on the sacrifice. The
human flesh that is eaten then is held as sacred, . . . the object
is "forbidden," sacred, and the very prohibition attached to it is
what arouses the desire. Religious cannibalism is the elementary
example of the taboo as creating desire: the taboo does not create the flavour and taste of the flesh but stands as the reason why
the pious cannibal consumes it. This paradox of the attraction of
forbidden fruit will be seen again when we come to eroticism.[24]

However, Bataille, whose imagination has been shaped by Roman
Catholic ritual and doctrine, denies any "reality" in the ritual representation of Christ's sacrifice in the Mass. In contrast to "primitive" religions
that might have actually engaged in cannibalism or actually offered human
beings as sacrifices to the gods, it is Bataille's observation that "Christians
have only ever known symbolic sacrifice."[25] In this, Bataille indicates the
irreducible mediacy to which all our primary interlocutors (Pickstock,
Chauvet, Ward, Power, even Altizer and Derrida) would attest as well. He
declares that "The sacrifice of the Mass is a reminder but it only rarely makes
a deep impression on our sensibility. However obsessive we find the symbol of the cross, the Mass is not readily identified with the bloody sacrifice.
. . . Essentially in the idea of sacrifice upon the cross the very character of
transgression has been altered."[26] This alteration is the reduction of the real
to the symbolic—transgression as symbolized in the sacramental act. Furthermore, one intuits that to Bataille, this is to the overall impoverishment
of the Christian religion: "It is the common business of sacrifice to bring life
and death into harmony, to give death the upsurge of life, life the momen-
tousness and the vertigo of death opening on to the unknown. Here life is
mingled with death, but simultaneously death is a sign of life, a way into the
infinite."[27] Yet, Christianity, according to Bataille, has forsaken this essential
aspect of the transgression. He sets about reinstantiating this transgression
in his fiction—an ironic avenue of exploration, given the metaphoric or
symbolic operation of fiction itself. But perhaps that is the only possibility
ever available to us to truly explore the extreme transgression of the God incarnate in Christ, who invites us to feed on his flesh and drink of his blood:

24. Bataille, *Eroticism*, 71–72.
25. Ibid., 88.
26. Ibid., 89.
27. Ibid., 91.

through the mediation of the imaginative arts of fiction, poetry, painting, film, and so on.

Caroline Walker Bynum has given considerable attention to medieval artistic depictions of the body of Christ as food. Typically associated with woman, construing the body of Christ as food is one way of conceiving the femininity of Christ's transcorporeal body. To illustrate this, we turn again with Bynum back to Herlin' fifteenth-century painting *Schmerzensmann* (Man of Sorrows) (see the front cover), which is a medieval vision of Christ's eucharistic body from which we can learn a great deal.[28] Herlin's vision is, as Bynum notes, "a striking illustration of the medieval conception of Christ as food. From the wound in Christ's right foot a stalk of wheat grows and pierces his left hand. A grapevine grows from his left foot"[29] penetrating his right hand. The stalk of wheat and the grapevine do not simply sit atop his feet, as if placed there, but *grow* from the wounds in his feet and grafted into the wounds in his hands. In this particular painting, these are not cryptic signs. The eucharistic symbolism is made explicit by the artist: a branch from each stalk protrudes and hangs over a figure of the chalice and elevated host that sits at Christ's right foot. Jesus' decimated, eucharistic body is presented to be eaten and drunk, the food of eternal life. The grapevine which springs forth from the body of the "true vine" (John 15:1) is heavily laden with succulent fruit, the stalk of wheat bent over under the weight of the grain. The life that is almost absent from Christ's human body is paradoxically transfigured in the produce of his wounds.

Bynum also highlights artistic renderings of Christ's flesh as food in which the wound in Christ's side is presented as a lactating breast, given as nourishment, a theme appearing not only in medieval art, but in mystical writings as well.[30] She alludes to such writers as St. Anselm, Julian of Norwich, and Catherine of Siena who envision Christ nursing humanity at his side, which metaphorically becomes life-giving milk to the suckling Church.[31] Christ is often depicted indicating or offering the wound in his side with gestures which explicitly mirror the Virgin Mary's offering of her breast to the infant Christ in other Christian art. In fact, the experience of the body of Christ as food is not even limited to Christ's physical body present in the Eucharist; it extends to his scriptural body as well, as Bynum recalls Ida of Louvain, who "was able to eat Christ almost at will by recit-

28. This painting is reproduced in Caroline Walker Bynum's *Holy Feast, Holy Fast*, (plate 4) and *Fragmentation and Redemption* (fig. 3.9, 107).

29. Bynum, *Holy Feast*, plate 4 (after p. 142); cf. *Fragmentation*, 103.

30. See Bynum, *Holy Feast*, 270–76, passim.

31. Bynum, *Fragmentation*, 93–98, 205–6, passim.

ing John 1:14 ["And the Word became flesh and lived among us . . ."]. For, whenever she spoke the words *Verbum caro factum est* . . . she tasted the Word on her tongue and felt the flesh in her mouth; when she chewed it, it was like honey."[32]

This complex of signification, as depicted in these literary and artistic expressions, is present within the biblical narrative, and continues to capture the Christian imagination. But it continues to capture the postmodern, post-Christian imagination as well, where the link between eating, cannibalism, and a kind of secular sacramentality continues to hold a certain currency as a compelling image of the traditional eucharistic themes of celebration, real presence/absence, participation, interpenetration, and the body as a means of grace. This should become apparent as we turn now our attention first toward the text of the Fourth Gospel and then toward contemporary literary and philosophical texts that further engage this thematic.

"THE BREAD OF LIFE": INGESTING THE BODY

In light of Douglas Templeton's notion of "true fiction" previously described in this book, we shall undertake a reading of select passages of John's Gospel as literary explorations of the significance of the historical and sacramental bodies of Christ as food to be eaten and drunk. Experts continue to debate eucharistic origins, and for just about every theory one can imagine, it seems a scholarly text exists to defend it.[33] We will not mire this project in those discussions, for what we are interested in, as our title indicates, is the *Eucharist in literary and theological perspective.* As we stated in the introduction, this project, beginning to end, is a interdisciplinary hermeneutical exercise in reading widely across texts to locate both the tensions and the resonances in the ways in which the concepts of sacrament and sacramentality are explored and wrestled with in those texts. And so, whether reading liturgies, sacred Scripture or contemporary fiction, we engage them, as a reader, at the level of their *writing*.

One could argue (and indeed many have) that the "eucharistic" passages in the New Testament must be read against the backdrop of a forming

32. Ibid., 130.

33. For one work that seeks to bring as many possible theories and interpretations together, see Bradshaw, *Origins*; as regards the New Testament origins of the Eucharist, see esp. 61–72. Liturgical studies is a demanding and detailed field which admittedly exceed our grasp by a wide margin. Bradshaw is an able guide as we attempt to navigate these waters.

liturgical practice.[34] In other words, the assumption is that the Gospels are not necessarily "historical" accounts of events as they actually took place, or prescriptions dictating praxis, but more likely *reflect* the existing practices (and beliefs) of the Christian context at the time of their composition. The letters and epistles are a slightly different matter, as they address specific contexts and so *do* in some cases give us clues about and prescriptions for worship in certain early Christian communities. However, we would rather turn these usual debates between liturgical scholars inside-out and suggest that, instead of reading the texts *either* for reflections of or clues about existing practices, *or* reading them historical or instructional, our suggestion is that an *intertexutal* reading is the most fruitful way to read the New Testament texts under consideration here. Another way of putting this would be to say we read them as "fictions"—true fictions to be sure, but fictions all the same. As we discussed in chapter 2, according to Templeton, "Literature differs from history as fiction differs from fact."[35] John's Gospel,[36] which is the subject at hand, does not appear to be particularly interested in "facts," but rather is deeply engaged from the outset in a full-scale interpretation of Jesus' life, death, and resurrection. This is evident from the prologue (1:1–18—"In the beginning was the Word . . ."), which is indisputably a poetic and intertextual gloss on the creation account of Genesis 1 ("In the beginning God . . .") intent to narrate *everything*, the whole of creation, in accordance with the Christ event. And so we propose here to take a text which is already an interpretive text, and interpret it further to illuminate the scandal of sacramentality.

It appears to us that the whole of John's text is an intertext opening onto itself, in some cases onto the Synoptic accounts, and perhaps even onto the still-forming liturgy of late-first-century churches. In our reading, which is but one possible reading, the Gospel according to John is as a highly eucharistic text, keenly interested in interpreting Christ's historical and sacramental bodies throughout its narrative. In chapter 3 we made reference to the conclusion to John's Gospel—its climax in Thomas's declaration of faith, having placed his hand in the gaping hole in the side of Jesus' resurrection

34. Cf. Bradshaw, *Origins*, 47–56, on "panliturgism," harmonization, etc. Reading Bradshaw, one wonders if arrival at any certainty is even possible in the study of early Christian liturgy. Our inference from his exposé of the problems inherent to every major approach is that *all is interpretation*. As Derrida famously declared, "*There is nothing outside of the text*" (*Of Grammatology*, 158). We hope this acknowledgment further defends our decidedly "non-expert" engagement with both biblical and liturgical sources.

35. Templeton, *True Fiction*, 305.

36. Acknowledging the contentious nature of this choice, for our purposes we prefer to address the author of the Fourth Gospel as "John."

body, and its figuration of Jesus' body as "the living bread that came down from heaven" (John 6:51), alluding to and superseding the manna of the Old Testament. Our focal point for this section is Jesus' scandalous "bread of life" discourse, recorded in John 6, in particular the metaphor of bodily consumption around which Jesus builds his entire speech.

This discourse must not be taken out of context, and is better served when viewed against the background of the multiplication of the loaves and fishes which immediately precedes it (6:1–15). The miraculous feeding follows what many would claim is a eucharistic pattern—"Jesus took the loaves, and when he had given thanks [eucharistēsas], he distributed them to those who were seated" (6:11), eliding Dix's four-fold shape (taken, blessed, broken, given) into a three-fold shape where the fraction and distribution are one and the same act. Despite the considerable surplus of food after this miracle, the implication of the crowd's pursuit of Jesus is that there is still a desire for more bread, as Jesus indicates in v. 26: "you are looking for me, not because you saw signs, but because you ate your fill of the loaves." Jesus begins to teach those who come to him seeking bread, like the bread that he (re)produced the previous day in such gratuitous measure, desiring food to fill their bellies. They request further signs that Jesus is sent by God, drawing an intertextual connection to the narratives of their tradition: "Our ancestors ate the manna in the wilderness; as it is written, 'He gave them bread for heaven to eat'" (6:31). Jesus gently corrects their interpretation, saying that it was God and not Moses who gave the bread, "For the bread of God is that which comes down from heaven and gives life to the world" (6:32–33). Just as circumcision can be seen as a Jewish prototype for the Christian sacrament of initiation (baptism),[37] so may the manna be regarded as a figure of sacramental grace and a prototype of the Eucharist, as Louis-Marie Chauvet has shown in some detail.[38]

When the crowd finally asks for this bread, Jesus identifies *himself*, his own body, as precisely that for which they ask—an identification that troubles them greatly, and causes them to "complain" (6:41). However, Jesus does not explain himself in such as way as to silence their complaints, but continues along the same line that has already caused their consternation:

37. "In him also you were circumcised with a spiritual circumcision, by putting off the body of the flesh in the circumcision of Christ; when you were buried with him in baptism, you were also raised with him through faith in the power of God, who raised him from the dead" (Col 2:11–12); Cf. Staples, *Outward Sign*, 124–25.

38. Chauvet, *Sacraments,* 87–88. See also Chauvet, *Symbol and Sacrament,* 44–45, 222–24, 279. Both works make similar observations. In *Symbol and Sacrament,* the passage connecting manna to John 6 is found on 222–24 in a section wonderfully titled "Chewing the Book."

"I am the bread of life. Your ancestors ate the manna in the wilderness, and they died. This is the bread that comes down from heaven, so that one may eat of it and not die. I am the living bread that came down from heaven. Whoever eats of this bread will live forever; and the bread that I will give for the life of the world is my flesh" (6:48–51). Jesus is doubly-offensive to his listeners' sensibilities: he not only makes the correspondence between himself and the manna in the wilderness—so significant a story of God's gracious action toward the people of Israel—but goes so far as to offer himself as a *replacement* for that bread of old, and a superior one at that. The manna, though graced and gracious, did not provide eternal life. *This* bread, which Jesus reveals as his own flesh, will cause those who eat it to live forever.

Scripture tells us that Jesus' words cause the Jews to dispute amongst themselves over the meaning of his statement: "How can this man give us his flesh to eat?" (6:52). Jesus heightens the scandal further by refusing to explain away his meaning in symbolic or metaphoric terms: "unless you eat [*phagēte*] the flesh of the Son of Man and drink his blood, you have no life in you. Those who eat [*trōgōn*] my flesh and drink my blood have eternal life, and I will raise them up on the last day; for my flesh is true food and my blood is true drink. Those who eat [*trōgōn*] my flesh and drink my blood abide in me, and I in them" (53–56). We could even regard Jesus' words as offensive on yet another level, for this blatantly (and, one assumes, *deliberately*) cannibalistic imagery would have been nothing short of horrifying in light of Jewish dietary customs, which forbade the consumption of blood. Indeed, taken literally, it is no less acceptable in the present day.

It is also of considerable interest that Jesus shifts his choice of verbs from *phagēte* ("to eat") at the beginning of the passage to *trōgōn* (lit. "to chew, gnaw, nibble, munch") at the end, and continues to use this form throughout vv. 57–58. This semantic shift appears to function to "offset any Docetic tendencies to 'spiritualize' the concept so that nothing physical remains in it, in what many hold to be the language of the Lord's Supper."[39] Whatever the intention, Jesus' words conjure for his listeners a noisy, animalistic manner of eating, like cattle chewing their cud. Jesus confronts them, through his choice of words, with a repulsive image: the physical, bodily—and not merely metaphoric—consumption of his flesh.

In the sacrificial system of old, the blood of the creature was synonymous with its very life; the spilling of blood is the outpouring of life. For this reason, Jews were forbidden to consume blood—the animal had to be drained of its blood before its flesh could be consumed as food. But Jesus scandalizes the sensibilities of his religious zeitgeist: "unless you eat the flesh

---

39. See "τρώγω" in Arndt et al., eds., *Greek–English Lexicon*.

of the Son of Man and drink his blood, you have no life in you" (6:53). Jesus knows the dietary customs of his own religion, and knows this teaching will offend his listeners, including his faithful twelve. Many of his disciples turn away at this point and follow him no longer (6:66). Jesus further elaborates, but far from explains, his meaning to the twelve: "It is the spirit (*pneuma*) that gives life (*zōopoieō*);[40] the flesh (*sarx*) is useless. The words that I have spoken to you are spirit and life" (6:63). It would be easy to interpret these words of Jesus as an admission of his "secret" meaning, reserved only for his closest disciples: after all of his emphasis on the physical eating of his bodily flesh, Jesus' intention seems at first to turn out to be spiritual rather than physical. It is not flesh he is concerned with after all, but spirit. However, the relationship between flesh and spirit in John's Gospel must not be regarded as a dichotomy. Instead, the ontology at work here is one of unity: the flesh animated by the creative spirit/breath/speech of God.

Let us look even more closely into the biblical text. As we have already established, John's prologue makes clear from the outset the symmetry he is drawing between his Gospel narrative and the creation narrative(s) in Genesis. In the priestly creation account in Genesis 1, the spirit/wind (*ruwach* in Heb.; *pneuma* in the *LXX*) of God sweeps over the face of the waters, animating them and co-participating in God's creative speech. The Yahwist account in Genesis 2 depicts God forming man from dust, but his body remains inanimate apart from the creative and life-giving spirit/breath of God.[41] In light of the prologue—*The Word became flesh, sarx*—Jesus' statement that "the flesh is useless," cannot be taken to mean that only the spirit, and *not* the flesh, is all that really matters. *Matter matters* in John's Gospel. Thus it appears Jesus' conception of the flesh as useless apart from the spirit is by no means a negation or denigration of the flesh but rather an affirmation of the animating breath of the spirit *in-dwelling* the flesh.[42] Death is the

40. It appears here that the spirit is a *poet* (*zōopoieō*) of sorts, perhaps justifying at least a thematic link with the creative Word (*Logos*) of John's prologue.

41. It is noteworthy that the animating "breath" of God in Gen 2:7 is not *ruwach* as in Gen 1:2 (cf. Ezek 37:8–9, 14) but *nĕshamah* (*pnoen* in the LXX; used also in Acts in ref. to the Holy Spirit). The verb *naphach* ("breathed into his nostrils") is translated *enephusesen* in the LXX (used also in Ezek 37:9: "O breath (*ruwach*) . . .breathe (*naphach*) upon these slain"). The only time this verb is used in the New Testament is at the conclusion of John's Gospel, when Jesus appears to the disciples post-resurrection: "he breathed (*emphusao*) on them and said to them, 'Receive the Holy Spirit (*pneuma*)'" (John 20:22). Cf. Pink, *Gospel of John*, 1100. The deliberate intertextuality in John is perhaps clearest here, emphasizing in his Prologue the connection to the first creation, and now the new creation in Christ.

42. Cf. Jesus' words to Nicodemus in John 3:6: "What is born of the flesh is flesh (*sarkos sarx*), and what is born of the Spirit is spirit (*pneumatos pneuma*)."

rending apart of flesh and spirit, a perversion of God's intention for creation, as we see in John 19:30 when Jesus gives up his spirit (*pneuma*), leaving only his useless, destroyed body stretched upon the cross. Furthermore, a purely spiritualist reading of Jesus' words here is unsustainable after Jesus' *bodily* resurrection, where flesh is restored and (re)inhabited by the spirit. However, just as Jesus' wounds remain part of his resurrection body, the separation between flesh and spirit which death effects is not entirely overcome in by the resurrection, as Chauvet reminds us: "The word does not come forth except as fractured, just as the Word of the cross is fractured, even when this Word is expressed, as it should be, starting with the resurrection. For the resurrection creates a *tear* in the fabric of language. One cannot speak of it without leaving open the interstice which both *separates and unites opposites: flesh and spirit*, to appear and to disappear, to touch and not to touch, presence and absence."[43] The cross of Jesus is the *coincidence* of such opposites as flesh and spirit, life and death. *Flesh is (not) spirit, and spirit is (not) flesh.* The spirit gives life to the flesh, and the flesh is the living bread gives life to all who consume it. On the other hand, the flesh *is* useless in that it exists outside the provinces of use and function. As we discovered in chapter 3, it is nothing, literally *no-thing* that can be appraised of value or commodified for exchange. Like the manna of old, it is pure gift, and can only be received as grace. His body is broken so that it may be eaten as food. His blood is shed that its life may flow into all who drink it. And even in the resurrection—*especially* in the resurrection—the body of Jesus maintains this transcorporeality, so that even raised to new life, flesh and spirit restored, his flesh and blood may be perpetually dismembered and disseminated as food and drink for the life of the world.

We have given considerable attention to the text of John's Gospel as a highly eucharistic text, one intensely determined to interpret to its reader Jesus' body, his flesh and blood, as existing beyond the normal limits of bodies: as water (John 7:37–39), as light (John 1:4–5, 8:12, 9:5), as the creative Logos (1:1–4), and most centrally to this chapter, as food to be eaten.[44] The

---

43. Chauvet, *Symbol and Sacrament*, 527 [italics added].

44. Lest we focus all our attention on bread, note that John 6 should be viewed against the backdrop of John 2, wherein Jesus performs his first miracle by turning water into wine at the wedding at Cana (2:1–11); no other account of this miracle appears in the Gospels. It is significant here because while the narrative gives greater attention to Jesus' body as both one that *makes* bread (the miraculous feeding of the 5,000) and *is* bread, the "living bread that came down from heaven" (6:51), this vignette connects Jesus body to *wine* as well. This connection is again made during Jesus' last supper discourse (John 15:1–6) where Jesus narrates his body as the "vine"—again, calling forth the image of the Friedrich Herlin painting considered previously. Jesus reads the text of his own body as the "water of life" (John 7:37–39). We have already seen that water

cannibalistic connotations are not buried at all, but are inscribed precisely at the surface of the text: the Eucharist as cannibalism, a scandalous transgression of the most fundamental of social and religious taboos. If the Eucharist is paradigmatic of sacramentality, as the Christian sacrament *par excellence*, this transgression must be viewed as central to sacramentality. Our point is not to argue that the description or experience of the sacramental must imply or employ the theme of cannibalism *per se*, but rather that, as evident in the cannibalistic connotations of the Eucharist, the sacramental stumbling-block is in part a stumbling over the a body which transgresses the discreet and comfortable limits placed upon bodies by the power structures of this-worldly kingdoms. This is a body which consumes, even as it is consumed. And this mutual consumption we call communion must never stray from its transgressive, de/constructive core, where the gift of the body is fulfilled in the body's consumption. We turn now turn to a contemporary literary text which explores the theme of cannibalism in explicitly sacramental terms.

A FRINGE OF LEAVES: CANNIBALISM AS EUCHARIST

A Fringe of Leaves, English writer Patrick White's 1976 historical fiction, is on the surface an adventure tale. Set in Australia during the early Victorian era, it tells of a group of travelers making the sea voyage from Van Diemen's Land back to their home in England on a ship called the *Bristol Rose*. A shipwreck occurs near the start of the journey, and the protagonist, Ellen Roxburgh, along with the other survivors, becomes captive of an aboriginal tribe. Although not an immediately obvious theme in the work, White's incorporation of sacramental imagery into the narrative is of interest to us, especially as it is linked to cannibalism and the consumption of the body as food. Early in the novel, as we are becoming acquainted with Ellen's character, the third-person omniscient narrator describes a childhood incident which alludes, indirectly, to the sacramental with imagery that is at once baptismal and eucharistic: "Once as a girl Ellen Gluyas had set out walking to St Hya's Well.... She walked all morning in what was heat for those parts, and tore her stockings on brambles, as well as her flesh, till blood ran."[45] On this childhood sojourn, which culminates in a baptism, Ellen's body is

---

can become wine, to say nothing of the commingling of water and blood that flow from Jesus' pierced side, a detail which only appears in Scripture in John 19:34. This symbolism, the flow of blood and water, emerges as a prominent theme in medieval theology and art as the dual figures of baptism (water) and the Eucharist (blood) are construed as the allegorical "birthing" of the Church from the wound/womb in Christ's side.

45. White, *Fringe of Leaves*, 97.

broken, her blood is shed. The implication that something mystical is likely to come is indicated by the association of this well with Saint Hya.[46]

> She found the well (or pool, rather) in the dark copse where they told her it was, its waters pitch black, and so cold she gasped as she plunged her arms. She was soon crying for some predicament which probably nobody, least of all Ellen Gluyas could have explained: no specific sin, only presentiment of an evil she would have to face sooner or later. Presently, after getting up the courage, she let herself down into the pool, clothes and all, hanging by a bough. When she had become totally immersed, and the breath frightened out of her by icy water, together with any thought beyond that of escaping back to earth, she managed, still clinging to the bough, to hoist herself upon the bank.
> . . .
>
> For the first time in many years she remembered this incident, and how her presentiment of evil had oppressed her over months, and then come to nothing, or else she had exorcised the threat by immersion in the pool.[47]

The reference to exorcism (a traditional component of the rite of baptism) solidifies the baptismal imagery of this vignette, as do the two references to her 'immersion' in the waters. Also, a "presentiment of evil" is mentioned twice in consecutive paragraphs, the first time in association with "sin." As well as a foreshadowing of the shipwreck to come, which will be for Ellen another plunge into the icy depths, this act is also an unorthodox baptism, a self-baptism of sorts, the significance of which is not altogether clear, but which in these first hundred or so pages alerts our sensibilities to a sacramentality which permeates the narrative, and which will become a defining experience for Ellen in particular. The sacramental quality of this impressionistic scene leads us to read Ellen's presentiment of evil as a foreboding of her later confrontation with the ultimate taboo: her participation in cannibalism, which is framed in explicitly sacramental terms as well.

46. According to Elizabeth Rees, St. Hya (also "Ia" or "Ives") of Cornwall was a 5th century Irish nun who was supposed to accompany St. Gwinear to Cornwall, but arrived late and was left behind. However, "a leaf enlarged itself to the size of a boat and carried her there . . . Ia's tomb was in St. Ives church, and her holy well is in a stone building outside the lower wall of the cemetery"; Rees, *Celtic Sites*, 215. Taking into account that St. Hya was a sea-farer, the foreshadowing of the shipwreck to come is even clearer. Further, establishing the proximity of this "holy well" to the nearby church and to the cemetery reinforces on several levels the baptismal imagery at work in this scene.

47. White, *Fringe of Leaves*, 97–98.

Bodies play a significant role in White's novel, both in how they mediate experience and their potential to be used as food. Ellen is pregnant when she begins her journey to Van Diemen's Land. Her condition makes her very aware of her corporeality. After the shipwreck, her body, host to the life within, impedes her escape to the lifeboats: "Physically she was at her lowest. She had the greatest difficulty in preventing her head from being dragged by its unnatural weight down upon her slack breasts, above her swollen belly."[48] The traumas of the shipwreck and its aftermath induce labor prematurely, which Ellen feels within her body before it becomes apparent to everyone else. As the waters overtake their lifeboat and swirl around her, she recognizes that the child she has carried as part of herself has become something foreign, a "creature which had begun to persecute her in its increasingly remonstrative form undulating out of time with her own somewhere in the folds of her petticoats bunting nibbling at her numb legs this slippery fish was pushing in the direction of a freedom to which she had never yet attained."[49] The lack of punctuation in the sentence lends to its sense of urgency, of breathless panic as the unborn child is lost. In the pain of delivery and the degradation of her body, Ellen reverts to her lower, "primitive" self. She instantaneously unlearns all that her snobbish, aristocratic mother-in-law has taught her about being a "lady": "'Ohhh!' she moaned, or lowed rather. . . . 'Aw, my Gore!'" The bovine connotations of "lowed" could be seen to imply the reduction of Ellen's body to a piece of meat. Further, her physical anguish in this moment robs her of the linguistic faculty, consistent with Elaine Scarry's analysis of the body in pain: "Whatever pain achieves, its achieves in part through its unsharability, and it ensures this unsharability through its resistance to language. . . . Physical pain does not simply resist language but actively destroys it, bringing about an immediate reversion to a state anterior to language, to the sounds and cries a human being makes before language is learned."[50] In this moment of betrayal—*is her body abandoning the child, or the child abandoning her?*— she is stripped of speech, unable to communicate, incapable of communion.

As she is reduced to an almost animalistic existence in this circumstance, the gap between Ellen and her calloused husband is greatest. She cries out in primeval, incomprehensible speech, while Mr Roxburgh longs for "his journal, to discuss his mood in rational terms, and thus restore a moral balance."[51] This profound lack of empathy, which is more savage

---

48. Ibid., 200.
49. Ibid., 203.
50. Scarry, *Body in Pain*, 4.
51. White, *Fringe of Leaves*, 202.

than the savages with whom Ellen will soon commune, is also revealed by his inner response to her "positively bestial" sounds which "His sensibility would have shut . . . out had it been at all possible."[52] Mr Roxburgh is more concerned with pretense and appearances than he is with his wife's laboring to deliver their still-born child: he is "startled by her unwonted use of his Christian name," and reacts harshly to Ellen's "whimpering and muttering childishly" with stark indifference toward the miscarriage: "'Then what is it?' he hissed, as desperate as he was irritated."[53] The lifeless infant body is laid to rest in an abandoned piece of luggage, shrouded in a canvas sack, and given a prayer-book funeral by the ship's Captain.

Ellen's still-born child is not part of the *dramatis personae* of the novel, and yet the body of this child haunts her. In a tragedy over which she had no control, this life inside her womb, with which she had lived for months, is converted into death almost without her knowing. The life-giving body of the mother becomes the sepulcher for an infant corpse. The baby she has carried within her, a felt presence inside her body, she now is only able to know as absence and death.

An abundance of other bodies pass from life to death. The loss of the child is followed immediately by the death of the ship's steward, Spurgeon, Mr Roxburgh's "recently acquired, unsavoury friend."[54] Spurgeon's disposal stands in stark contrast to that of the child. It is accompanied by no ceremony whatsoever: "Spurgeon the steward, already stiff, was pitched overboard by his crew mates. . . . Spurgeon, some of those present suspect, is the corpse the sharks get. But who cares, finally?"[55] As their situation worsens, the survivors gradually abandon societal formalities. The tragedy of the shipwreck and the ensuing trials degrade and dehumanize all of them to the point that dignified funerary rites become irrelevant. In this way, the novel is overtly a kind of regression back toward, but never quite arriving at, a state of primal innocence. The title's "fringe of leaves" draws a direct reference to Eden and the attempt of our First Parents to conceal their nakedness from their Creator and from one another after their tragic loss of innocence. However, it is a post-lapsarian Eden to which the characters return, cast out from their innocent idyll.

As Spurgeon's body is tossed into the waters to be food for sharks, Austin Roxburgh's hidden inner monologue foreshadows the cannibalism to come. His thoughts make explicit the novel's sense of the sacramentality

52. Ibid., 203.
53. Ibid.
54. Ibid., 206. The association of *(un)savoury* with food/taste should not be missed.
55. Ibid., 206.

of the body as food: "As one who had hungered all his life after friendships which eluded him, Austin Roxburgh did luxuriate on losing a solitary allegiance. It stimulated his actual hunger until now dormant, and he fell to thinking how the steward, had he not been such an unappetizing morsel, might have contributed appreciably to an exhausted larder. At once Mr Roxburgh's self-disgust knew no bounds."[56] He immediately recoils at his own indulgence in this secret cannibalistic fantasy, and yet does not restrain his indulgence, as his thoughts pass into a dream-like sequence: *"This is the body of Spurgeon which I have reserved for thee, take eat, and given thanks for a boil which was spiritual matter. . . .* Austin Roxburgh was not only ravenous for the living flesh, but found himself anxiously licking the corners of his mouth to prevent any overflow of precious blood."[57] In Austin's fantasy, Spurgeon's "unsavoury" body—disintegrous, permeable, grotesque—becomes the eucharistic host. Even a fluid-filled boil is "spiritual matter." The sacramental cannibalism, considered here but not yet enacted, functions in an explicitly nutritional sense, as it will later for Ellen amongst the Aborigines. As hunger takes over and the living body withers, the body of the other becomes the object of desire as a potential source of sustenance. Cultural taboos may be suspended in such desperation as one hungers and thirsts for the life-giving body and blood of an other.

Continuing this theme, we are moved to the central sacramental scene of the novel, which will profoundly shape Mrs Roxburgh and our reading of the narrative as a whole. Mr Roxburgh has been murdered; we find Ellen reduced to her most primal, fallen state as a captive of the savages. This prim Victorian lady now runs naked with "innocent savages"[58] through the Australian wilderness. She accepts and eventually embraces her savage existence, for however long it may last. Unlike the brambles that tear her flesh on the occasion of her childhood baptism at St. Hya's well, now even the wildness of nature caresses her as she gives herself over to it: "Where she had been slapped and scratched at first, she was now stroked by the softest fronds. Shafts of light admitted between the pinnacles and arches of the trees were directed at her path, if the hummocks and hollows had been in any way designed to assist human progress. But she left accepted, rejuvenated. She was the 'Ellen' of her youth, a name they had attached to her visible person at the font, but which had never rightfully belonged to her . . ."[59] Here Ellen is Eve, the first woman, the name "attached to her" at

56. Ibid., 206.
57. Ibid., 206–7.
58. Ibid., 243.
59. Ibid., 242.

her Christian baptism is finally, fully accepted and acceptable. No longer is she troubled by a disconnection between her body (her "visible person") and her name—through this regression to primitivism, she becomes a self.

Soon she is confronted with the very reality suggested by those secret thoughts that earlier had simultaneously obsessed and repulsed her husband. She awakes one morning and stumbles upon the remnants of ritual cannibalism:

> . . . a most delectable smell mingled with the scent of drifting smoke. She altered course in the direction of the voices, and eventually came upon a party of blacks whom she recognized as members of her tribe. . . . [T]heir faces when turned toward the intruder wore expressions which were resentful and at the same time curiously mystical. She realized she had blundered upon the performance of rites she was not intended to witness. There was no immediate indication of what these were; most likely the ceremony was over, for she sensed something akin to the atmosphere surrounding communicants coming out of church looking bland and forgiven after the early service.[60]

The reference here ("communicants") to the Eucharist is unmistakable, and Ellen's (and White's) sensitivity to the shaping influence of Anglican liturgy makes the allusion almost second-nature. Still, Ellen does not yet realize upon what precisely she has stumbled. The previous evening, she had observed an elaborate ritual murder, in which two young women in the tribe had fought and one was killed. The following morning, however, she must interpret the aftermath of the ritual. She notices "an object not unlike a leather mat spread upon the grass. She might have remained puzzled had she not identified fingernails attached to what she had mistaken for fringes, and at one end, much as a tiger's head lies propped on the floor at one end of a skin rug, what could only be the head of the [slain] girl. . . . Women rolled up the dark skin, as well as gathering the head and what she saw to be a heap of bones. It was easy to guess from the greasy smears on lips and cheeks how the flesh had disappeared . . ."[61] Shockingly, cannibalism, the only cultural taboo to rival incest in extremity and universality, is here framed in spiritual and even sacramental terms. Of course, as has been discussed in the practices and Scriptures of Christianity, this scandalous and scandalizing aspect of the Eucharist has always been part of a Christian sacramentality; despite efforts to renarrate it as something else, any attempt to erase it entirely would be impossible (perhaps even heretical). As with her childhood

60. Ibid., 243.
61. Ibid., 243.

self-baptism at St Hya's well, Ellen exercises her own volition and initiates herself more fully into the tribe by partaking of the remnants of the ritual feast. The scene is narrated masterfully and deserves quotation in full.

> she looked down and caught sight of a thigh-bone which must have felled from one of the overflowing dillis. Renewed disgust prepared her to kick the bone out of sight. Then, instead, she found herself stooping, to pick it up. There were one or two shreds of half-cooked flesh and gobbets of burnt fat still adhering to this monstrous object. Her stiffened body and almost audibly twangling nerves were warning her against what she was about to do, what she was, in fact, already doing. She had raised the bone, and was tearing at it with her teeth, spasmodically chewing, swallowing by great gulps which her throat threatened to return. But did not. She flung the bone away only after it was cleaned, and followed slowly in the wake of her cannibal mentors. She was less disgusted in retrospect by what she had done, than awed by the fact that she had been moved to do it. The exquisite innocence of this forest morning, its quiet broken by a single flute-note endlessly repeated, tempted her to believe that she had partaken of a sacrament.[62]

As the early Christian Eucharist was (mis?)construed as a cannibalistic feast, here we conversely encounter the act of cannibalism construed as sacrament. The novel is finally ambiguous about the motivation behind the act, for although Ellen would have certainly been hungry, this tiny morsel of meat left on the bone does not indicate that her motivation was to fill her belly. Rather, it appears both a profane sort of Eucharist *as well as* a sacrament of initiation, driven by a desire to be part of the community of the tribe, to be "one *of* them" and "one *with* them." Her relational ties to the "civilised folk" on the *Bristol Rose* having been obliterated, she desires to speak the food-language of the tribe, even if she cannot speak their spoken language. Also, in this passage, White seems to use Mrs Roxburgh's "proper" name to highlight just how far this lady has erred from her standing in Victorian society. Her eating is narrated in language that recalls that of Jesus in latter part of John 6, not the polite *phagēte* eating but *trōgōn*, munching, gnawing, "tearing at it with her teeth, spasmodically chewing, swallowing by great gulps."

Ellen is unable to put the incident out of her mind. She is later forced to recount it in a kind of inquisition after her rescue. And while in her account she (re)narrates her complicity, her willing participation in the act,

---

62. Ibid., 244.

she is unable to speak of the incident in any fully intelligible way, for like any Eucharist, it is beyond communicability or comprehensibility.

> "I came across some of the members of my tribe, in a forest clearing. I never understood so deeply, I believe, as then."
>
> "What were the blacks doing?"
>
> "It was a secret ceremony. They were angry with me and hurried me away."
>
> "Because you saw what they were at?"
>
> "It was too private. For me too, I realized later. A kind of communion."
>
> "If it made such an impression on you, I should have thought you'd be able to describe it."
>
> "Oh, no!"[63]

Thus we grasp that Ellen is unable to convey "the sacramental aspect of what could only appear a repellent and inhuman act."[64] A true encounter with the unconditioned, the sacred which is absolutely profane, reduces one to incommunicability. We see that, in the final instance, sacramentality is not so much about articulation as participation, even and especially when it involves a participation in such a deep and all-consuming scandal. Patrick White's vision maintains an element of mystery: Ellen's participation in the cannibalistic ritual may appear repellent to an outsider, and yet, deep within the act is a sacramental aspect that affects her profoundly and haunts her continually. She cannot explain it or describe in language, but receiving the body into her own body has left its mark on her. Even as she has consumed the morsel of human meat in the ritual, so her body has been consumed by the tribe—not just held captive by force, but now captivated by the sacrament: "*Made one . . . we offer you these gifts, and with them ourselves, a single, holy, living sacrifice.*"[65]

A Fringe of Leaves admits the possibility that cannibalism can be both construed and experienced as sacrament, bringing into sharper focus one aspect the scandal of sacramentality: the symbolism of the body as food to be eaten must not be too easily domesticated. We turn now, albeit briefly, to another contemporary fiction which is captivated by the body—the sensuality of the body, in the sense of both the body's *senses* and the sensual body. Again, an extreme and depraved act of consumption of the body is cast in a

63. Ibid., 328–9.
64. Ibid., 283.
65. *SL 1982*, 8.

eucharistic light in a way that confounds our understanding of sacraments and sacramentality.

PERFUME: THE EUCHARISTIC BODY OF A MURDERER

Patrick Süskind's *Perfume* is a unusual novel on a number of levels. It has a fabulous quality, like a myth or parable. It is also a highly sensuous novel, in that it brings alive the most overlooked, and certainly least theorized of the five senses: the olfactory. Süskind brings the sense of smell alive through language in a way that is unparalleled in literature, writing a central character who literally apprehends the world first and foremost not through the eyes but the nose. Set in eighteenth-century France, the story revolves around the character of Jean-Baptiste (John the Baptist) Grenouille, who is both protagonist and antagonist.

Simultaneously recalling and perverting the Nativity, Grenouille is born into horrendous and utter degradation: his unwed mother, a fishmonger in the marketplace of Paris's underlings, hardly breaks from her work to deliver him into the filth and fish guts on the ground beneath her. He is born with a gift that is paradoxically also a curse: he has an extraordinary sense of smell, but his own body is itself odorless. These two unique but interrelated bodily traits, combined with his humble beginnings, isolate him from society. As a child, he is maligned by the priest to whom his mother abandons him, and he is maltreated by the wet-nurse who takes him in, as well as by the other children in her charge. He is, as the narrator states near the novel's conclusion, "raised without love, with no warmth of a human soul, surviving only on impudence and the power of loathing, small, hunchbacked, lame, ugly, shunned, an abomination within and without."[66]

As a young man, Grenouille's olfactory gift leads to an obsession with fragrances, and eventually he becomes an apprentice to a famous perfumer named Baldini, who teaches Grenouille the art of distilling the fragrances of inanimate objects such as flowers, fruits, and so on. However, Grenouille is not only interested in pleasant smells—he is fascinated by *all* smells, including those which society would regard as repulsive. Baldini's method of "capturing" fragrances fails to allow the distillation of certain scents Grenouille would like to collect, so he seeks out alternative methods, arriving at one that allows him to capture the essence of human beings, but only during cellular breakdown shortly after death. Thus beings the "story of a murderer" indicated by the novel's subtitle.

66. Süskind, *Perfume*, 248.

As Grenouille's begins his murderous career, his endgame and artistic vision is to create an extraordinary perfume which will invoke true love. He concludes that such a perfume must be mixed from the essences of virgin girls, who embody purity in their undefiled flesh. His nose tells him that with such a fragrance, he will be able to control the entire world. And while a single drop of his concoction saves him from execution for the many murders he has committed, in the end he is despondent. The fragrance which has been his all-consuming passion exonerates him but still brings about his destruction.

The novel does not explicitly frame its final few scenes, which we will consider here, in sacramental terms, but the implication is present and has been noted by theological thinkers who have transgressed these boundaries before.[67] After Grenouille is caught by the civil authorities and charged with the crime, it is determined that his execution be carried before a large crowd, comprised of gentry and common folk alike. Dignitaries and ecclesiastical officials are present and eager to witness the particularly inhuman method of human disposal planned for Grenouille, whose body will be affixed to a St. Andrew's cross and dealt twelve blows with an iron rod, smashing all his joints, before then being hanged. His body, in his death as in his birth, is an object of utter revulsion. Of his origin, the narrator tells us his mother "wanted to put this revolting birth behind her as quickly as possible."[68] He is held in similar regard by the executioner, who is "disgusted by the murderer. He did not want to regard him as a human being, but only as a victim to be slaughtered."[69] Süskind's narrator inscribes on Grenouille's body total rejection as less than human. He is not a person, he is a victim. In the narrative, no explanation is given for this. Prior to his murderous acts, what cause could there be for the loathing to which he is subjected? Is there something about his lack of personal odor that makes him so detestable to everyone around him? Perhaps the absence of an aroma symbolizes that Grenouille is less than human: for humans eat and excrete, they sweat and seep and bleed, and all the while, they give off odors. The question is left unresolved.

At the execution, Grenouille orchestrates his escape with but a single drop of his love-inducing perfume, which actually simply conceals his own *lack* of a personal scent. As he enters the arena of the execution, "a miracle occurred. Or at least something so incomprehensible, so unprecedented and so unbelievable that everyone who witnessed would call it a miracle

---

67. Detweiler, "Torn by Desire," 60–77; Jasper, *Sacred Body*, 26 and 191, n. 40; cf. Ledbetter, *Victims and the Postmodern Narrative*.

68. Süskind, *Perfume*, 5.

69. Ibid., 240.

afterwards if they had taken the notion to speak of it at all."[70] The miracle
is that the crowd's loathing for Grenouille is mystically transformed into
adoration: "They were overcome by a powerful sense of goodwill, of tenderness, of crazy, childish infatuation, yes, God help them, of love for this little
homicidal man. . . . They loved him."[71] An orgiastic scene ensues as these
good and noble people "abandoned themselves to their emotions . . . gave
free rein to the urges" of their hearts.[72] Even the Bishop is powerless over
Grenouille's sensuous spell: "for the first time in his life basking in religious
rapture, for a miracle had occurred before their very eyes."[73]

While Grenouille has succeeded in his effort, his life spared and in
the perfume in his hands all the power of a god "to command the love of
mankind,"[74] he remains unsatisfied. In spite of his intensely gifted nose,
Grenouille's inability to smell himself and thus "know"/perceive himself
in the primary way he himself apprehends the world—through his nose—
makes him doubt, and indeed hate, his own flesh. The odorless Grenouille is
separated from himself, his body something foreign and despicable to him,
however loved it might be by those under the spell of his perfume. Despite
the overflowing "love" (we should perhaps interpret this "love" as at best
ironic, based as it is upon the artifice of the perfume) of his intoxicated Mass
of devotees, Grenouille "could not enjoy one second of it. . . . What he had
always longed for—that other people should love him—became at the moment of its achievement unbearable, because he did not love them himself,
he hated them. And suddenly he knew that he had never found gratification
in love, but always only in hate—in hating and in being hated."[75] As a "god"
in this moment of supreme control, Grenouille discovers the divine basis
for the gift of free will: for this offering of love is hollow, without content or
meaning, because the crowd gives it only under duress of the perfume. Their
senses are as corrupt as Grenouille's soul. Like a perverted, blasphemous
figure of Marion's "God without Being," whose very being is the *kenotic* out-
pouring of Love, Grenouille "wanted only to empty himself. For once in his
life, he wanted to be like other people and empty himself of what was inside
him—what they did with their love and their stupid adoration, he would do
with his hate. For once, just for once, he wanted to be apprehended in his
true being, for other human beings to respond with an answer to his only

70. Ibid., 244.
71. Ibid., 244–45.
72. Ibid., 246.
73. Ibid.
74. Ibid., 260.
75. Ibid., 249.

true emotion, hatred."[76] Grenouille's hate, the novel implies, is the result of the maltreatment and estrangement to which he has been victim throughout his life, and so, while his character is clearly diabolical, he becomes in the end an object of at least our pity, if not our empathy. His crowning achievement, the master perfume which simultaneously reveals his artistry and his evil, only further isolates him from the world around him: "The only one who has ever recognized it for its true beauty is me, because I created it myself. And at the same time, I'm the only one that it cannot enslave. I am the only person for whom it is meaningless."[77] Paradoxically, his gift is a curse that renders him utterly alone, immersed in (self)loathing and the desire for death.

In the novel's final scene, he returns to the place of his birth, "the most putrid spot in the whole kingdom,"[78] which is populated after dark by "thieves, murderers, cut-throats, whores, deserters, young desperadoes."[79] In this stinking charnel house overlooking a cemetery, he empties the nearly-full bottle of perfume, anointing (baptizing? he is *Jean-Baptiste* after all . . .) his body head to toe in the eroticizing scent, only to be dismembered and consumed by these filthy outcasts of society, who are his people, in a way, his (non)community, bound together only by their common degradation and alienation. The Mass divides him into thirty pieces, a clear allusion to Judas Iscariot, the one whom "Satan entered" to carry out Jesus' betrayal.[80] But this is not a betrayal of Grenouille's body; instead it is the fulfillment of his desire. Grenouille's body, almost imperceptible in life due to the absence of odor, is finally presented as absent in this final consummation, which is narrated as a mystical communion of sorts: "When the cannibals found their way back together after disposing of their meal, no one said a word."[81] Like Ellen Gluyas after her experience of ritual cannibalism, and like Mariette, rendered speechless in the ravages of religious ecstasy, the crowd cannot speak of this unspeakable act. However, they feel no guilt: "On the contrary! Though the meal lay rather heavy on their stomachs, their hearts were definitely light. All of a sudden, there were delightful, bright flutterings in their dark souls. And on their faces, was a delicate, virginal glow of happiness. . . . For the first time they had done something out of Love."[82] The capitaliza-

76. Ibid., 250.

77. Ibid., 260.

78. Ibid., 4.

79. Ibid., 261.

80. cf. Matt 26:14–16; Luke 22:3–6; John 13:2.

81. Süskind, *Perfume*, 263.

82. Ibid., 263.

tion of the this final word of the narrative—"Love"—calls attention to its significance while remaining ambiguous in its meaning. *Is* Süskind construing the "Love" induced by Grenouille's perfume, which drives the crowd to excessive debauchery at the would-be execution, and which motivates the mob of criminals to feast upon his body, in an ironic way after all? Or is this presented as a real possibility of communion, of these degenerate societal outcasts brushing up against the sacramental in this most profane experience? Is Grenouille's body host to some experience of the sacred that he, in his abandonment, has never been afforded? Or is it simply the victim of suicidal self-destruction?

Robert Detweiler interprets the novel as functioning on one level as "an allegory of how cultural achievements are attained at the expense of human lives and often accomplished by obsessive personalities whose behavior denies the very grandeur of their art."[83] However, his analysis is more deeply theological when he points out that "The particularly audacious aspect of this final scene of *Perfume* is that it is presented as having the effects of a Eucharist. . . . If the conclusion of *Perfume* shocks the reader—a finale in which a corrupt man dies in style, is dismembered and eaten in an ecstatic ceremony that brings communion to those who devoured him—the scandal one feels may be a signal that the scandal of Christianity has been interpreted too narrowly. . . . The celebration of the Eucharist is, after all, at heart an intensely erotic act that marks both the presence and the triumph of the scandalised and transformed body."[84] Like Süskind's text itself, Detweiler's insightful questioning of our hermeneutical limitations leaves open the possibility of how we might interpret "the scandal of Christianity" more broadly. He hints at the unexplored, or at least under-explored, erotic content of the eucharistic symbol, which will be the topic of the next chapter. However, the body of Grenouille is, as David Jasper points out, at best the "perverse opposite" of "the eucharistic banquet whereby, out of pure love, there is mutual consuming and consumption."[85] Yet this perverse opposite is not a negation of the symbol of the Eucharist, in Jasper's reading, but rather is a perverse opposite contained within the symbol itself, in a "marriage of heaven and hell" (quoting Blake), a *coincidentia oppositorum*. Noting the parallel between our consumption of this distasteful text and the consumption of the distasteful body contained in the narrative, Jasper suggests: "Even to read this passage is hard enough, shocking and indigestible to the sensitive reader. But if to consume an angel (and a murderer) is utterly nau-

---

83. Detweiler, "Torn by Desire," 71.

84. Ibid., 72–73.

85. Jasper, *Sacred Body*, 11; cf. 191 fn. 40.

seating, what of Christ himself? Yet only in this utterly profane, liturgical moment of pure *kenosis,* of pure consumption as sacrament of the actual body, can be glimpsed the kingdom of God . . ."[86] What kind of kingdom is this, where the most universally taboo, the most "utterly profane," human act is transfigured as sacred? Is it only through a kind of domestication of the symbol, a watering down of the living metaphor until it is drowned and dead? In John 6, Jesus does not seem to shy away from the visceral, "utterly nauseating" image of eating his flesh and drinking his blood, which given Jewish dietary customs would have been *more than* shocking, As we have seen, neither does Tertullian recoil from the startling characterization of the Eucharist as cannibalism in his *Apology.* All of this begs the question: if the Eucharist as the eating and drinking of the *real* flesh and blood of Jesus is *really* "just a symbol," so easily misapprehended and potentially controversial—*why has it been maintained, practiced, theorized, debated, and defended for two millennia? Why has it been so extensively drawn upon as a literary, poetic, and artistic motif?* Could it be in some sense due to the way that the Eucharist, as the sacrament *par excellence,* scandalously holds together the sacred and the profane, wholeness and brokenness, holiness and depravity, presence and absence, immanence and transcendence, the material and the spiritual, and so on? We suggest that this is precisely the case.

CONSUMING THE BODY AS AN ACT OF LOVE

Elaine Scarry observes that "[Christ] himself, of course, in the Last Supper and in the communion ceremony enters the food chain, allowing himself to be taken in, now not just as the object of perception but as an object of sustenance."[87] But Christ's body is not the only eucharistic, edible body to which we can point. A clear tradition in Christian mystical writings can be traced which emphasize the body as food to be taken into oneself as an act of holy communion. Almost invariably, the image of eating the body is simultaneously an erotic figure of interpenetration, of the exchange of bodily fluids, or of domination and subjugation. In *The Second Sex,* Simone de Bouvoir, discussing the phenomenon of female mystics, provides particularly striking accounts of Angela of Foligno and St. Catherine. The former "drank with delight the water in which she had just washed lepers' hands and feet"; quoting Angela, she recounts: "This beverage flooded us with such sweetness that the joy followed us home. Never had I drank with such pleasure. In my throat was lodged a piece of scaly skin from the lepers'

86. Ibid., 26.
87. Scarry, *Body in Pain,* 216.

sores. Instead of getting rid of it, I made a great effort to swallow it and I succeeded. It seemed to me that I had just partaken of communion."[88] Beauvior is of course critiquing and challenging a religion that elicits these sorts of practices, wherein women especially are found to be "imitating the Redeemer who saved the flesh by the degradation of his own flesh."[89] She also tells us of Marie Alacoque, who licks up the vomit of a patient she nurses, and of St. Catherine, to whom Jesus gives the foreskin removed at his circumcision as a wedding ring.

What might it mean to give, or receive, the body as food in an act of love? In the previous chapter, we considered Ron Hansen's novel *Mariette in Ecstasy* as a literary instantiation of the broken body—in this case the stigmatic body—as sacramental. Mariette's body is also consumed in the narrative—not ripped apart and eaten like Grenouille, but tasted—by Sister Hermance, who we know has a sexual attraction to Mariette. In the central scene where Mariette's body is revealed as sacramental, her broken body is being nursed my Sister Hermance, who unwraps the bandages from her hands, unveiling the wounds of Christ, and "With reverence Sister Hermance licks the blood inside the hand wound. 'I have tasted you. See?'"[90] Mariette's body, broken, her blood, the blood of Christ, poured out for the sake of many. *The blood of Christ, shed for you.* Sister Hermance tastes, drinks the miraculous blood, incorporating Mariette into her own body. "'Ever since I first met you, I have loved you more than myself,'" she tells the semi-conscious Mariette. She partakes of the offering of Mariette's body as a sacrament—"You have been a sacrament to me"—and as an act of love. Yet there is another sense in which Mariette's body is consumed in the novel in an act of love. As Mariette presents her body to Christ—"*Even this I give you*"[91]—she is simultaneously consumed by him.

In this chapter, we have examined writings that are concerned with the body that eats and is eaten, especially the Body on the altar, the transcorporeal body which presents itself to us to be eaten as bread and drunk as wine. This body, the edible body, is part of the scandal of sacramentality, because it is bound up with the *skandalon* of the Word made flesh, which was stretched on to a cross, poured out for the life of the world. This *kenosis* is the nature of Love, the nature of the God who is love. In the next and final chapter, we shall explore one more theme related to the scandal of sacramentality, manifest in the symbolic matrix of the Eucharist: that of the erotic body.

---

88. Beauvoir, *Second Sex*, 676.

89. Ibid., 676.

90. Hansen, *Mariette*, 121. The quotes that follow are all from this page.

91. Ibid., 9.

6

Penetrating
Eroticism and Sacrament

Penetrating things and bodies—that is, body contact and sexuality, aggression, destruction, and murder—constitute a second type of world appropriation, in which the merging of bodies with other bodies or with inanimate things is always transitory and therefore necessarily opens up a space of distance for desire and for reflection. This, I think, is the context that explains why sexuality allows for such a strong connotation of death, of overwhelming another body or of being overwhelmed by it.[1]

EROS: THE EUCHARIST AS AN EROTIC ACT

Although we have thus far avoided the language, it should be clear by now that the mediacy and materiality of sacramentality is another way of saying that sacraments are *sensuous*—they engage us, and we participate in them, at the level of our senses. We see, taste, touch, and smell the bread and the wine; we hear the fraction of the host and the pouring of water and wine into the chalice. And relatedly, sacraments are *sensual*—they *gratify* the senses, in a way that might almost connote carnality. As we concluded the previous chapter, we began to move from the conception of the body as food and drink, received for sustenance, life-giving nourishment, to the

1. Gumbrecht, *Production of Presence*, 87.

consumption of the body as an act of communion based upon and evocative of *love*. Indeed, to take the body of another into oneself is the deepest form of human intimacy, and in this way, ritual cannibalism, even when the victim is an enemy, is a deeply sacred act.

However, eating is not the only way to receive another's body into one's own body. In the interpenetration of bodies, including but not limited to sexual intercourse, we encounter the profound paradoxes of closeness and distance, life and death, violence and intimacy, and sacrality and profanity. Bodily interpenetration is also a central characteristic of the Eucharist. As we have seen that eating Christ's flesh and drinking his blood is not reducible to a "spiritualist" interpretation—the materiality of Christ's body and our bodies, made one metabolically in our consumption of the physical bread and the wine—neither is our consumption of His body reducible to a utilitarian meal. The mystics *savor* Christ's flesh, tasting its sweetness. In communion, bodily fluids are exchanged, our saliva, his blood, commingled in our mouths. Recall from our discussion in chapter 4 that, following Bakhtin, the orifices of the body, as the liminal spaces where the body opens itself to the world, are the locus of the body's degradation, which is also to say, its incarnation. This is the coincidence of the most profane—the body eating, drinking, excreting, sweating, seeping, bleeding—and the most intimately sacred—the body kissing, caressing, making love. So it seems appropriate for our discussion of sacrament and sacramentality to consider the erotic encounter between bodies.

As we have indicated, experience of the divine as an erotic experience is not foreign to Christian mysticism. Saint Thérèse describes her experience of First Communion as an overtly erotic event. Upon receiving the host, she recounts, "'Ah! how sweet was that first kiss of Jesus! It was a kiss of *love*; I *felt* that *I was loved*, and I said: 'I love You, and I give myself to You forever!' . . . [I]t was a fusion; they were no longer two, Thérèse had vanished as a drop of water is lost in the immensity of the ocean. Jesus alone remained."[2] Thérèse's religious fervor is a startling confluence of eroticism and violence, as when she writes: "In order to love in one single act of perfect Love, I OFFER MYSELF AS A VICTIM OF HOLOCAUST TO YOUR MERCIFUL LOVE, asking You to consume me incessantly, allowing the waves of *infinite tenderness* shut up within You to overflow into my soul, and that thus I may become a *martyr* of Your *Love*, O my God!"[3] This powerful expression indicates another corresponding theme of the present chapter: the hidden violence that accompanies the erotic. René Girard attests to this in *Violence*

---

2. Thérèse de Lisieux, *Story of a Soul*, 277 [caps and italics in original].

3. Ibid., 77 [italics in original].

and the Sacred, which bears witness to the inseparable relationship between the sacred and sacrificial violence. According to Girard, "The connection between sexuality and religion is a heritage common to all religions."[4] However, "Sexuality is impure because it has to do with violence."[5] Violence is bound up with the sacred, and sexuality, with its violent connotations, is encompassed as well.[6] Of course, it is impossible to talk about sacramentality independently of the sacred, and so Girard's thesis is clearly relevant.[7] When we look to the symbolic matrix of the Eucharist, violence and sacrifice are at the surface, pointing to the cross and the passion narrative, the violence inflicted on Christ's *broken* body and *shed* blood. Indeed, Catholic eucharistic theology maintains the Mass *as a sacrifice*.[8]

Georges Bataille, whose fiction we will consider shortly, has also provided us with a theoretical foundation for our discussion of the erotic as it relates to sacramentality. First, Bataille and Girard are in agreement that "the domain of eroticism is the domain of violence, of violation."[9] Bataille also recognizes that eroticism—as we have been claiming with regard to sacrament—"always entails a breaking down of established patterns, the patterns . . . of the regulated social order."[10] In Bataille's thinking, human life is characterized by discontinuity; only in death do human beings have a sense of continuity. When Bataille writes of *continuity*, he appears to mean something similar to *communion*—the bond or connection between persons, in contrast to our in-born *discontinuity* or fragmentation. From the perspective of the Eucharist, viewed through the lens of Zizioulas and others whose thought figures heavily in this study, this is not far off the notion that we are born into sin, which is manifest as individualism, but are redeemed through/into communion and relationality, which is manifest as true "being" or authentic personhood. However, in Bataille's more nihilistic view, this is only possible in death. "Eroticism opens the way to death," he

4. Girard, *Violence*, 36. Girard goes on to catalogue all the ways in which sexuality manifests its inner violence, ranging from rape and sadism to the bloody processes of menstruation and childbirth to lovers' quarrels and jealous rages. Furthermore, "Thwarted sexuality," writes Girard, "naturally leads to violence" (37).

5. Ibid., 35.

6. This is evident in the French phrase *la petite mort* ("little death"), a metaphor for orgasm.

7. Chauvet's notion of (anti)sacrifice in his sacramental theology (discussed previously) is drawn explicitly from Girard; see *Symbol and Sacrament*, 303–7.

8. cf. McGuckian, *Holy Sacrifice*.

9. Bataille, *Eroticism*, 15.

10. Ibid., 18.

writes, and "Death opens the way to the denial of our individual lives."[11] This "denial of our individual lives" is, for Bataille, desirable, for it is the condition of possibility for any continuity (at one point he calls it "liberating continuity"[12]), which is to say communion, to occur between persons.

Most importantly for our purposes, Bataille acknowledges that "all eroticism has a sacramental character."[13] Bataille is a strange and difficult thinker—like Nietzsche, it is at times difficult to distinguish between playfulness and insanity. While we will reflect upon his fictional instantiation of these ideas regarding sacrality, sacrifice, eroticism and violence, we are not ultimately undertaking an analysis or critique of Bataille's theoretical work. However, his prose expresses much of the inner erotic scandal of sacramentality that we wish to explore in this chapter: "Only in violation, through death if need be, of the individual's solitariness can there appear that image of the beloved object which in the lover's eyes invests all being with significance. For the lover, the beloved makes the world transparent. . . . There is something absurd and horribly commixed about this conception, yet beyond the absurdity, the confusion and the suffering there lies a miraculous truth. There is nothing really illusory in the truth of love; the beloved being is indeed equated for the lover . . . with the truth of existence."[14] Bataille, like several of the authors considered thus far, is shaped by a Catholic imagination, and so the appearance of an explicitly eucharistic term in this passage ("commixed") should not surprise us. Further, Bataille seems to be brushing up against the kind of experience that in Christian practice is associated with sacramentality—indeed the Eucharist could be described as an absurd yet miraculous truth, i.e., that the divine became incarnate in Jesus Christ, who died and was raised, and who now offers his resurrection body as bread and wine to be eaten and drunk.

However, in all of this exists something shocking, as we have seen already in our examinations of the broken body and the body as food. We again run into the *skandalon* of sacramentality, and must pause to collect ourselves. The living metaphor Christ establishes is irreducibly transgressive, not only in its (il)logic—bread and wine *are* not and do not *become* body and blood—but in its prescription as well: human flesh and blood are not to be consumed. To do so is a violation of a nearly universal taboo. Yet, as Bataille explains, "Transgression is complementary to the profane world, exceeding its limits but not destroying it. . . . The profane world is the world

11. Ibid., 24.
12. Ibid., 21.
13. Ibid., 15–16.
14. Ibid., 21.

of taboos. The sacred world depends on limited acts of transgression."[15] The Eucharist, as part of the sacred world, which is naturally intertwined with the profane, is such a limited act of transgression, for we *celebrate* the sacraments—the Eucharist (*thanks-giving*) in particular—and as Bataille points out, celebration is "the time of transgressing taboos."[16]

We have drawn upon Bataille to get us to this point in the discussion, and to be fair to his theory, we should make mention of his view of the Christian religion as it relates to eroticism—for it differs substantially from our own. To Bataille, Christianity fails, and reveals itself to be "the least religious"[17] of the religions of the world, because of the symbolic character of the Mass. Bataille concludes, therefore, that Christianity has a fundamental misunderstanding of the sacrality of sacrifice and transgression, rooted in Christianity's aversion to law-breaking, which domesticates the original transgression, the *sin*, of the cross: "the sin of the crucifixion is disallowed by the priest celebrating the mass. . . . The echoing liturgy is in harmony with the deeps of primitive human thought but strikes a false note."[18] This is a contentious claim on a number of levels, and a full critique of Bataille's reading of Christianity lies outwith the scope of this project. However, we would register our disagreement with Bataille, suggesting instead that the bloodless sacrifice of the Mass is in fact an enactment of transgressive sacrifice, including the connotations of violence and eroticism which are exalted in his essay. Our close readings of three fictional texts should demonstrate this far better than any theological argument.

THE SACRAMENTAL BODY AS EROTIC BODY: MARIETTE AND GRENOUILLE

We should take a moment to recall two of the fictional bodies considered thus far in our literary explorations which, while selected for the ways they respectively embodied the brokenness of the body and the body as food, also capture the sacramentality of the erotic body. In *Mariette in Ecstasy*, Catholic novelist Ron Hansen portrays the body of Mariette Baptiste as

15. Ibid., 67–68.

16. Ibid., 258; quoted in MacKendrick, *Counterpleasures*, 11.

17. Ibid., 32. Indeed, Bataille confesses, "If it were not for the fact that Christianity is a religion after all, I should even feel an aversion for Christianity. That this is so is demonstrated by the subject of the present work. . . . Christianity sets its face against eroticism and thereby condemns most religions" (32).

18. Ibid., 89–90. He writes elsewhere: "Christianity has created a sacred world from which everything horrible or impure has been excluded" (135).

both a broken body, wracked by the stigmata, but also as an intensely sexual body, which does become the object of erotic desire and pleasure for some of the sisters of the Crucifixion. Nowhere is this more evident than in the "playlet" that Mariette and the sisters put on for one another, acting out the Song of Songs. Hansen's language conjures the violence we have been discussing as well as the stigmata that colonize and define Mariette's body in the narrative. As the play begins, he writes: "Mariette is glamorously there, her great dark mane of hair in massacre, like the siren pictures of Sheba. She's taken her habit and sandals off and shockingly dressed her soft naked-ness in a string necklace of white buttons that are meant to seem pearls and red taffeta robe that is like a bloodstain on linens."[19] This scene, with its ab-surd dramatic subject matter and gender-bending, is simultaneously natural (they are all women, after all), comedic (i.e., Sister Geneviève's penciled-in mustache and put-on deep voice), and scandalous: "'We shouldn't be doing this,' Sister Philomène says, but no one pays her the slightest attention."[20] The scene is representative of the mystery and ambiguity with which Han-sen has deliberately written Mariette's character—the vignette from the Song of Songs concludes not with consummation but desire unfulfilled, and Mariette turns the attention of the sisters away from the sensual whimsy of the playlet toward fervent desire for Christ: "she gets to her knees below Christ on the crucifix, and one by one the novices get to their knees, too."[21]

However, we know that Mariette is the object of sexual desire for Sister Hermance at least, who is in love with Mariette. Considering the novel in its entirety, it is difficult to conclude otherwise than that Sister Hermance's love extends beyond *agape* and indeed transgresses the limits of *eros*. The scandal that Mariette creates at the priory, leading to her eventual dismissal, at first appears to be a result of the stigmata, but in the end, we wonder if it is not also related to her brimming sexuality, which arouses erotic desire amongst some of the sisters. The wounds of Christ are a blessing and a curse to she who receives them, but as a visible manifestation of the presence and blessing of Christ, should be received by the community as a means of grace. However, erotic desire of sister for sister places the stability of the entire convent at considerable risk, a risk that simply cannot be afforded.

In chapter 4, we attended to the brokenness of the stigmatic body of Mariette, and in chapter 5, she appeared again briefly as a fictional instance of the body as food, when Sister Hermance licks the wound in her hand,

---

19. Hansen, *Mariette*, 82–83.
20. Ibid., 83.
21. Ibid., 85.

tasting her blood as a sacramental participation in the body of the beloved.[22] In this way, Mariette's body is a counterpart to the body of Jean-Baptiste Grenouille, whose body is consumed as a love feast by the ravenous mob intoxicated by his perfume. It is purely coincidental, of course, that they share in common the name *Baptiste*, a reference to the ascetic cousin of Jesus, "the voice of one crying out in the wilderness" (Mark 1:2). However, both Mariette and Grenouille can be understood as ascetic—*sacrificial*—bodies, and so the connection to John the Baptist, while unrelated between the two novels, is not insignificant. Like John *Baptiste*, Mariette is a harbinger of Christ. She places herself in the role of his unworthy servant. She claims no carnal desire for the attention her wounds bring her, but only desiring to embody "Christ's own plainness and humility."[23] Jean-Baptiste Grenouille, like the Baptizer, is an outcast from mainstream society, a perceived wild man, encapsulated most fully in *Perfume* in his sojourn to the wilderness of his cave, where he transforms himself into the mad genius who will emerge to create the monstrous, love-inducing perfume. Süskind makes the reference explicit only once: "We are familiar with people who seek out solitude: penitents, failures, saints or prophets. They retreat to deserts, preferably, where they live on locusts and honey. . . . They act in the belief that they are living a life pleasing to God."[24] However, our narrator assures us that for Grenouille it is nothing of the sort; his nominal reference to the one who announced the coming of the Messiah is, at best, ironic, and at worst, demonic: "There was not the least notion of God in his head. . . . He had withdrawn solely for his own personal pleasure, only to nearer to himself. No longer distracted by anything external, he basked in his own existence and found it splendid. He lay in his stony crypt like his own corpse."[25]

Ultimately Grenouille's body, whatever challenge it might pose to our thinking about sacraments and sacramentality, reveals itself to be an anti-sacrament—not a means of grace, but a means of damnation, to the scent-drunk horde of criminals who tear him apart and consume his thirty pieces of flesh. He is Judas Iscariot, Christ's betrayer, not the one who proclaimed his coming. And the one he betrays is ultimately himself, for he is the only one for whom he exists. Grenouille is the personification *in extremis* of the kind of individualism and solipsism that is called into question by the trans-corporeal body of Christ, which extends beyond itself and gives itself to and for others. This individualism is the carnal state into which we are thrown

22. Ibid., 121.

23. Ibid., 12.

24. Süskind, *Perfume*, 127.

25. Ibid., 128.

at birth, but following Zizioulas, Pickstock, Chauvet, and many of our key interlocutors, this isolated individualism is transformed into authentic personhood, received as gift, in the act of communion (construed here as widely as possible). Sacramentality as we are conceiving it may hold together the paradoxes of sacred and profane, life and death, presence and absence, and so on, but we finally are able to determine that Grenouille's body is not sacramental but anti-sacramental, for it only embodies the negative terms of the paradox. There is, in the end, no paradox, but only nihilism. There is, in the end, no *eros*, not even amongst those who consume his body "out of Love," but only Grenouille's hatred for himself and for all humankind—the "Love" of the mob is at best artificial, their murderous criminality disguised by the perfume with which he baptizes himself. Their insanity is only renarrated as Love after the fact. To use Bataille's terms, Grenouille's existence is discontinuous in the most profound way, and even in his spectacular death fails to become continuous, for his is self-sacrifice, carried out by those who know not what they do, only to satisfy his own desires. It is a loveless suicide containing no redemptive or grace-giving value whatsoever.

We have (re)considered the fictional bodies of Mariette and Grenouille as bodies which are broken and consumed out of love (or "Love"). We will now undertake close readings of three fictional texts which take us further in our understanding of the erotic body as sacramental, and of the eroticism of sacramentality.

COUNTERPLEASURES: BALLARD'S *CRASH*

We turn our attention to J. G. Ballard's novel *Crash*,[26] a nightmare vision of violent, post-human sexuality arising from the automobile as a prosthetic extension of the human body. Ballard's novel contains virtually nothing that we would associate with erotic or pornographic literature. The sensuous language characteristic of such work is replaced instead with a sterile, objective, mechanistic voice indicative of the technological landscape that provides the backdrop for the novel. Throughout the text, sexual acts and organs are consistently referred to not in the seductive, colloquial manner often characteristic of erotic literature, but rather in purely technical, even clinical terms: *breast, buttocks, penis, clitoris, vulva, perineum, rectum, anus* (and so forth) are the human anatomical equivalent to the automobile's *bonnet, instrument panel, binnacle, dashboard, steering wheel, seat belt,* etc.

---

26. The novel was later adapted for the screen and directed by David Cronenberg, starring James Spader and Holly Hunter. For the purposes of this essay, we will consider only the novel.

The novel's aim, it would seem, is not to entice or arouse, but provoke and perhaps even to repulse and repel. Furthermore, as these technologies strip the human body of its humanity, any hint of romance is absent; several times Ballard describes the sexual rituals as "devoid of ordinary sexuality . . . divorced from all feeling,"[27] "conceptualized acts abstracted from all feeling."[28] Love barely enters into the discussion, and the amorous is replaced by violence. And yet, certainly *Crash* still should be understood as an erotic novel, for as Bataille (to whose fictional work we will turn next) has noted, "the domain of eroticism is the domain of violence, of violation."[29] This reminder from Bataille serves to illuminate *Crash*'s difficult and disturbing vision. The author's words in the introduction are essential to unlocking the riddle of the novel:

> Throughout *Crash* I have used the car not only as a sexual image, but as a total metaphor for man's life in today's society. As such the novel has a political role quite apart from its sexual content, but I would still like to think that *Crash* is the first pornographic novel based on technology. In a sense, pornography is the most political form of fiction, dealing with how we use and exploit each other, in the most urgent and ruthless way. Needless to say, the ultimate role of *Crash* is cautionary, a warning against that brutal, erotic and overlit realm that beckons more and more persuasively to us from the margins of the technological landscape.[30]

The author acknowledges the novel's pornographic quality. Yet it is pornography in service of politics, pornography meant to provoke and even forewarn.

    Crash's plot is difficult to summarize. In many ways, it breaks the rules of fiction by failing to follow the traditional narrative arch of rising and falling action, of conflict and resolution. The key characters consist of a

---

27. Ballard, *Crash*, 161; also 212: "By some paradox, this sex act between us had been devoid of all sexuality." In the novel, Ballard speaks also of the possibilities of a "new sexuality" emerging (e.g., 35, 102, 119). It appears that, in the novel, reference to sexuality connotes a certain "human-ness" that is lost—or transformed—due to the automobile's technological colonization of the human body. The novel's "post-human" themes (body modification and extension, automobile as prosthetic, etc.) and their political significance merit further exploration, but lie outwith the scope of the present study.

28. Ibid., 127

29. Bataille, *Eroticism*, 15.

30. Ballard, *Crash*, 6.

narrator (called "Ballard"),[31] his wife Catherine, and Vaughan, whose perverse desires and wild genius generate the momentum of the narrative. As the characters engage in their violent, erotic play, wherein sexual desire is consummated in automobile collisions, the reader should become aware of the ways in which her body has been, and is being, colonized by technologies like the automobile, which become extensions of our bodies, inserting an additional layer of mediation to our already mediate (bodily) experience of the material world. Now "relationships," as Ballard observes, are "mediated by the automobile and its technological landscape."[32] The novel's *erotic liturgies* (as we shall call them) are as incomprehensible as the world the author has created. Again, as he writes in the introduction, "*Crash* is . . . an extreme metaphor for an extreme situation."[33]

The novel begins with Ballard's account of Vaughan's (sacrificial) death, and then backs up to chronicle the events leading up to his death. From the first paragraph, Ballard's narration employs language that invokes the liturgical: "During our friendship [Vaughan] had *rehearsed* his death in many crashes, but this was his only true accident."[34] As the narrative unfolds, it becomes apparent that Vaughan's dual-obsession is with collisions as well as with the wounds and scars resulting from this violence. Even the terms by which the narrator describes the collisions that obsess Vaughan, and into which Vaughan draws his small band of disciples,[35] bear resemblances to eucharistic theology. For example, Vaughan is obsessed with "two cars meeting head-on in complex collisions endlessly repeated in slow-motion films, by the identical wounds inflicted on their bodies,"[36] just as theologians have asserted that even as the Eucharist is repeated in local churches across time and space, history and geography, it is yet one identical Eucharist that is being celebrated, which shares symbolically in Christ's Last Supper with his disciples and in the sacrificial body of the incarnate Christ.[37] Vaughan's

31. We presume this is a "fictional" imagining of the author. In fact, the character of the narrator is not named as "Mr Ballard" until chapter 6 (59). We shall differentiate between "the author" (who will be referred to as such) and "the narrator" (Ballard).

32. Ibid., 101.

33. Ibid., 6.

34. Ibid., 7 [italics are mine]. In the following paragraph, the narrator refers to the "formula" of death, reinforcing this liturgical quality.

35. Ballard refers to Vaughan's "success in converting me into an eager disciple" (190).

36. Ibid., 8.

37. When we refer to Christ's body as "sacrificial," we do not mean to limit this reference to Christ's crucifixion. Indeed, the "sacrificiality" of Christ's body begins with the incarnation of God the Son, as indicated by the Christ Hymn of Phil 2:5–11 ("[He] emptied himself, taking the form of a slave . . . he humbled himself and became

violent rituals, like the Eucharist, are also *erotic* rituals: "He talked of these wounds and collisions with the erotic tenderness of a long-separated lover."[38]

Further, Vaughan is an evangelist for these obsessions; he is the high priest over what emerges as a sort of erotic liturgical community of car-crash junkies. The narrator recounts that "Vaughan unfolded for me all his obsessions with the mysterious eroticism of wounds: the perverse logic of blood-soaked instrumental panels, seat-belts smeared with excrement, sun-visors lined with brain tissue."[39] It is clear that the author is at least sensitive to the religious themes buried deep within his profane imagination, and is able to draw upon religious/liturgical language to convey his pornographic vision. With language that recalls sacramentality (*mystērion*), this "mysteri-ous eroticism" is opaque to outsiders, but to those who have been initiated—have embraced through practice and participation—into its inner logic, this mystery edges nearer to reality. The novel's first chapter, which itself (and the novel as a whole) is a kind of *anamnēsis* (remembrance) of Vaughan's life after the event of his death, concludes with a vision of "the speeding cars, moving together towards their celebration of wounds"[40]—celebration serv-ing as a central feature of the Eucharist, as Paul Bradshaw has thoroughly explicated in his essay on the topic.[41]

Ballard's obsession with the synthesis of sex and car crashes begins with his auto collision with Helen Remington and her husband, who dies in the crash. After the accident, as Helen is helped from the car, the narrator offers this reflection: ". . . all I could see was the unusual junction of her thighs, opened towards me in this deformed way. It was not the sexuality of the posture that stayed in my mind, but the stylization of the terrible

---

obedient to the point of death"). Christ's death *is* indeed sacrificial, but His incarnate life should be regarded as sacrificial *en toto*.

38. Ibid., 8.

39. Ibid., 10.

40. Ibid., 18. The language/theme of *celebration* something of a leitmotif through-out the novel; cf. ". . . celebrated in her husband's death the unity of our injuries and my orgasm" (75); "The junction of her mucous membranes and the vehicle, my own metal body, was celebrated by the cars speeding past us" (113); ". . . as if in celebration, their figures were taking up ever more eccentric positions" (126); ". . . celebrating a new technology" (161); ". . . celebrating in this sexual act the marriage of their bodies with this benign technology" (162); ". . . celebrating the marriage of his own genitalia and the skull-shattered dashboard binnacle . . ." (169). Perhaps the most richly liturgical reference appears on p. 187: ". . . the *entrances* of her flesh to a *wedding* with himself already *celebrated* across the bloody *altar* of Seagrave's car" [italics added]. Compare the notion of *anamnēsis* within celebration: "In our wounds we celebrated the re-birth of the traffic-slain dead, the deaths and injuries of those we had seen dying by the roadside and the imaginary wounds and postures of the millions yet to die" (203).

41. Bradshaw, "Celebration," in Jasper, ed., *Eucharist Today*, 130–41.

events that had involved us, the extremes of pain and violence ritualized in this gesture of her legs, like the exaggerated pirouette of a mentally defective girl I had once seen performing in a Christmas play at an institution."[42] The reference to the Christmas play in this passage (one assumes a nativity play, although this may not be the case) immediately invokes Christianity; suddenly key words of the passage—*pain, violence, ritualized*—beg to be read through the lens of Christian imagination. Clearly, Ballard is hinting at the resonance between Christian ritual and this profane, erotic ritual that replaces the symbols of Christ's body and blood, or even the cross and the other traditional symbols that comprise Christian worship, with automobiles, seat belts, hood ornaments/emblems, instrument panels, and human bodies and their interior fluids, made exterior by the penetration of the human body by the car's appendages and extremities. Even the actions of the rescue crews, cutting bodies from the cars which have become metal sarcophagae, are perceived in liturgical terms: "Even their smallest movements seemed to be formalized, hands reaching towards me in a series of coded gestures"[43]—much as the ceremonial preparation for the Eucharist. The narrator comments that not long after the incident, "Already I felt isolated from the reality of this accident." And so his quest begins to reclaim some connection to the *res*, the reality, the transcendence that he experienced in this most immanent of bodily experiences, where *eros* and *thanatos* converge in the stylized ritual of the auto crash. Gazing at Helen, "Seated like a demented madonna between the doors of the second ambulance," the narrator reflects: "Already I was aware that the interlocked radiator grilles of our cars formed the model of an inescapable and perverse union between us. I stared at the contours of her thighs. Across them the grey blanket formed a graceful dune. Somewhere beneath this mound lay the treasure of her pubis. Its precise jut and rake, the untouched sexuality of this intelligent woman, presided over the tragic events of the evening."[44] When considered in relation to ritual theory, the idea of *presidency* has a strong eucharistic connotation. As the priest *presides over* the liturgy, the narrator suggests that, under his gaze, Helen's sexuality (in general) and genitalia (in particular) somehow occupy a presiding role in his narration of the crash. This significant placement of the erotic—of the sex-act, the collision and interpenetration

42. Ballard, *Crash*, 22.

43. Ibid., 23.

44. Ibid., 24–25. The image of "presidency" over the collision ritual appears throughout the novel, e.g., "These amiable young women ministered within a cathedral of invisible wounds, their burgeoning sexualities presiding over the most terrifying facial and genital injuries" (27); "Over the profiles of her body now presided the metallized excitements of our shared dreams of technology" (41).

of human and automotive bodies—in the violent liturgies of Vaughan and his disciples is, according to Ballard's vision, precisely that which brings a certain (albeit perverse) sacramentality to the car crashes. We might, then, call this assemblage of "techo-erotomanes" a liturgical community of sorts: their eucharistic ritual is indeed a sharing of body and blood, a communion of bodies, broken and spilled. However, instead of the "wonderful exchange" in which the divine and human life (and *bodies* human and divine: recall that the risen Christ remains *incarnate,* bodily) are brought together in the Christ event, the divine is replaced here with the technological body of the automotive machine.

The novel is far too full of words and phrases that connote Ballard's quasi-sacramental vision for all of them to be recounted and considered here. The following passage reveals the resonance between the eucharistic doctrine of the real presence and the existential reality of the narrator and his fellow techo-erotomanes: "The crash was the only real experience I had been through for years. For the first time I was in physical confrontation with my own body, an inexhaustible encyclopedia of pains and discharges, with the hostile gaze of other people, and with the fact of the dead man."[45] In a perverse way, the violent ritual of the collision, and the presence of death therein, brings the narrator into deeper communion with his own body— but it fails to achieve anything that could be described as communion with the body of an other—at least in this instance. This brush with the possibility of death—the extinguishing of life, the damaging of the body beyond repair—becomes for the narrator a "real experience."

The resonance with eucharistic theology that the author is exploring in the text is made most explicit in a passage recounting the characters happening upon a horrific interstate car crash. The scene is littered with spectators, including Vaughan, Catherine and Ballard, who cannot help but take in the aftermath of the crash. As the ambulances pull away and the scene is cleared of the bodies and detritus of the crash, Ballard narrates: "This pervasive sexuality filled the air, as if we were members of a congregation leaving after a sermon, urging us to celebrate our sexualities with friends and strangers, and were driving into the night to imitate the bloody eucharist we had observed with the most unlikely partners."[46] The author's post-ecclesial, yet still thoroughly Christian, imagination cannot avoid fusing and *con*-fusing the traditional rituals of the Christian faith with the violent, mechanistic rituals of contemporary life, which take us to the point of death. Altizer's voice echoes here: "Christianity, even as all religious ways, knows death as the way

45. Ibid., 39.
46. Ibid., 157.

to life, and knows an actual passage through death as the way to an actual realization of life. Of course, this way is a universal way, and perhaps it is most powerfully present in ritual, and above all in that pure or archaic ritual which is uncontaminated by modernization, a ritual wherein resurrection is wholly illusory and unreal apart from its manifestation and realization as crucifixion."[47] Even the most perverse sexual practices explored in the novel are infused with a language and a sacrality drawn from the liturgical and theological arena. Furthermore, in connection with our earlier discussion in chapter 4, the sacramentality of the broken, wounded body emerges as a strong theme in the narrative. Vaughan, whose body permanently carries the marks of the many car crashes he has (intentionally) experienced, is described in raw, visceral terms:

> He lounged back, legs apart, one hand adjusting his heavy groin. The whiteness of his arms and chest, the scars that marked his skin like my own, gave his body an unhealthy and metallic sheen, like the worn vinyl of the car interior. These apparently mean- ingless notches on his skin, like the gouges of a chisel, marked the sharp embrace of a collapsing passenger compartment, the cuneiform of the flesh formed by shattering instrument dials, fractured gear levers and parking-light switches. Together they described an exact language of pain and sensation, eroticism and desire.[48]

The *textuality* of the wounded, disfigured body is depicted here not merely as a personal narrative, but as representative of the entire erotic language that emerges from the violent collision of the human body with the automo- bile. Further, not only does the wounded body possess a language and tell a story, but it also represents an entirely different aesthetic which breaks with the traditional understanding of beauty in terms of purity, completeness, wholeness, etc. Both Ballard and his wife, Catherine, become scarred in car crashes, and these marks as well become "sacred" sites, the focus of erotic desire. After watching Catherine and Vaughan engage in violent sex in the backseat of the automobile he pilots, Ballard says of his wife, "I saw the weals on her cheek and neck, the bruised mouth that deformed her nervous smile. These disfigurements marked the elements of her real beauty."[49] He continues: "I held Catherine closely, loving her for the blows Vaughan had struck her body. Later that night, I explored her body and bruises, feeling them gently with my lips and cheek, seeing in the rash of raw skin across her

47. Altizer, *Total Presence*, 92.

48. Ballard, *Crash*, 90.

49. Ibid., 165.

abdomen the forcing geometry of Vaughan's powerful physique. My penis traced the raw symbols that his hands and mouth had left across her skin . . . marking out the contact points of the imaginary automobile accident which Vaughan had placed on her body."[50] Vaughan's body is also a body of desire to Ballard and the other characters. He is horrifically disfigured, deeply scarred from countless car crashes. Ballard remarks, "Vaughan's body, with its unsavoury skin and greasy pallor, took on a hard, mutilated beauty within the elaborately signalled landscape of the motorway."[51]

Another body in the narrative, that of a minor character named Gabrielle, is unique in that her extensive injuries have crippled her legs, requiring elaborate mechanical braces to allow any mobility. Gabrielle's mechanized body is most like the automobiles that the novel romanticizes, making her an object of particular desire. In once scene, the narrator accompanies Vaughan and Gabrielle to an auto showroom filled with new cars. Ballard confesses, "My eyes were fixed on her leg brace, on her deformed thighs and knees, her swinging left shoulder, these portions of her body that seemed to beckon toward the immaculate machines on their revolving stands, inviting them to confront her wounds."[52] Later Ballard and Gabrielle make love in the rear seat of her car, which has been customized to compensate for her physical limitations. "Each of her deformities became a potent metaphor for the excitements of a new violence. Her body, with its angular contours, its unexpected junctions of mucous membrane and hairline, detrusor muscle and erectile tissue, was a ripening anthology of perverse possibilities."[53] As Ballard undresses her of her braces and harnesses, he discovers "marked depressions, troughs of reddened skin hollowed out in the forms of buckles and clasps . . . corrugated skin . . . these were the templates for new genital organs, the moulds of new sexual possibilities yet to be created in a hundred experimental car crashes."[54] Further, Ballard acknowledges that arousal and excitement is not, for them, the product of "the nominal junction of points of the sexual act" but rather the exploration of the wounds and marks and disfigurements of one another's bodies:

> Her fingers found the small scars below my left collar bone, the imprint of the outer quadrant of the instrument binnacle. . . . [She] began to explore the other wound-scars on my chest and abdomen, running the tip of her tongue into each one. In turn,

50. Ibid., 166.
51. Ibid., 171.
52. Ibid., 174.
53. Ibid., 175–76.
54. Ibid., 176–77.

one by one, she endorsed each of these signatures, inscribed on
my body by the dashboard and control surfaces of the car. . . . I
moved my hand . . . to the scars on her thighs, feeling the tender
causeways driven through her flesh by the handbrake of the car
in which she had crashed. . . . I explored the scars on her thighs
and arms, feeling for the wound areas under her left breast, as
she in turn explored mine, deciphering together these codes of a
sexuality made possible by our two car-crashes.[55]

Ballard finds sexual fulfillment in "the deep wound on her thigh," and states
that he "felt no trace of pity for this crippled woman, but celebrated with her
the excitements of these abstract vents let into her body by sections of her
own automobile. . . . in these sexual apertures formed by fragmenting wind-
shield louvres and dashboard dials in a high-speed impact. . . . I dreamed of
other accidents that might enlarge this repertory of orifices."[56]

As horrific as these images are of the wounded, damaged body, which
is eroticized precisely in its brokenness, we suggest that a novel like *Crash*
warrants a "liturgical" reading. By this, we mean that the characters and
their practices, as depicted in the narrative, are best understood, and in
many ways only begin to make sense, when considered through a liturgical lens. We are not referring to the eucharistic liturgy *per se*, but rather
to the ritual forms by which the characters that inhabit the literary world
"make sense" of their existence. Certainly by now it is apparent that liturgies
and rituals grant to a people the ability to narrate their identity, and this
ability is especially powerful in the case of groups, cultures, and societies
that are particularly disparate or atomized.[57] Ballard's parable describes a
thoroughly diasporic culture, wherein every person is disconnected from
every other. In response to this given condition, the characters of the novel
seek to overcome their fragmentation through sacrificial rituals wherein
the violent interpenetration of bodies in automotive collisions and sexual
intercourse comprise the liturgies by which these characters glean meaning
and "make sense" of their otherwise solitary lives. While we do not find
it particularly useful to make assertions or assumptions about the author's
intentions, Ballard's employment of theological and liturgical language and
images indicates that he is not oblivious to the many parallels highlighted
here. Perhaps more than most, Ballard's literary art is keenly aware of the

55. Ibid., 178–79.

56. Ibid., 179.

57. Here we could consider as one example the conclusions William Cavanaugh
arrives at in *Torture and Eucharist*, viz. the Chilean Catholic Church's recovery of the
Eucharist as a ritual means by which to resist the social fragmentation wrought by the
tortuous dictatorship of General Pinochet.

resonance between these myriad expressions of sacramentality, juxtaposing and confusing (seemingly deliberately) the sacred and the profane, the immanent and the transcendent, the corporeal and the incorporeal, and so on. And so we emerge with a dystopian, horrifying vision of the broken, erotic body, yet one that is still conceived as profoundly *sacramental*. We will reserve judgment about the value and validity of this vision of sacramentality until after our discussion of Bataille's fiction, to which we now turn.

PROFANING THE EUCHARIST: BATAILLE AND THE LIMITS OF LANGUAGE

Georges Bataille's scholarly work, which is itself a strange confluence of philosophy, theology, anthropology, and cultural history, bears a fascinating relationship to his fiction. It occurs to us that Bataille's literary (fictional) language seeks to *perform* that which his scholarly (non-fictional) writings theorize. And in a certain sense, his fiction succeeds—or more nearly approaches its mark—where his scholarly language falls short. As Karmen MacKendrick writes, "It is Bataille who breaks language apart to show us why the erotic and the sacred are the same at base, wildly sacrificial and incomprehensibly joyous."[58] Bataille's *Story of the Eye* pushes the symbol of the Eucharist to its erotic extreme. The story, which has been heralded as a masterpiece of pornographic literature, demonstrates the ultimate inability of language to convey both religious and erotic experience. It also, in its stunning and disturbing conclusion, seeks to unveil a common sacramentality shared between sex and the sacred, which as we have established encompasses violence, sacrifice, and death as well. The experience of each of these is, of course, inexpressible and unsharable. It is as though Bataille is keenly aware of—and intent on exploring in his fiction—the way that each of these experiences are universal (at least potentially), and yet at the same time they are also deeply isolated and isolating, insofar as no one is able to truly share in the religious or sexual experience of any other person; and certainly one cannot experience any death but her own. This is similar to what Elaine Scarry describes in her masterful study, *The Body in Pain*: all humanity is united in the common experience of bodily pain, and yet at the same time, bodily pain is absolutely individual and unable to be shared or experienced by any other body.[59]

The narrative of *The Story of the Eye* chronicles the sexual escapades of a woman named Simone and an unnamed male narrator, who recounts

58. MacKendrick, *Counterpleasures*, 4.

59. Cf. Scarry, *Body in Pain*.

the events of the novel from a vantage point later in life. An additional male character, Sir Edmund, a wealthy and voyeuristic Englishman, enters the narrative midway and plays a significant role in the horrific final scene, which will be the subject of our discussion here. The structure is episodic, with little besides the growing depravity and intensity of the sexual acts providing cohesion from one vignette to the next. After several chapters providing remembrances of various exhibitionist sexual scenarios, we arrive at chapter 12, entitled "Simone's Confession and Sir Edmund's Mass," and the thirteenth and final chapter ("The Legs of the Fly") where the story ends unresolved; the author (Bataille, or perhaps a fictive "Bataille") providing the final postscript connecting certain characters and events of the novel to his own childhood and family relations.

Throughout the novella, each of the narrator's remembrances of his sexual history with Simone seems to involve an increased degree of violence. The pair's early sexual experiences are relatively innocent, but their practices soon turn to scatological play, sado-masochistic mutilation, and eventually murder and necrophilia. In the final two chapters, the three main characters—the narrator, Simone, and Sir Edmund—have absconded to Spain, where they visit Madrid, take in a bullfight and witness the castration of a bull and the death of a toreador, both of which incite erotic pleasure in Simone. Shortly thereafter, they travel to Seville, which Simone wishes to visit "because of it's reputation as a city of pleasure."[60] Simone seems to float through the city as an object of arousal; the narrator recounts "Indeed, we virtually never stopped having sex."[61] However, the descriptions of sex in the story eventually begin to lose all meaning; they become numbed and numbing repetitions of depravity, in no way sensual or arousing. The trio eventually enters an empty Catholic church, which according to legend (and appropriately to the narrative) was founded by the fabled lover Don Juan, whose tomb is said to be located beneath the threshold of the church. Entering the sanctuary, the confessional chamber in the church is found occupied, and the trio sit and wait for the penitent—an attractive young woman—and the priest, to emerge. The narrator describes the two in highly erotic terms: the woman is "enraptured: with her head thrown back and her eyes white and vacant" and the priest is "blond . . . very young, very handsome, with a long thin face and the pale eyes of a saint . . . still gliding in his ecstasy."[62] The sacrament of reconciliation which has taken place inside the chamber is thus conceived as an erotic interaction between the penitent and

60. Bataille, *Story of the Eye*, 55.

61. Ibid., 55

62. Ibid., 57–58.

her confessor, perhaps implied as a kind of power play wherein each party in the exchange is gratified—spiritually but also perhaps sexually—despite the absence of touch.

Simone expresses her desire to confess, so she enters the confessional chamber, and the profane sex-play ensues. Unbeknownst to the priest, but apparent to the narrator and Sir Edmund, Simone pleasures herself whilst giving her confession. She eventually reveals this perversion to the confessor, and then begins to perform fellatio and other sexual acts on the passive, unresisting priest. It is clear that here Bataille, through his narrator, is exploring the subversion and utter degradation of the Eucharist, as the central act of the Catholic worship that defines his own experience of Christianity. The narrator speaks of the priest in contemptuous terms: he is "lugubrious," a "sordid creature," a "dreadful phantom," a "larva," a "vile priest," a "wretch," a "swine," a "sacerdotal pig" with a "moronic face," "monster," "imbecile," "beast" and so on. However, it is noteworthy that Bataille, in describing the pitiful, despicable priest, places this piece of dialogue in the narrative:

"*Senores*," the wretch snivelled, "you must think I'm a hypocrite."

"No," replied Sir Edmund with a categorical intonation.

It as though the unresisting priest is giving himself over/up as the sacrifice in this erotic liturgy, to be raped, tortured, killed, and mutilated. However, while the priest perceives his willing participation in the eroto-drama as hypocritical and irreconcilable with his religious vocation, Sir Edmund admits no such disconnection; to Sir Edmund and the other two players, his passivity and non-interference is most natural. This key passage could be easily passed over without comment, except that in the final chapter, the priest is referred to several times as "victim,"[63] recalling the association of Christ as the victim—the subject of sacrifice, but also the *victual* given as food—of the Mass. Bataille tests the ability, or inability, of language to profane the most sacred of things, and to *con-fuse* the sexual with the religious.

As the drama unfolds, the characters drag the priest out of the confessional chamber and to the sacristy. While Simone and the narrator defile the unprotesting priest, Sir Edmund discovers the key to the tabernacle, and retrieves the ciborium filled with the eucharistic wafers, and the chalice used to hold the wine. Thus ensues the most comprehensive and explicit profanation of the Eucharist found in modern literature. The trio force the priest to urinate into the chalice, which he is then commanded to drink. The

---

63. Ibid.: "Next, Sir Edmund, slipping under his victim . . ." (64); "At last, she squeezed so resolutely that an even more violent thrill shot through her victim" (65).

narrator's description of this event is paradoxical: "The paralyzed wretch drank with well-nigh filthy ecstasy at one long gluttonous draft . . . gurgling desperately and revelling in it."[64] Here again, the passive priest is perceived to be enjoying this torturous degradation, these "miserable sacrileges." This parallel defilement of both the vicar and the Eucharist finally reaches its extreme when the priest ejaculates onto the wafers contained in the ciborium. In many ways this orgasm is also the climax of the narrative; the final chapter is a decrescendo after "Sir Edmund's Mass." The ritual concludes with Simone strangling the priest to death during intercourse; Sir Edmund extracting the priest's eye; and the narrator and Simone engaging in additional perverse sex-play with the eye.[65]

Bataille could be commended for his daring exploration of this most profane imagery bound up together with the sacrality of the Eucharist; for the ritual undertaken by the characters in the novella is certainly a liturgy, just as their sexual acts have held a certain liturgical quality throughout the narrative (albeit rituals largely devoid of any love or passion). We wish to assert that what Bataille accomplishes is actually a demonstration of the utter *failure* of these sexual liturgies to fulfill, to satisfy. If desire is not the desire of fulfillment but rather the desire for desire,[66] so the sexual acts in the narrative *obliterate* desire by exploring the relentless pursuit of desire even as every desire in the narrative, however perverse and carnal, is almost fully instantaneously *fulfilled*. As a consequence, the accounts of the sexual acts in this pornographic novel are devoid of any eroticism whatsoever—far from titillating, the vignettes of the novel are, like Ballard's *Crash*, a horrifying and nauseating experience to read and imagine.[67]

64. Ibid., 62.

65. Much could be made of the symbolism of eggs and eyes throughout the narrative, as demonstrated by Roland Barthes' critical essay "The Metaphor of the Eye," included in the Penguin Classics edition of *Story of the Eye*. However, this symbolism is not of significant interest to the discussion at hand of the confluence of the sacred and profane, of the erotic and the sacramental. We note the multiple possibilities of such interpretations (the relationship between eggs, testicles, and eyes; the similarity in French between *oeil and oeuf*; etc.), but elect instead to focus on the story's profanation of the vicar and the Eucharist, and in particular Bataille's disclosure of the utterly depraved and sacrilegious lurking just beneath the surface of the most sacred of rites.

66. Bataille writes: "How sweet it is to remain in the grip of the desire to burst out without going the whole way, without taking the final step! How sweet it is to gaze long upon the object of our desire, to live on in our desire, instead of dying by going the whole way, by yielding to the excessive violence of desire" (*Eroticism*, 141–42).

67. In fact, in attempting to categorize the novel according to conventional genres, it may not be inappropriate to describe the novel as not only as "pornography" but also as "horror/fantasy." The gruesome violence of the novel's final scene bears striking similarities to a recent trend in the cinema of horror that has been described as

Bataille's depiction is a horrific dystopia of unbridled sexual depravity, which in the end proves to be all-consuming, insatiable, self-destructive. In the final scene, even the most sacred is profaned; the vicarious, gracious presence of Christ, represented by the priest who in the Eucharist acts *in persona Christi,* and embodied in the eucharistic elements, is raped, degraded, massacred, mutilated. Or, perhaps better put, the most sacred of acts—the sexual and the sacramental—are simultaneously revealed to be *indistinguishable* from the most utterly profane. For this reason, it seems to us, Roland Barthes describes *Story of the Eye* as "not a deep work. Everything in it is on the surface. There is no hierarchy. The metaphor is laid out in its entirety; it is circular and explicit, with no secret reference behind it. It is a case of signification without a thing signified (or in which everything is signified), and it is not the least beauty nor the least novelty of this text that it constitutes . . . a kind of open literature out of reach of all interpretation."[68] In this sense, it is a novel that destroys interpretation. It is "anti-hermeneutical." But in a sense, this could be said of the Eucharist itself, which resists—not just confounds but renders useless—our most nuanced attempts to interpret. The Eucharist, in other words, is not an object for hermeneutical inquiry: it *is* a hermeneutic, an interpretive grid through which to interpret all of life, yet itself resistant to interpretation.

In her essay "The Pornographic Imagination," Susan Sontag comments that Bataille's "intellectual project [is] to explore the scope of transgression."[69] Sontag's essay looks further into literature that we will not examine in this study, most notably Pauline Réage's *The Story of O.*[70] We will however consider Sontag's comment upon this literary work, for it is in her consideration of this work that Sontag takes note of the sacramental quality of the sexual liturgies recounted in such works of pornographic fiction. She writes: "Religious metaphors abound in a good deal of modern erotic literature . . . and in some works of pornographic literature, too. *The Story of O* makes heavy use of religious metaphors for the ordeal that O undergoes. O 'wanted to believe.' Her drastic condition of total personal servitude to those who use her sexually is repeatedly described as a mode of salvation. With anguish and anxiety, she surrenders herself. . . . When she has, to be sure, entirely lost her freedom, O has gained the right to participate in what is described as

---

"torture–porn"; films exemplary of this genre include *Hostel,* the *Saw* franchise, and several recent Asian horror films (*Old Boy*), characterized by liturgies of sexualized/ eroticized and voyeuristic violence, dismemberment, cannibalism, etc.

68. Barthes, "The Metaphor of the Eye," 123.

69. Sontag, "The Pornographic Imagination," 107.

70. Robert Detweiler gives an insightful theological (or, rather, "religious") reading of Réage's *The Story of O* in his seminal volume *Breaking the Fall,* 136–45.

virtually *a sacramental rite*."[71] As referenced earlier in this chapter, Bataille acknowledges that "all eroticism has a sacramental character,"[72] and in *Story of the Eye*, he attempts to demonstrate that there is indeed no limit to this claim: *all* eroticism, no matter how perverse, profane and depraved.

It is apparent that the limits of language, located and transgressed in erotic or pornographic literature, bear much resemblance to those boundaries transgressed in the symbolic grammar of sacramentality. From the perspective of Christian faith, that salvation explored in Réage's fiction, wrought by sado-masochistic submission, mirrors almost precisely, albeit perversely, the traditional Christian understanding of salvation: one must lose one's life to find it; one must take up one's cross and die to self to gain eternal life, for, following St. Paul, to live is Christ and to die is gain. We are baptized into Christ's vicarious death and resurrection; we give up our freedom and become willing slaves to the gospel; we carry on our bodies the marks or wounds of Christ; and so on. In the Eucharist, we *enact* this visceral image of salvation.

No matter how hard Christian theology tries to domesticate this image or make it more palatable, the scandalous core of sacramentality will rise to the surface again and again. If theology cannot bear this thought, the *skandalon* will surface in literary and artistic utterances not constrained by or beholden to ecclesiastical dogma. It is our assertion that this is *precisely* what Bataille and Réage accomplish in their pornographic fictions: transgressing boundaries that theology cannot bear; *speaking* (and in godlike fashion, in speaking, *creating*) that which Christian theology considers unspeakable. To illustrate this, we turn once again to Bataille's narrative: when Sir Edmund draws an explicit connection between the whiteness of the eucharistic wafer and that of male ejaculate (and even more shockingly, *Christ's* sperm!), "The lucidity of this logic was so convincing that Simone and [the narrator] required no further explanation."[73] In many ways, this is the linchpin of novella's entire finale, in our view, for here Bataille sums up in one brief statement our entire thesis regarding the confluence of the sacred and the profane in the inter-relationship between the erotic and the sacramental: this connection, so jarringly sacrilegious and abhorrent to the reader, is accepted and dismissed as the most sane and obvious sort of common sense. To the characters engaged in this profane erotic liturgy, which culminates not simply in aberrant sex-play but in death and dismemberment, the symbolic level on which one would connect the eucharistic host to

71. Sontag, "Pornographic Imagination," 112–13 [italics are mine].

72. Bataille, *Eroticism*, 15–16.

73. Bataille, *Story of the Eye*, 62.

semen (a kind of hyper-literalization of the *logos spermatikos*), or the chalice holding tawny wine to urine, requires no stretch of the imagination whatsoever, but instead emerges as primary even to the point of being unworthy of significant comment, explanation, or interpretation by the characters.

In this sense, Bataille succeeds in bringing to light the horrifying commingling of the sacred and the profane, of the erotic and the sacramental, of life and death, bound up in the Eucharist itself. By subverting the Eucharist, by profaning its ritual, by perverting its liturgy and slaying its principle actor (the priest/vicar), Bataille reveals not so much the *sacramentality of sex* as the *eroticism of sacramentality*—although of course both observations are appropriate. His narrative *both* elevates the erotic to the level of the liturgical and sacramental, even as it degrades the Eucharist to the level of carnality. And yet, is the former truly an *elevation*? Is the latter a *degradation*? Perhaps these spatial metaphors are no longer useful in this coincidence of opposites where each infuses the other: elevation is degradation and vice versa. The Second Person of the Triune Godhead becomes incarnate, flesh and blood, in Jesus of Nazareth; as divinity assumes humanity, humankind is subsumed into the life of the Divine, even as human beings *consume* the physical body of the Divine in the Eucharist itself.

LIPSTICK ON THE HOST: THE SACRAMENTALITY OF SEX

Ballard's and Bataille's fictions present us with horrific visions of bodies engaged in aberrant erotic activity. In the cases of both their fictions, the erotic, no matter how perverse and depraved, is construed in sacramental and even liturgical terms. We want to be clear that our use of these novels in the present discussion is *not* a glorification of violent, pornographic fictions, an attempt to baptize these two novels or novelists in sacramentality, nor is it an effort to radicalize our understanding of sacramentality such that it may indeed include the kinds of extreme practices depicted in these two novels. Rather, our incorporation of these narratives into the discussion is motivated by the way both works draw upon more (Bataille) or less (Ballard) overt sacramental and even eucharistic language and imagery to present similar-yet-distinct visions of the sacramentality of the erotic body which are unbearable for Christian theology of any sort. The challenge presented to Christian sacramental and liturgical thinking (and practice!) by these fictions must not be passed over, even though we finally ascertain that the "sacramental" visions contained in these novels is at best, like *Perfume*'s Grenouille, *anti*-sacramental—for how can we accept these visions as part of our understanding of sacramentality when they are devoid of any sense of *love* or authentic, embodied *koinōnia*?

We will conclude this chapter, and this study, by engaging a fictional narrative that we believe offers a constructive and profound vision of the sacramentality of the erotic body, and the inner eroticism of the Eucharist, which points the way forward in our thematic exploration of sacrament. Irish author Aidan Mathews' novella *Lipstick on the Host* tells the story of Margaret (Meggie), an unmarried woman of about forty. Meggie, a Roman Catholic herself, teaches literature at a Catholic school. Struggling with her hypochondriac mother, her age, her loneliness and desire for romance, and her compulsion to make up stories, our narrator reveals herself to the reader through a series of sixteen journal entries, spanning nearly two months of her life around the time of her forty-first birthday. Throughout her journal entries, Meggie is especially candid about her insecurities with her body. However, she does meet and form a romantic relationship with Antony, and this encounter, however brief, sets in motion the events into which the story draws us.

The religious and the sensual are never far apart in this story, a hint into the sacramentally-steeped, incarnational Catholicism of the Irish literary imagination. During Meggie and Antony's first date, their conversation ranges widely: "We touched on just about everything, and just about everything touched us."[74] Antony happens to be a gynecologist and several years Meggie's senior. Writing about their date, Meggie reflects on Antony's body, and her own, in relation to his profession:

> He is a gynaecologist. I should have guessed from his hands. His hands are thoughtful and cared-for. No woman would be afraid of them. They are too fatherly for that. Instead of being afraid, you would be the opposite. You would buy new underwear and a new outfit for each visit, and spray the inside of your thigh with an atomizer when the nurse called you in. He would stroke your bump, and beam. Then, as his fingers slipped ever so quietly inside you, you'd read the Latin diplomas and degrees that hung from the picture railing on the opposite wall, and wonder why his name didn't have a H in it.[75]

On their date, they also discuss their religious faith and backgrounds; Meggie is "Dublin Catholic," while Antony is low-church Protestant. Antony gives insight into his very this-worldly, non-supernatural spirituality: "Of course I'm spiritual. . . . But spirituality . . . has more to do with my brother

74. Mathews, *Lipstick*, 240.

75. Ibid., 240–41.

scampering round the house when he was four, shouting 'Easter eggs. Christ
has risen. Easter eggs.' It's very down to earth, you know. It's got its feet
on the ground. It's soiled. The odour of sanctity is the stink of the laundry
bin."[76] Antony here articulates a kind of pervasive spirituality or sacramentality that comprises everyday life. Distinct from Meggie's high-sacramental
Catholic tradition, Antony represents something less mystical, or perhaps
rather, mystical chiefly in its mundaneness—"the stink of the laundry bin."
His faith, his religious practice, is incarnate, "soiled"—dirty perhaps, but
only in the way that is unavoidable and fully a part of our humanity. There
is nothing sinful, after all, about having to wash sweaty clothes; it is simply
a consequence of being in-the-body.

In class the following day, Meggie makes a questionable remark to her
high school students about Milton and "how his use of lovely, long Latin
words is a compensation for no sex. It is, actually, a kind of cunnilingus."[77]
She later questions the wisdom of making such a sexually charged comment
to her class, but her musings cut right to the heart of the story, the intermingling of the sacramental and the sexual, the sacred and the profane, in
the "wonderful exchange" equally present in Holy Communion and human
coitus. She writes: "Should I have said that? Perhaps I shouldn't have said
that. You can show them pictures of the electric chair or a baby eating blue-
bottles in a back-street in Bangladesh, but you can't tell them that people
receive each other like Holy Communion."[78]

Later in the story, Meggie accompanies Antony on an errand, after
which he decides he wants to buy her a dress. Antony peeks into the dress-
ing room where Meggie is changing, and she unflinchingly discloses her
naked body to him:

> I opened my bra and took it off, and hung it on a hanger. It bal-
> anced beautifully, one cup on each side of the wire. It didn't tilt,
> and slip to the ground. I was so grateful. . . .
>
> I gathered the flowing folds of the gown from where they
> had run like water to my pleated waist, and I drew them up
> slowly over my stomach and the cove of my ribs and my bare,
> unbearable breasts, until I was decent again. . . .
>
> He had seen them. He had wanted to touch them; not to test
> them, not to handle or manhandle them with brisk, cellophane
> fingers, palpating for lumps; but to touch them, to squeeze them,
> to leave the marks of his fingernails around the wet stub of the

76. Ibid., 241.
77. Ibid., 249.
78. Ibid., 249.

nipple. He was not thinking of lactation then; he was thinking of milk and honey.[79]

Meggie presents her body to Antony as a visual feast. Her body, which has troubled her in its age and its isolation, becomes under her lover's gaze a promised land, a garden of delight. It is almost as if through his gaze, but not yet his touch, Meggie receives the gift of her own body—her body as an object of desire, but at this stage, desire unfulfilled. Describing these events in her journal, Meggie concludes thus: "I am very near the world. I can almost smell it."[80] The sensuous image recalls Antony's brand of spirituality: earthy, grounded, the "odour of sanctity," the smell of the human body. Here once again we are flung into not the carnality of this world, in the sinful sense, but its in/carnality, its incarnation. Desire, sacred and profane, infuses every action with deeper significance for these two characters and their commingled passions. Like the individual words of a poem, mundane if interpreted on their own, the actions and events of life during this phase of newly germinating love all become plurisignificant. For this brief period, particularly because of her growing intimacy with Antony, Meggie experiences life with a heightened awareness of its wonder, its mystery. Not that everything is perfect—to the contrary—but everything is a swirl of communion, God's love (*agape*) and the love of God commingling with Antony's love for her, and her for him (*eros*)—to the point when, in fact, one cannot be distinguished from the other.

At the end of chapter 5, we briefly considered Simone de Beauvoir's accounts of women mystics St. Angela of Foligno, who happily drank the wash-water of the lepers she bathed, consuming bits of dead skin like communion, and Marie Alacoque, whose love for a patient she nursed led her to clean up vomit with her tongue. In our story, Meggie becomes like these women mystics when she cleans up the morning-sickness of a secretly pregnant student in her class: "I picked up the vomit with my bare hands. . . . But I wasn't disgusted. I wasn't even indifferent. Actually, I was quite happy. It made such perfect sense, really. . . . And I think I felt joy for the time that it took for the classroom to empty around me. I am not quite certain what joy feels like, but I think I felt joy."[81]

Following this epiphanic experience, a sacred celebration of bodily filth, Meggie runs errands and makes preparation for the Antony's visit to her home and the inevitable sexual consummation she desires. She is keenly aware of her body: "I sat in the bath for an hour. I've never been so clean.

79. Ibid., 268.
80. Ibid., 269.
81. Ibid., 272.

... I shaved a lot of myself; I could wear a thong, almost. ... Then I got hard skin off the side of my foot with the edge of the scissors."[82] Meggie is readying her body to be presented as an offering to her lover. She is caring for it—grooming it, removing dead skin and hair, soaking and softening it—as a way of caring for him. When he receives her "like Holy Communion," she wants to be a pleasing sacrifice to his senses. In her journal entry for Sunday, 25 February, Meggie makes her confession about her first love-making with Antony. She conceives her body as text to be read, and as food to be tasted and savored: "My body was Braille to his blindness. He read me everywhere. There are so many parts of my body I have never touched, unless they are ill. They are sick from not being touched. But his tongue toured me. He opened me like a book, and smelled the pages."[83] Meggie's body occupies several different metaphors in this passage. She is Braille, a sign system that is interpreted by touch rather than sight. She is a book, but not one that is read, but rather smelled. Again we are taken to the image of the laundry bin, the musty bookstore smell of pages which have absorbed the odors of their surroundings. She is a map, or a road—a journey to be taken—"his tongue toured me." This complex of metaphors reveals both the ability and inability of language to express erotic experience. The same is true, of course, with religious experience, experience with the sacred, which encompasses the sexual. The best that she can do, with language, with her writing, is tell it in metaphors.

Bringing to a close what we assume is a lengthy period of sexual deprivation, Meggie is confronted with feelings—physical, emotional, spiritual?—long since forgotten: "I can still feel him inside me. Antony, I mean. I had forgotten that, too: the feeling of being filled. I had forgotten how quickly you itch afterwards, and how warm the sperm is, and the lines of noughts and crosses on your breasts from the weight of their bodies. ... [T]he theologians and the pornographers only know the half of it. ... How long do you feel a man inside you? It will be twelve hours in two hours' time."[84] The communion between their bodies brings Meggie more fully into communion with her own body: its openings and aporias, the impressions on skin, the lingering sensation of touch removed. Her conjoining of the sacred (theologians) and the profane (pornographers)—or perhaps it is the dichotomy between theory (theology) and practice (pornography)—is both ironic and profound. What she seeks, what she has found, is a third-way, a

82. Ibid., 275.

83. Ibid., 277.

84. Ibid., 278.

kind of *doxic* experience which is more akin to worship or mystic ecstasy than anything else.

After their sexual consummation, a few days pass without Meggie hearing from Antony, and she reflects in her journal. "It is twenty-four hours since I stopped feeling him inside me. Now I can only feel his absence. It's not as nice."[85] Her experience of being filled by him, of what must seem to her, despite the body's mediation, like im-mediacy, is replaced by an experience of absence. Toward the end of this entry, she reveals that a pregnant fellow-teacher (and sometimes-rival) from her school—who shares her name ("the other Meggie")—has suffered a late-term miscarriage. Our narrator writes of it in gut-wrenching terms that indicate this is a pain that perhaps she has experienced herself; and although she never verifies this fact, earlier comments about mid-life child-bearing, and her attempts to convince herself, through the popular wisdom of magazine articles, that she is not past her prime, seem to disclose a desire—almost an obsession—rooted in loss. Despite her occasional hostility toward the other Meggie, she is clearly touched on a deep level, and writes about it in painful, visceral terms:

> Meggie's baby will not be born. It will be disinterred, and buried again somewhere else, with the skeletons and the signet rings of great-grandparents. It will never kick her again; it will only trample her into the ground. It had the lifespan of a laboratory mouse or a tin of pears. It was alive; now it's dead. And the little semi-colon in between, that tough and tiny waterway between the one and the other, like the Panama Canal between the Atlantic and the Pacific, will never see it throw a stone and watch the circles spread.
>
> They say it's been dead for a week. . . . He has been decomposing inside her suntan for seven days and seven nights, with his thumb in his mouth and his ankles crossed . . .[86]

Mathews' poetics in this passage, inscribed in Meggie's voice, are as devastating as they are remarkable. David Jasper wrote of reading the final scene of *Perfume* that it is hard, shocking, "indigestible."[87] This passage is exceedingly more intolerable—excruciating to read. Meggie's experience, coping with the absence of Antony, in the aftermath of their erotic communion—her feeling of being filled, now feeling only the presence of his absence—is juxtaposed with the other Meggie's experience of losing the life which filled her womb. Like Ellen Gluyas' miscarriage and stillbirth in *A*

85. Ibid., 284.
86. Ibid., 284–85.
87. Jasper, *Sacred Body*, 26.

Fringe of Leaves, the *corps* of the mother has become the host to a corpse, "decomposing inside her." Mathews, via Meggie, even gives us an additional punch when the pronoun shifts—"it's been dead for a week. . . . *He* has been decomposing inside her." The child, the *son*, is dead—"*it is finished*." Lest this excursus on the miscarriage seem like a detour from our discussion of the sacramentality of the *erotic* body, let us call to mind the erotic act that led to this pregnancy. The maternal body here, as Caroline Walker Bynum has amply demonstrated, is associated with food to be consumed, nursing and nourishing the newborn.[88] Additionally, Girard has called attention to the relationship of the female body, which spills blood in menstruation and is distended and torn in childbirth, with sacred/sacrificial violence.[89] However, this account of profound abandonment cannot be theorized or circumscribed. The body of the child is simultaneously present and absent: present body, absent life. "*Why do you look for the living among the dead? . . . He is not here*" (Luke 24:5). Like the crucified, transcorporeal Christ, he is neither here, nor there—a displaced body.[90]

The day following this journal entry is Ash Wednesday, which is of course not insignificant—it is the start of Lent, the liturgical season leading up to Easter during which the faithful participate in ascetic practices of self-denial and renunciation for the sake of deepening their relationship to Christ, participating in his forty-day wilderness sufferings, and in preparation to celebrate the Church's greatest feast of Christ's Resurrection. Meggie still has not heard from Antony—their sexual consummation was the previous Saturday, and she is anxious and frustrated by his silence. On Ash Wednesday, Meggie confesses that she is late for chapel and presents herself to receive communion only to realize she is wearing lipstick, and does not feel comfortable to partake of the host over painted lips. She takes the host in her hand, and secretly returns to her seat with it to receive after she has wiped her lips clean, but she is interrupted and forgets about the wafer, wrapped in a tissue in her handbag. Later that evening, it occurs to Meggie: "I had brought the host home with me. Jesus of Nazareth had been in the car beside me all the time[,] . . . the mystery of the world in the palm of my hand. . . . The car-keys had bashed it a bit. One of the sweeteners that I use instead of sugar had stuck to it, but I got it off with my nail. . . . I had never really looked at a host before. They are very delicate. They break at the wrong touch; they break at a touch, even. If you dropped them, they would

88. Bynum, *Holy Feast*, 269–76, passim.

89. Girard, *Violence*, 34–37.

90. Cf. Ward, *Cities*, 81–116.

not fall; they would flutter, like flakes of snow."[91] The fragility of the Eucharist is striking in this passage; not only the delicacy of the Eucharist, but of the eucharistic body of Christ in particular. Not much explication is required to bring to the surface the significance of this vignette in the novella to the present discussion. Meggie is amazed by the delicacy, the wispy translucence, of the very sacrament which forms the basis for not only her spirituality, but her entire faith tradition, her very Church. She continues to reflect upon the host as she prepares to celebrate her own solitary Mass: "Nuns make them. They are made by hand. I wonder did the nun who made my host ever love a man, apart from Our Lord, apart from the God who mingled with the crowd . . . that was what God did, I think. He became naked so that we could be nude again."[92] The God who is present in the sacrament is the God who walked this earth, who denuded himself to restore us to innocence and regain paradise, yet with a second naiveté where we must wrestle with the paradoxes of our language, broken and yet meaning-full—and of our bodies, sexual and spiritual, sacred and profane. Meggie questions, "Wouldn't it be terrible if my hands still smelled of Antony, while I was holding the host in them? Or would it?"[93] As her makeshift Mass unfolds, she administers the sacrament to herself, only to realize that yet again, she has forgotten to wipe off her lipstick—the story's title now clearly a symbol of the confluence of the sacramental and the sexual. In her journal, she writes: "I went to Holy Communion then, more than I have ever gone before in my life; and it was too late by the time I realised that I had completely forgotten to wipe the lipstick off my lips. There is another world, and it is this one."[94]

As should be clear by now, for a relatively short piece of fiction, *Lipstick on the Host* is overflowing with sacramentality, constantly testing and exploring the visceral and bodily character of sacramental spirituality, while simultaneously presenting the sacramentality of bodily and erotic experience. Much more could be said about this remarkable story, but we shall attempt to draw our discussion of these themes to a close. The day after her Ash Wednesday Communion, Meggie visits Antony's office and discovers the reason for his silence: he has been killed in an auto accident. She grieves his loss, his absence, set against the backdrop of the other Meggie's still unfolding miscarriage. Meggie's pain erupts in an exchange with her mother: "I want to start from the beginning[;] . . . I want to be conceived. . . . Then I want to be passed as a heavy period. . . . I want to be blood in the

91. Mathews, *Lipstick*, 288.

92. Ibid.

93. Ibid.

94. Ibid., 288–89.

pedal-bin."[95] Later, she struggles with her doubt, her grief, her loss, reminiscent of the ending of *Monsignor Quixote*, where the Mayor experiences in the absence of his *compañero* the haunting present absence of God. Meggie writes: "At weekends, I met with God; always at his place, never at mine. We had an arrangement. Only at the weekends. He was not to ring me at home; he was not to contact me at work. He was not to leave messages. There was a place and a time, for everything. Now he's broken the rules. Now he wants more. He wants more than my lips and my tongue. He wants me."[96] Her world is turned upside-down, as much by God as by this amorous encounter with a man who is now a corpse, who can only be experienced as an absence . . . much like the God she experiences in the Eucharist. "I feel him in me like a phantom limb. My toes itch at the end of no leg."[97] Who is the "*him*" in this sentence? The lover, or God?

95. Ibid., 292.
96. Ibid., 301.
97. Ibid., 307.

Conclusion

In-Conclusion

TOWARD A POETICS OF SACRAMENTALITY

THROUGHOUT THIS BOOK WE have wrestled with the question of how to conceive of sacrament and sacramentality in a way that consists with the postmodern imagination. We have seen that the meaning of the Eucharist, and by extension sacramentality, may be derived from the endless matrix of signification within which it exists. In this sense, the Eucharist is not "rooted" in its history, but rather *extends across history* as an endlessly sprawling, endlessly relevant *living* metaphor. It recalls the Last Supper; it (re)presents Christ's sacrificial death on Calvary; it is ratified by the living Tradition of the Body of Christ called Church. But it is linked as well to any "thanksgiving" meal, every break-breaking or cup sharing. It exists within the genealogy of sacrifice and ritual slaughter while also subverting and overcoming those structures. The Eucharist connects us across time and space, history and geography, by the incessant relatability of *bread,* the basic unit of human subsistence, and *wine,* the drink classically related to celebration and revelry but also linked to extravagance and *gratuity* (grace!).

To reiterate, then, this network of meaning is not founded upon or rooted in a singular, originary event or meaning or character (etc.) but rather demonstrates a polyvalence of significance, a *transignificance,* which still resonates profoundly within the postmodern milieu. The depth of signs, symbols, and by extension sacraments (and the Sacred in general) has been *emptied* in postmodernism. This kenosis has already taken place— has *always already* taken place, even in and before the beginning when the

Spirit of God hovers over the *surface of the deep* and the creative *Logos* of God speaks into existence all that is. Therefore, when discussing sacraments and sacramentality, we have endeavored to be cautious about the language of *root* and *grounding* and so on. As we are interested in the question of how sacrament appears within the postmodern zeitgeist, and of why the notion of sacrament (re)emerges so powerfully and appears so compelling to the postmodern consciousness, the conception of sacrament as a more traditional/stable concept whose roots can be traced back to some singular source is somewhat contradictory to our purpose. Following Nathan Mitchell, who borrows from Deleuze and Guattari, the notion of sacrament is truly *rhizomal*. The anatomy of sacrament we have attempted to explore looks more like a web of connections, which is truer to form in the postmodern imagination. The Eucharist, for example, is connected to myriad "nodes" in this network of meaning: the Jewish Passover, Jewish table ritual in general, the Last Supper, Jesus' miraculous feedings of the multitudes, Jesus' "scandalous" bread-breakings and meals with sinners, the Emmaus encounter (Luke 24), Jesus' "bread of life" discourse (John 6), Jesus physical flesh and blood, the crucifixion, the Church, etc. And yet, as we have seen, the Eucharist is also infinitely relatable to the poetic discourses of literature, the arts, and cultural practice. All of these coalesce somehow to comprise the transignificance of the Eucharist. To prioritize any one of these connections as primary or foundational is precisely to miss why sacrament continues to capture the postmodern imagination, whether theological or poetic. But none of these "defining" connections (moments, events, entities, etc.) toward which the Eucharist points is "foundational" in the strict sense; none is the "root" or the singular "Signified." They all comprise the matrix of connections by which the Eucharist continues to derive its meaning, a process which is ever-shifting and never-ending. As all sacramental liturgies are the result of their own unique histories, and as all are located within culture(s), this matrix of connections can be, and indeed *is*, altered and added to as the Eucharist is practiced (recited) and interpreted (re-sited) within ever-changing cultures and by bodies, individual and corporate, which are never circumscribed but always opening out onto new possibilities of sacramental living.

Even as the *ecclesia* is circumscribed and constituted by its sacraments (especially Baptism and Eucharist, but Holy Orders cannot be minimized either) and derives its sacramental structure from these practices, sacramentality cannot and will not be circumscribed by the Church. And for this reason we might call sacramentality "post-ecclesial," not because it has left the *ecclesia* behind, but because it is constantly moving beyond the ecclesia, superseding and transcending its (seemingly necessary) limits. As Graham

Ward writes, "The institutional churches are necessary, but they are not ends in themselves; they are constantly transgressed by a community of desire, an erotic community, a spiritual activity. . . . The body of Christ desiring its consummation opens itself to what is outside the institutional Church; offers itself to perform in fields of activity far from chancels and cloisters. In doing this certain risks are taken and certain fears can emerge within those who represent the institution."[1] Throughout this book, we have witnessed ways in which the (il)logic of the Eucharist spills over into a kind of post-ecclesial sacramentality. It produces paradox, the bringing together of seemingly opposing or contradictory notions, and holding them together in an ineradicable tension. But at the heart of paradox is *doxa*, like *orthodox* (right belief/worship) and *doxology* (words of glory/praise). Therefore, when we speak of the incarnation of God in Christ as a paradox, or of the paradoxical nature of the Eucharist, we use this term in a qualified sense. While it does stand to reason that the idea of the God becoming human, being born of a virgin's womb, and suffering death is indeed paradoxical in the common sense of the term—contrary to the opinion or expectation of what constitutes divinity—we employ this term also to mean going *beyond belief* or *beyond glory*—another way of writing about the im/possibility of liturgy, which derives from the nature of sacrament itself, by which we are confronted as well with the im/possibility of the Church and of every "eucharistic community."

By this, we wish to indicate the uncircumscribable character—a certain "beyond" or "outside"—as well as an internal tension or contradiction inherent to every act of doxology, which is at the same time signified or made manifest by that act of doxology. Every utterance of theology or worship, at least from the standpoint of Christian sacramentality, necessarily involves ascribing seemingly contradictory "glories" to the God revealed in Christ, for this God's presence is known in and as absence; greatness is personified in becoming least, in becoming empty; to be filled and full-filled is to be eaten, consumed; real life is achieved and actualized in the most real and horrible of deaths. In other words, the "glory" (*doxa*) of this God is paradoxical and uncircumscribable. Death is swallowed up in life as true life is revealed as possible only by the passage through death. Absence is negated by presence (resurrection), and this negation of absence is revealed as the negation of the negation of presence.

As we trace this "poetics" of sacramentality, the only judgement that this essay wishes to pass on the forms of worship undertaken by any particular Christian community is based upon a rather simple criteria. In this

1. Ward, *Cities*, 180.

thesis we have endeavoured to unearth the scandalous nature of the broken body of the Crucified One, which is participated in and celebrated in the Church's eucharistic liturgy. This broken body constitutes the very unity of the Christian Faith, as indicated by the words said at the Fraction in the Scottish Episcopal liturgy: "The living bread is broken for the life of the world: *Lord, unite us in this sign.*" "In the breaking," writes Graham Ward, "the fracturing, the extension beyond a concern with one's own wholeness, is a sharing that will constitute our own true wholeness."[2] This sign of brokenness which is wholeness is an insuppressible scandal for the Christian and for the Church, for it indicates an economy that has no place in this world. In this divine economy, to invoke Meister Eckhart, all distinctions are lost: absence and presence are seen as co-participants in one another, as are immanence and transcendence, or materiality and imagination. Even the distinctions between fact and fiction, faith and doubt, sacred and secular become not simply blurred, and certainly not eliminated, but mutually inscribed into each other. The symbolic depiction of this is the cross of Jesus, which stands eternally as a *coincidentia oppositorum,* a coincidence of opposites, which is not a simple harmonization of antithetical elements, but a *chiasmic* holding together in tension of those contradictions. This is the anatomy of paradox. Our assessment, then, on any particular liturgical formula that calls itself Christian is this: worship that has lost this element of paradox, or worse, which seeks to domesticate the scandal of the Crucified, fails to offer a true participation in the God who was in Christ in his passion and death, his offering of the gift of his very brokenness, his sacrifice of ultimate separation from God. We must realize the truth of what Žižek writes about God, and find ways of applying and embodying it in worship, in language and body: "We are one with God only when God is no longer one with Himself, but abandons Himself, 'internalizes' the radical distance that separates us from Him. Our radical experience of separation from God is the very feature which unites us with Him[;] . . . only when I experience the infinite pain of separation from God do I share an experience with God Himself (Christ on the Cross)."[3]

Worship is ultimately about communion with God, and with our fellow creatures. Therefore, if liturgy is "the school of the church,"[4] this means that the Church learns not only what it believes but receives who it is in its very act of worship. The problem arises when the Church's worship has silenced and eventually forgotten altogether Jesus' cry of dereliction, which

2. Ibid., 174.
3. Žižek, *Puppet,* 91.
4. Cf. Pfatteicher, *School of the Church.*

is central to the Church's identity as the Body of Christ. The church as the Body of Christ is the Body of the Crucified One. This Body is exalted as it hangs dead and bloody from a Roman cross; this Body reveals itself for who and what it really is—the incarnate *logos* of God, the eternally begotten Son and creative Word of the Father—in its moment of profoundest annihilation, and again in the most aching absence of the empty tomb. How does the Church re-present this body, this body that is most present in its very absence? We assert that the Church does this, becomes this body, by subjecting itself fully and without restraint to the scandal of the broken body of God, our participation in which is fully, though not exclusively, made possible in the sacrament of the Eucharist. As Henri de Lubac and John Zizioulas have shown, the Eucharist makes the Church.[5] However, what the Eucharist makes the Church *into* is often a matter of discrepancy, with often much variety from church to church. What the Eucharist *should* make the Church into is a community of dispossession, a community which unites itself to broken bodies everywhere, a community which risks certainty and stability and even life itself to *be(come)* the Crucified and Risen (Absent-Present) Body of Christ. Eucharistic liturgies which exclude or gloss over this danger, this scandalous risk, offer less than full participation in the story of the salvation of the world, the climax of which is Christ's paradoxical death and resurrection.

THE (IM)POSSIBILITY OF "EUCHARISTIC COMMUNITY"

To understand the Church as a "eucharistic community" is on the simplest level to conceive of the Church's identity as the Body of Christ as that which is received as gift through the Eucharist. This sacramental celebration takes atomized individuals and makes a community: takes "*I*"s and makes a "*We.*" Graham Ward well articulates the uncircumscribability of the Eucharistic, and by extension the Church: "The eucharistic We is a pluralised and pluralising body that overspills defined places, opening up another space . . . [and] transgresses institutional bodies that assist in defining, but can never confine, the body of Christ."[6] Ward describes the body of Christ as "transcorporeal," as "displaced," a body which passes from the cradle to the cross, from the cross to the tomb to the heavens, and is finally (re)incarnated as the Church, the universal body of Christ, an erotic community[7] existing to

5. Cf. McPartlan, *The Eucharist Makes the Church.*
6. Ward, *Cities,* 176.
7. Ibid., ch. 3, "Transcorporeality: The Ontological Scandal" (81–96), and also ch. 4,

celebrate, to reveal and revel in the mystery of incarnation. In concluding this study, we wish to suggest something like Ward's vision, one which is correlational or analogical, one which seeks to place the Christian Church and its practices in constructive, redemptive (which is to say *loving*) engagement with the culture which the Church so often seems to desire to convert but also, paradoxically, holds contemptuously and defensively at bay.

In this way, might we see the practices of other texts, bodies, rituals, communities, etc., as participating in the same sacramentality that defines (but cannot be *defined by*) the Christian faith? Cavanaugh has made an excellent point of seeing "the world in a wafer,"[8] locating in the Eucharist the entire significance of the worshiping Church as Christ's body, God's vehicle of redemption in the world. His insight is considerably important, but our interest is slightly different. We wish to explore the possibility of seeing not "the world in a wafer" but *the wafer in the world*. Are there other communities, other bodies, other texts and rites outside the walls of the Church, which bear traces or echoes of the body of Christ and which therefore might also be regarded as eucharistic? Although more could be suggested, we will briefly propose two broad categories of such cultural incarnations of the body of Christ, instances of the wafer in the world—one *literary* and the other *literal*—which are identified by the sharing of communion and which conform, we propose, to a eucharistic shape.

First, as we have seen in this book, there is something sacramental about our participation in the world(s) of fiction—even when these fictions do not explicitly explore sacramentality. Communities which converge around and within fictional narrative worlds—what Stanley Fish calls "interpretive communities,"[9] communities gathered in celebration of story—might serve as a point of departure for a concept of post-ecclesial eucharistic community. Communal reading necessitates discussion, communication, and communion. But there exists also an invisible community of readers, one which transcends space and time. It has been said that "we read to know we are not alone,"[10] and indeed, when we read a story we join the ranks of all those who have ever participated in its narrative world. We commune with readers past and present, with characters fictional and real

---

"The Displaced Body of Jesus Christ" (97–116), an earlier version of which is published in Milbank et al., eds., *Radical Orthodoxy*, 163–81.

8. Cavanaugh, "World in a Wafer," 181–96.

9. Fish, *Is There a Text*, 14: "Indeed, it is the interpretive communities, rather than either the text or the reader, that produce meanings and are responsible for the emergence of formal features."

10. *Shadowlands* (Price Entertainment/Shadlowands Productions/Spelling Films, 1993). Screenplay by William Nicholson, directed by Richard Attenborough.

(again, the distinctions become difficult to trace). This invisible community is an impossible community, one which can never meet together in the material world but is able to experience a sort of mystical fellowship within the space of the page, which becomes then a sort of sanctuary, not as an escape from reality but as a portal to a parallel reality, a fantastic place barely hidden beneath the veneer of the ordinary.

Our every attempt to capture meaning or truth from a text is ill-advised; we do not capture the text, but rather the text *captures* us, holds us captive. Neither do we *consume* a text without it consuming us. The hermeneutical task flows in both directions: we are read and interpreted, even in our most secret places, as we read and interpret. We are not, however, trapped within "the prison-house of language"[11] or bound within the "reading gaol."[12] Rather, we are set free, sent on a journey in the bound-*less* wilderness of the page. The thrill of entering into the fun-house of reading is precisely the possibility of getting lost within the text, the narrative world wherein our mundane certainties disappear. As we get lost on this journey of reading, we discover that, in Christian terms, the only way to be found is finally to be lost (Matt 16:24–25)—abandoning all hope of ever being found. We wrestle with the text in the wilderness, and like Jacob's encounter with the angel, this wrestling inevitably wounds us. As with every encounter with the Divine, there is a sacrifice, and we come away altered. But "it is no sin to limp," as Valentine Cunningham points out, for the wound we receive is also a blessing: "Encounters with *this* mystery, with such mysteries, with stories and texts . . . are the kind of necessary, painful, laming, struggle that . . . can be redemptive, saving, transforming, healing."[13] A hint of violence occurs on both sides—the writer's pen, which penned the words we read, is a blade that cuts into us, pins us to the page, exposing our weaknesses and leaving us scarred. But we also wield the invasive scalpel of criticism with our interpretive endeavors, tearing into the text, sacrificing it on the altar even as it alters us. Yet, kenotically, the text always invites us: "Take, read—this is my body, my corpse, my corpus, broken for you."[14]

The narrative worlds generated by fictions grab hold of us, transport us from the ordinary into the extraordinary. We might describe this in terms of *rapture*, from the Latin "raptus," meaning to carry off, or to be abducted, carried away by force or seized violently (the same root as *rape*),

11. Jameson, *Prison-House.*

12. Cunningham, *Reading Gaol.*

13. Cunningham, "No Sin to Limp," 309.

14. The reflections in the paragraph are inspired by Stephen D. Moore and Mark C. Taylor. See Moore, *Mark and Luke in Poststructuralist Perspectives*, 11–18, and *God's Gym*, 37–39. Also Taylor, *Erring.*

a duplicitous word—the violent sense conjuring up horrific images, of us or a loved one raptured, captured, brutalized. But this stands in stark contrast to the more common usage of *rapture* in Christian terminology, the dreamy sense which calls to mind the promise of heaven, our reward for keeping it clean in this life. This is *anamnēsis*, a memory of the future, a remembrance of that of which we have no memory.

Perhaps a qualification is in order, for not every fictive work is equally sacramental in the sense we are tracing. For a story, a work of fiction, to generate such a eucharistic community it must be what Stanley Fish calls a "self-consuming artifact," one which "signifies most successfully when it fails, when it points *away* from itself to something its forms cannot capture."[15] Fish has elsewhere reminded us that the work (for him, literary, but for our broader purposes, narrative) "is not constrained by something in the text, nor does it issue from an independent and arbitrary will; rather, it proceeds from a collective decision as to what will count, . . . a decision that will be in force only so long as a community of readers or believers continues to abide by it."[16] The status of the work, like the relationship between the interpretative community and the narrative world within which it congregates, is tenuous, vulnerable. It never escapes a degree of risk, the risk of its own (the work's and the community's) dispossession and de-stability. To embrace *poiesis*, then, is to accept risk, and so these literary communities join the ecclesial community to form "a community that produces and occupies a space transcending place, walls and boundaries, a liturgical, doxological space opening in the world onto the world."[17]

In this way, the Church as a eucharistic community "is itself a fractured and fracturing community, internally deconstituting and reconstituting itself."[18] This fractured and fracturing character places the Church in an inextricable bond with all fractured bodies, wherever they may be found. Hence we suggest a second possibility of the "sacrificial" community, which shares in common physical suffering, as a post-ecclesial eucharistic community. The experience of pain—physical, mental, emotional—is something that all of humankind shares in common, and yet, in our moment of pain, we are the most profoundly isolated. In *The Body in Pain*, Elaine

15. Fish, *Self-Consuming Artifacts*, 4. The quality I am attempting to express could also be put in Jean-Luc Marion's terms: to bring about the emergence of a eucharistic community, the work must be an *icon*, that which directs the gaze beyond itself by becoming invisible, rather than an *idol*, that which freezes the gaze on the object. See Marion, *God without Being*.

16. Fish, *Is There a Text*, 11.

17. Ward, *Cities*, 258.

18. Ibid., 154.

Scarry explains that no one can experience the pain of another. "To have great pain," she writes, "is to have certainty; to hear that another person has pain is to have doubt. (The doubt of other persons, here as elsewhere, amplifies the suffering of those already in pain.)"[19] In this way, one of the few experiences that unites all of humanity is at the same time the loneliest and most isolated (and isolating) of experiences. We hear the echoes of Jesus' words to his disciples: "Where I am going, you cannot follow" (John 13:33–36). Pain captures the imagination and excises a part of the sufferer, which is why torture is so effective as a measure of social fragmentation. Think of the politically disappeared in Latin America: wives, mothers, children, returning to empty houses where fathers or brothers should be—bodies that have vanished, as if into thin air, usually never to be seen again. No one touched by torture, which touches not only the subject but also every person to whom the subject is connected, is ever left unchanged.[20]

Communities joined by common suffering congregate in emergency rooms and AIDS clinics, in support groups that meet in church rec halls or civic centres. In many cases, these might be created or even imposed community—the l'Arche community, the cancer ward, even the leper colony, as recently portrayed in the film *The Motorcycle Diaries*, in which young Che Guevara breaks the rules and the gloves come off, literally, so as to share, simply by touch, in the broken bodies of these exiles.[21] On one hand, society tends to cordon off such broken bodies into groups, for it is easier to deal with "the handicapped" or "the mentally ill" as categories than to personally and lovingly engage with "the least of these" (Matt 25:31–46). But this is a tragic act, for the denial of death, the denial of our mortality, is paradoxically the very thing that makes us human. Scarry notes that the "unsharability" of pain obliterates language, rendering suffering incommunicable, and yet, as "the act of verbally expressing pain is a necessary prelude to the collective task of diminishing pain,"[22] we wish to suggest that eucharistic language (word bodied-forth in action) works toward overcoming the isolation and atomization of pain. It renders the boundaries between our bodies permeable, making possible the impossible act of not just experiencing one another's burdens but also bearing them. Because Christ suffered "once, for all" (1 Pet 3:18), the impossible is made possible: we are able to share in one

19. Scarry, *Body in Pain*, 7.

20. Torture—not only its social impact but its character as a "liturgy" of the state—is a central theme in William Cavanaugh's *Torture and Eucharist*, to which we are indebted for these insights.

21. *The Motorcycle Diaries* (*Diarios de motocicleta*, FilmFour/South Fork, 2004). Screenplay by Jose Rivera, directed by Walter Salles.

22. Scarry, *Body in Pain*, 9.

another's suffering by our common participation in his suffering, which is memorialized and incarnated in the eucharistic sacrifice.

Further, Christian participation in the Eucharist (not to mention the teachings of Jesus) necessarily imposes a responsibility upon the ecclesial community to care for and include such suffering bodies within the scope of their fellowship. Again echoing Graham Ward, we assert that communion with suffering communities is necessary, for the "racked and viral-ridden bodies of the sick"[23] and downtrodden serve as visible symbols of the eucharistic sacrifice, Christ's broken body and spilt blood which mystically and *real*-ly binds us each to another and together to God. Since we cannot truly experience their pain or share in their suffering, we must "bear something of their body weight (with something of its pain) within our imaginaries."[24] The ecclesial community, to be truly eucharistic, must be and become one which continually seeks to discover, as David Toole proposes, "what it might mean to view suffering through the lens of the Crucified."[25] Given our common brokenness, we cannot afford to ignore such bodies, for we are inextricably bound together in Christ's body, indelibly marked with his wounds.

The character of sacramentality that we have been tracing is therefore finally, as James White puts it, "taking fully seriously our full humanity."[26] We agree with White entirely when he attests that we must develop a sense of sacramentality, that is, "a special language in which objects and actions provide a new vocabulary." To arrive at this sense of sacramentality, which should inform all sacramental celebration and participation, "One must begin by observing how humans relate to one another in nonverbal ways. Love, in its demand for visible expression, is our best guide. In this sense, we are dealing with the humanity of the sacraments."[27] This love *must* be self-emptying, existing for the other, existing for the body broken even as it is fuelled by the body broken. It must manifest itself in language, in words and texts which express a divine, selfless love to those who do not know love. It must write itself upon the body, which is taken, blessed, broken and given for the other. While inscribed in language and embodied in the flesh, this sense of sacramentality can never be circumscribed or contained. As the foundation of the Church (or any community) it is a shaky, unstable foundation at best. But as Graham Ward has observed, "The body of Christ

23. Ward, *Cities*, 82.

24. Ibid., 96.

25. Toole, *Godot in Sarajevo*, 87.

26. White, *Introduction to Christian Worship*, 201.

27. Ibid., 200.

lives on, beyond its precincts: each member of the eucharistic We writing God's name elsewhere in the world—redeeming it through desire."[28] In this way, the community gathered around the Eucharist *is* an (im)possible community—it is possible, yet only by living on *beyond itself*, transgressing its own boundaries, following the sacramental out from the Church and into the world.

And so it seems fitting to conclude, inconclusively perhaps—for if we have established anything it is that there is no final word on sacrament—with these words from Teilhard de Chardin:

> As our humanity assimilates the material world, and as the Host assimilates our humanity, the eucharistic transformation goes beyond and completes the transubstantiation of the bread on the altar. Step by step, it irresistibly invades the universe. It is the fire that sweeps over the heath; the stroke that vibrates through the bronze[;] . . . in a true sense, the sacramental Species are formed by the totality of the world, and the duration of the creation is the time needed for its consecration.[29]

28. Ward, *Cities*, 181.
29. Teilhard de Chardin, *Milieu Divin*, 125–26.

Bibliography

PRIMARY TEXTS

Ballard, J. G. *Crash*. London: Vintage, 1995.

Bataille, Georges. *Eroticism*. Translated by Mary Dalwood. London: Boyars, 2006.

———. *Story of the Eye, by Lord Auch*. Translated by Joachim Neugroschal, with essays by Susan Sontag and Roland Barthes. London: Penguin, 2001.

Greene, Graham. *Monsignor Quixote*. Harmondsworth, UK: Penguin, 1983.

Hansen, Ron. *Mariette in Ecstasy*. London: Macmillan, 1991.

Mathews, Aidan. *Lipstick on the Host*. London: Vintage, 1998.

Metzger, Bruce M., and Roland E. Murphy, editors. *The New Oxford Annotated Bible with the Apocryphal / Deuterocanonical Books*. New Revised Standard Version. New York: Oxford University Press, 1994.

Palahniuk, Chuck. *Fight Club*. London: Vintage, 1996.

Süskind, Patrick. *Perfume: The Story of a Murderer*. Translated by John E. Woods. London: Penguin, 1986.

White, Patrick. *A Fringe of Leaves*. Harmondsworth, UK: Penguin, 1976.

SECONDARY TEXTS

Altizer, Thomas J. J. *The Gospel of Christian Atheism*. London: Collins, 1966.

———. *Living the Death of God: A Theological Memoir*. Albany, NY: SUNY Press, 2006.

———. *The Self-Embodiment of God*. New York: Harper & Row, 1977.

———. *Total Presence: The Language of Jesus and the Language of Today*. New York: Seabury, 1980.

Altizer, Thomas J. J., and William Hamilton. *Radical Theology and the Death of God*. Harmondsworth, UK: Penguin, 1966.

Altizer, Thomas J. J., et al. *Deconstruction and Theology*. New York: Crossroads, 1982.

Aristotle. *Poetics*. Translated by Malcolm Heath. Penguin Classics. Harmondsworth, UK: Penguin, 1996.

Arndt, W., F. W. Gingrich, F. W. Danker, and W. Bauer, editors. *A Greek-English Lexicon of the New Testament and Other Early Christian Literature*. 1979. Reprint. Chicago: University of Chicago Press, 1996.

Augustine, Saint, Bishop of Hippo. *On Christian Teaching*. Translated by R. P. H. Green. Oxford: Oxford University Press, 1997.

Austin, J. L. "Performative Utterances." In *Philosophical Papers,* 2nd ed., edited by J. O. Urmson and G. J. Warnock, 233–52. London: Oxford University Press, 1970.

Baillie, D. M. *God Was in Christ: An Essay on Incarnation and Atonement.* London: Faber and Faber, 1977.

Bakhtin, Mikhail. *Rabelais and His World.* Translated by Hélène Iwolsky. Bloomington, IN: Indiana University Press, 1984.

Barthes, Roland, "The Death of the Author." In *Image Music Text,* translated by Stephen Heath, 142–48. London: Fontana, 1977.

———. "The Metaphor of the Eye." In *Story of the Eye, by Lord Auch,* by Georges Batille, 119–27. London: Penguin, 2001.

Bataille, Georges. *Theory of Religion.* Translated by Robert Hurley. New York: Zone, 1989.

Bauman, Zygmut. *Imitations of Postmodernity.* London: Routledge, 1992.

Beauvoir, Simone de. *The Second Sex.* Translated and edited by H. M. Parshley. New York: Vintage, 1989.

Belcher, J. David. "Baptism into the Poor Body of Christ: or, How to Possess Nothing and Yet Have Everything." MA diss., Vanderbilt University, 2007.

Blanchot, Maurice. *The Writing of the Disaster.* New edition, translated by Ann Smock. Lincoln, NE: Nebraska University Press (Bison Books), 1995.

Blond, Phillip, editor. *Post-Secular Philosophy: Between Philosophy and Theology.* Lincoln, NE: Nebraska University Press, 1998.

Blumenberg, Hans. *The Legitimacy of the Modern Age.* Chicago: University of Chicago Press (Reaktion Books), 1983.

Boeve, Lieven. "Postmodern Sacramento-Theology: Retelling The Christian Story." *Ephemerides Theologicae Lovanienses* 74.4 (1998) 326–43.

Boeve, Lieven, and Kurt Feyaerts, editors. *Metaphor and God-Talk.* Bern: Lang, 1999.

Boeve, Lieven, and Lambert Leijssen, editors. *Contemporary Sacramental Contours of a God Incarnate.* Louvain: Peeters, 2001.

———, editors. *Sacramental Presence in A Postmodern Context.* Leuven: Peeters, 2001.

Boeve, Lieven, and John C. Ries, editors. *The Presence of Transcendence: Thinking "Sacrament" in A Postmodern Age.* Leuven: Peeters, 2001.

Bond, H. Lawrence, editor and translator. *Nicholas of Cusa: Selected Spiritual Writings.* Classics of Western Spirituality. Mahwah, NJ: Paulist, 1997.

Bradshaw, P. F. "Celebration." In *The Eucharist Today,* edited by R. C. D. Jasper, 130–41. London: SPCK, 1975.

Bradshaw, Paul F. *Eucharistic Origins.* Oxford: Oxford University Press, 2004.

———, editor. *The New Westminster Dictionary of Liturgy and Worship.* Louisville, KY: Westminster John Knox, 2002.

———. *The Search for the Origins of Christian Worship: Sources and Methods for the Study of Early Liturgy.* 2nd ed. Oxford: Oxford University Press, 2002.

Breton, Stanislas. *The Word and the Cross.* Translated by Jacquelyn Porter. New York: Fordham University Press, 2002.

Brown, Callum G. *The Death of Christian Britain: Understanding Secularisation, 1800–2000.* London: Routledge, 2001.

Brown, David. *God and Grace of Body: Sacrament in Ordinary.* Oxford: Oxford University Press, 2007.

Brown, Peter. *The Body and Society: Men, Women and Sexual Renunciation in Early Christianity.* London: Faber and Faber, 1990.

Bruce, Steve. *God is Dead: Secularization in the West.* Oxford: Blackwell, 2002.

Buber, Martin. *I and Thou.* 2nd ed. with a Postscript by the author. Translated by Ronald Gregor Smith. London: T. & T. Clark, 1994.

Bynum, Caroline Walker. *Fragmentation and Redemption: Essays on Gender and the Human Body in Medieval Religion.* New York: Zone, 1991.

———. *Holy Feast and Holy Fast: The Religious Significance of Food to Medieval Women.* Berkeley, CA: University of California Press, 1988.

———. *The Resurrection of the Body in Western Christianity, 200–1336.* New York: Columbia University Press, 1995.

Caledott, Stratford, editor. *Beyond the Prosaic: Renewing the Liturgical Movement.* Glasgow: McLehose and Sons, 1998.

Caputo, John D. "After Jacques Derrida Comes the Future." *Journal of Cultural and Religious Theory* 4.2 (2003). No pages. Online: http://www.jcrt.org/archives/04.2/caputo.shtml. [Accessed March 15, 2010.]

———. *The Prayers and Tears of Jacques Derrida: Religion without Religion.* Bloomington, IN: Indiana University Press, 1997.

———. *The Weakness of God: A Theology of the Event.* Bloomington, IN: Indiana University Press , 2006.

Caputo, John D., and Michael J. Scanlon, editors. *Augustine and Postmodernism: Confessions and Circumfession.* Bloomington, IN: Indiana University Press, 2005.

———. *God, The Gift, and Postmodernism.* Bloomington, IN: Indiana University Press, 1999.

Cavanaugh, William T. *Torture and Eucharist: Theology, Politics, and the Body of Christ.* Oxford: Blackwell, 1998.

———. "The World in a Wafer: A Geography of the Eucharist as Resistance to Globalization." *Modern Theology* 15.2 (1999) 181–96.

Certeau, Michel de. *The Mystic Fable: vol. 1, The Sixteenth and Seventeenth Centuries.* Translated By Michael B. Smity. Chicago: University of Chicago Press, 1992.

———. "The Weakness of Believing: From the Body to Writing, a Christian Transit." In *The Certeau Reader,* edited by Graham Ward, 214–43. Oxford: Blackwell, 2000.

Chauvet, Louis-Marie. "The Broken Bread as Theological Figure of Eucharistic Presence." In *Sacramental Presence in a Postmodern Context,* edited by Boeve and Leijssen, 236–62. Leuven: Peeters, 2001.

———. *The Sacraments: The Word of God at the Mercy of the Body.* Translated by Madeleine Beaumont. Collegeville, MN: Liturgical, 2001.

———. *Symbol and Sacrament: A Sacramental Reinterpretation of Christian Existence.* Translated by Patrick Madigan, SJ, and Madeleine Beaumont. Collegeville, MN: Liturgical, 1995.

Church, F. Forrester, editor. *The Essential Tillich: An Anthology of the Writings of Paul Tillich.* New York: Collier / Macmillan, 1987.

Clark, Mary T., editor. *An Aquinas Reader: Selections From the Writings of Thomas Aquinas.* New York: Fordham, University Press, 1988.

Coleridge, Samuel Taylor. *Biographia Literaria.* London: Dent, 1997.

———. *Confessions of an Inquiring Spirit.* Philadelphia: Fortress, 1840.

———. *Lay Sermons.* The Collected Works of Samuel Taylor Coleridge, Vol. 6. London: Routledge and Kegan Paul, 1972.

Cox, Harvey. *The Feast of Fools: A Theological Essay on Festivity and Fantasy.* New York: Harper & Row, 1970.

Critchley, Simon. *The Ethics of Deconstruction: Derrida and Levinas.* Oxford: Blackwell, 1992.

Crockett, Clayton, editor. *Secular Theology: American Radical Theological Thought.* London: Routledge, 2001.

Culler, Jonathan. "Jacques Derrida." In *Structuralism and Since: From Levi-Strauss to Derrida,* edited by John Sturrock, 154–80. Oxford: Oxford University Press, 1979.

———. *On Deconstruction: Theory and Criticism after Structuralism.* Ithaca, NY: Cornell University Press, 1982.

Cummings, Owen F. *Eucharistic Doctors: A Theological History.* Mahwah, NJ: Paulist, 2005.

Cupitt, Don. *After All: Religious without Alienation.* London: SCM, 1994.

Davie, Grace. *Religion in Britain Since 1945: Believing without Belonging.* London: T. & T. Clark, 1994.

Davies, Horton. *Bread of Life & Cup of Joy: Newer Ecumenical Perspectives on the Eucharist.* Grand Rapids: Eerdmans, 1993.

Davies, J. G., editor. *A New Dictionary of Liturgy and Worship.* London: SCM, 1986.

Davies, Oliver. "The Sign Redeemed: A Study in Christian Fundamental Semiotics." *Modern Theology* 19.2 (April 2003) 219–41.

de Lubac, Henri Cardinal, SJ. *Corpus Mysticum: The Eucharist and the Church in the Middle Ages, Historical Survey.* Translated by Gemma Simmonds, CJ, with Richard Price; edited by Laurence Paul Hemming and Susan Frank Parsons. London: SCM, 2006.

Derrida, Jacques. *Dissemination.* Translated by Barbara Johnson. Continuum Impacts. London: Continuum, 2004.

———. "How to Avoid Speaking: Denials." Translated by K. Frieden. In *Languages of the Unsayable: The Play of Negativity in Literature and Literary Theory,* edited by S. Budick and W. Iser, 3–70. Stanford: Stanford University Press: 1996) .

———. *Margins of Philosophy.* Translated by Alan Bass. Chicago: University of Chicago Press, 1982.

———. *Of Grammatology.* Corrected edition; translated by Gayatri Chakravorty Spivak. Baltimore, MD: Johns Hopkins University Press, 1997.

———. *Positions.* Translated by Alan Bass. Chicago: University of Chicago Press, 1981.

———. "The Supplement of Copula: Philosophy *before* Linguistics." In *Textual Strategies: Perspectives in Post-Structuralist Criticism,* edited by J. V. Harari, 82–120. Ithaca, NY: Cornell University Press, 1979.

———. *Writing and Difference.* Translated by Alan Bass. Routledge Classics. London: Routledge, 2002.

Detweiler, Robert. *Breaking the Fall: Religious Readings of Contemporary Fiction.* London: Macmillan, 1989.

———. "Torn by Desire: Sparagmos in Greek Tragedy and Recent Fiction." In *Postmodernism, Literature and the Future of Theology,* edited by David Jasper, 60–77. London: Macmillan, 1993.

Dix, Dom Gregory. *The Shape of the Liturgy.* 2nd ed. New York: Continuum, 2003.

Docherty, Thomas, editor. *Postmodernism: A Reader.* Hertfordshire, UK: Harvester Wheatsheaf, 1993.

Dorado, Robert. "Loose Canons: Augustine and Derrida on Their Selves." In *God, The Gift, and Postmodernism,* edited by John D. Caputo and Michael Scanlon, 79–111. Bloomington, IN: Indiana University Press, 1999.

Drew, Mark. "The Spirit or the Letter?: Vatican II and Liturgical Reform." In *Beyond the Prosaic: Renewing the Liturgical Movement,* edited by Stratford Caledott, 48–68. Glasgow: McLehose and Sons, 1998.

Easton, Burton Scott, editor and translator. *The Apostolic Tradition of Hippolytus.* London: Cambridge University Press, 1934.

Eckhart, Meister. *Meister Eckhart: A Modern Translation.* Edited and translated by Raymond B. Blakney. New York: Harper & Row, 1941.

———. *Selected Writings.* Edited and translated by Oliver Davies. Harmondsworth, UK: Penguin, 1994.

Eliade, Mircea. *The Sacred and the Profane: The Nature of Religion.* Translated by Willard R. Trask. New York: Harcourt Brace, 1987.

Euripides. *The Bacchae and Other Plays.* Translated by Philip Vellacott. Harmondsworth, UK: Penguin, 1973.

Feeley-Harnik, Gillian. *The Lord's Table: Eucharist and Passover in Early Christianity.* Philadelphia, PA: University of Pennsylvania Press, 1981.

Fenn, Richard K. *Liturgies and Trials: The Secularization of Religious Language.* Oxford: Blackwell, 1982.

Fish, Stanley E. *Self-Consuming Artifacts: The Experience of Seventeenth-Century Literature.* Berkeley, CA: California University Press, 1972.

———. *There's No Such Thing as Free Speech, and It's a Good Thing, Too.* New York: Oxford University Press, 1994.

Flannery, Austin, O.P., editor. *Vatican Council II: The Basic Sixteen Documents.* Northport, NY and Dublin: Costello Publishing and Dominican Publications, 1996.

Fountain, J. Stephen. "Postmodernism, A/theology, and the Possibility of Language as Universal Eucharist." In *The Nature of Religious Language,* edited by Stanley E. Porter, 131–47. Sheffield, UK: Sheffield Academic Press, 1996.

Girard, René. *The Scapegoat.* Translated by Yvonne Freccero. Baltimore, MD: Johns Hopkins University Press, 1986.

———. *Violence and the Sacred.* Translated by Patrick Gregory. New York: Continuum, 2005.

Gregory Nazianzen, "To Cledonius the Priest against Apollinarius." In *Nicene and Post-Nicene Fathers,* Series II, Vol. 7, edited by Philip Schaff. Edinburgh: T. & T. Clark. No pages. Online: http://www.ccel.org/ccel/schaff/npnf207.iv.ii.iii.html. [accessed 28 Mar 2010]

Gumbrecht, Hans Ulrich. *Production of Presence: What Meaning Cannot Convey.* Stanford, CA: Stanford University Press, 2004.

Hampson, Daphne. *After Christianity.* Valley Forge, PA: Trinity, 1997.

Hansen, Ron. *A Stay Against Confusion: Essays on Faith and Fiction.* New York: HarperCollins, 2001.

Hardison, O. B. *Christian Rite and Christian Drama in the Middle Ages: Essays in the Origin and Early History of Modern Drama.* Baltimore, MD: Johns Hopkins University Press, 1965.

Hart, Kevin. "Jacques Derrida: The God Effect." In *Post-Secular Philosophy: Between Philosophy and Theology,* edited by Philip Blond, 259–80. Lincoln, NE: Nebraska University Press, 1998.

———. *The Trespass of the Sign: Deconstruction, Theology and Philosophy.* Cambridge: Cambridge University Press, 1989.

Hass, Andrew W. *Poetics of Critique: The Interdisciplinarity of Textuality*. Burlington, VT: Ashgate, 2003.

Hebert, A. G. *Liturgy and Society: The Function of the Church in the Modern World*. London: Faber and Faber, 1961.

Heidegger, Martin. *Poetry, Language, Thought*. Translated Albert Hofstadter. New York: Harper and Row, 1971.

Hughes, Graham. *Worship As Meaning: A Liturgical Theology for Late Modernity*. Cambridge: Cambridge University Press, 2003.

Huizinga, Johan. *The Autumn of the Middle Ages*. Translated by Rodney J. Payton and Ulrich Mammitzsch. Chicago: University of Chicago Press, 1996.

Hyman, Gavin. *The Predicament of Postmodern Theology: Radical Orthodoxy or Textual Nihilism?* Louisville, KY: Westminster John Knox, 2001.

Irvine, Christopher. *The Art of God: The Making of Christians and the Meaning of Worship*. London: Liturgy Training, 2005.

Irwin, Kevin W. *Models of the Eucharist*. Mahwah, NJ: Paulist, 2005.

―――. "A Sacramental World: Sacramentality as the Primary Language for Sacraments." *Worship* 76.3 (2002) 197–211.

Jameson, Fredric. *Postmodernism, or the Cultural Logic of Late Capitalism*. London: Verso, 1991.

Jasper, David. "'The Eucharistic Body in Art and Literature." In *Exchanges of Grace: Essays in Honor of Ann Loades*, edited by Natalie K. Watson and Stephen Burns, 213–23. London: SCM, 2009.

―――. "From Theology to Theological Thinking: The Development of Critical Thought and its Consequences for Theology." *Literature and Theology* 9.3 (1995) 293–305.

―――, editor. *Postmodernism, Literature and the Future of Theology*. London: Macmillan, 1993.

―――. *The Sacred Body: Asceticism in Religion, Literature, Art, and Culture*. Waco, TX: Baylor University Press, 2009.

―――. *The Sacred Desert: Religion, Literature, Art and Culture*. Oxford: Blackwell, 2004.

Jasper, Ronald C. D., editor. *The Eucharist Today: Studies on Series 3*. London: SPCK, 1975.

―――, editor. *The Renewal of Worship: Essays by Members of the Joint Liturgical Group*. London: Oxford University Press, 1965.

Jasper, Ronald C. D., and G. J. Cuming, editors. *Prayers of the Eucharist: Early and Reformed*. 3rd ed. Collegeville, MN: Liturgical, 1990.

Jencks, Charles. *The Language of Post-Modern Architecture*. Rev. ed. New York: Rizzoli, 1978.

Jenson, Robert W. *Visible Words: The Interpretation and Practice of Christian Sacraments*. Philadelphia, PA: Fortress, 1978.

Jeremias, Jochaim. *The Eucharistic Words of Jesus*. Translated by Norman Perrin. London: SCM, 1966.

Johnson, Thomas H., editor. *The Complete Poems of Emily Dickinson*. Boston: Little, Brown and Company, 1960.

Jones, Cheslyn, Geoffrey Wainwright, Edward Yarnold SJ, and Paul Bradshaw, editors. *The Study of Liturgy (Revised Edition)*. London and New York: SPCK and Oxford University Press, 1992.

Julian of Norwich. *A Lesson of Love: The Revelations of Julian of Norwich.* Translated by Father John-Julian, OJN. Lincoln, NE: Writers Club, 2003.

Kaufmann, Walter, editor and translator. *The Portable Nietzsche.* London: Penguin, 1982.

Kilpatrick, G. D. *The Eucharist in Bible and Liturgy.* Cambridge: Cambridge University Press, 1983.

Klauser, Theodor. *A Short History of the Western Liturgy: An Account and Some Reflections.* 2nd ed. Oxford: Oxford University Press, 1979.

Klemm, David E., editor. *Hermeneutical Inquiry, Vol. I: The Interpretation of Texts.* Atlanta: Scholars, 1986.

———. "'This is My Body': Hermeneutics and Eucharistic Language." *Anglican Theological Review* 64.3 (1982) 293–310.

Koerner, Joseph Leo. *The Reformation of the Image.* Chicago: University of Chicago Press (Reaktion Books), 2008.

Lacoste, Jean-Yves. *Experience and the Absolute: Disputed Questions on the Humanity of Man.* Translated by Mark Raftery-Skehan. New York: Fordham University Press, 2004.

Ledbetter, Mark. *Victims and the Postmodern Narrative, or, Doing Violence to the Body.* New York: Macmillan, 1996.

Loughlin, Gerard. *Alien Sex: The Body and Desire in Cinema and Theology.* Oxford: Blackwell, 2003.

Léon-Dufour, Xavier. *Sharing the Eucharistic Bread: The Witness of the New Testament.* Mahwah, NJ: Paulist, 1987.

Lyotard, Jean-François. *The Postmodern Condition: A Report on Knowledge.* Translated by Geoff Bennington and Brian Massumi. Manchester: Manchester University Press, 1984.

MacKendrick, Karmen. *Counterpleasures.* Albany, NY: SUNY Press, 1999.

———. *Word Made Skin: Figuring Language at the Surface of Flesh.* New York: Fordham University Press, 2004.

Marion, Jean-Luc. *The Erotic Phenomenon.* Translated Stephen E. Lewis. Chicago: University of Chicago Press, 2007.

———. *God Without Being: Hors-texte.* Translated Thomas A. Carlson. Chicago: University of Chicago Press, 1991.

———. *The Idol and Distance: Five Studies.* Translated Thomas A. Carlson. Stanford, CA: Stanford University Press, 2001.

———. "They Recognized Him; and He Became Invisible To Them." *Modern Theology* 18.2 (2002) 145–52.

Marsh, Clive. *Christianity in a Post-Atheist Age.* Edinburgh: T. & T. Clark, 2002.

Martos, Joseph. *Doors to the Sacred: A Historical Introduction to Sacraments in the Catholic Church.* Garden City, NY: Image, 1982.

Mauriac, François. *The Eucharist: The Mystery of Holy Thursday.* Translated Marie-Louise Dufrenoy. New York: McKay, 1944.

McGuckian, Michael. *The Holy Sacrifice of the Mass: A Search for an Acceptable Notion of Sacrifice.* Chicago: University of Chicago Press, 2005.

McPartlan, Paul. *The Eucharist Makes the Church: Henri de Lubac and John Zizioulas in Dialogue.* San Francisco, CA: Harper Collins, 1993.

Milbank, John. *Theology and Social Theory: Beyond Secular Reason.* 2nd ed. Oxford: Blackwell, 2006.

————. *The Word Made Strange: Theology, Language, Culture.* Oxford: Blackwell, 1997.

Milbank, John, Catherine Pickstock, and Graham Ward, editors. *Radical Orthodoxy: A New Theology.* London: Routledge, 1999.

Miles, Margaret. *The Word Made Flesh: A History of Christian Thought.* Oxford: Blackwell, 2005.

Mitchell, Nathan D. *Meeting Mystery: Liturgy, Worship, Sacraments.* Maryknoll, NY: Orbis, 2006.

————. "Mystery and Manners: Eucharist in Postmodern Theology." *Worship* 79.2 (2005) 130–51.

Moore, Stephen D. *God's Gym: Divine Male Bodies of the Bible.* London: Routledge, 1996.

————. *Post-structuralism and the New Testament: Derrida and Foucault at the Foot of the Cross.* Minneapolis, MN: Fortress, 1994.

Nicholas of Cusa. *Selected Spiritual Writings.* Edited, translated, and introduced by H. Lawrence Bond. Mahwah, NJ: Paulist, 1997.

Nichols, Bridget. *Liturgical Hermeneutics: Interpreting Liturgical Rites in Performance.* Frankfurt: Lang, 1996.

Osborne, Kenan B. *Christian Sacraments in A Postmodern World: A Theology for the Third Millennium.* Mahwah, NJ: Paulist, 1999.

Pagels, Elaine. *Beyond Belief: The Secret Gospel of Thomas.* London: Pan Macmillan, 2003.

Picasso, Pablo. ""Picasso Speaks (Statement to Marius de Zayas)." *The Arts,* May 1923, 315–26. No pages. Online: www.learn.columbia.edu/picmon/pdf/art_hum_reading_49.pdf. [accessed July 3, 2009]

Pickstock, Catherine. *After Writing: On the Liturgical Consummation of Philosophy.* Oxford: Blackwell, 1998.

————. "Thomas Aquinas and the Quest for the Eucharist." *Modern Theology* 15.2 (1999) 159–80.

Pink, Arthur W. *Exposition of the Gospel of John.* Grand Rapids: Zondervan, 1975.

Power, David N. *The Eucharistic Mystery: Revitalizing the Tradition.* Dublin: Gill and Macmillan, 1992.

————. *Sacrament: The Language of God's Giving.* New York: Crossroads, 1999.

Pseudo-Dionysius, the Aeropagite. *The Complete Works.* Translated and annotations by Colm Luibheid and Paul Rorem. Mahwah, NJ: Paulist, 1987.

Rahner, Karl. *The Church and the Sacraments.* Translated by W. J. O'Hara. Exeter, UK: Burns & Oates, 1986.

Raschke, Carl A. "À-Dieu to Jacques Derrida: Descartes' Ghost, or the Holy Spirit in Secular Theology." In *Secular Theology: American Radical Theological Thought,* edited by Clayton Crockett, 37–50. London: Routledge, 2001.

————. *Theological Thinking: An Inquiry.* Chico, CA: Scholars, 1988.

Rees, Elizabeth. *An Essential Guide to Celtic Sites and Their Saints.* London: Burns and Oates, 2003.

Ricoeur, Paul. *Oneself as Another.* Translated by Kathleen Blamey. Chicago: University of Chicago Press, 1992.

————. *The Rule of Metaphor: The Creation of Meaning in Language.* Translated by Robert Czerny with Kathleen McLaughlin and John Costello, SJ. Routledge Classics. London: Routledge, 1977.

————. *The Symbolism of Evil.* New York: Harper & Row, 1967.

Robinson, John A. T. *Honest To God*. London: SCM, 1967.

Rubin, Miri. *Corpus Christi: The Eucharist in Late Medieval Culture*. Cambridge: Cambridge University Press, 1991.

Saliers, Don E. *Worship as Theology: Foretaste of Divine Glory*. Nashville, TN: Abingdon, 1994.

Saussure, Ferdinand de. *Course in General Linguistics*. Edited by C. Bally and A. Sechehaye in collaboration with A. Riedlinger; translated by Wade Baskin. New York: McGraw-Hill, 1959.

Scarry, Elaine. *The Body in Pain: The Making and Unmaking of the World*. Oxford: Oxford University Press, 1985.

Scharlemann, Robert P. *Inscriptions and Reflections: Essays in Philosophical Theology*. Charlottesville, VA: University Press of Virginia, 1989.

———, editor. *Theology at the End of the Century: A Dialogue on the Postmodern with Thomas J. J. Altizer, Mark C. Taylor, Charles Winquist, and Robert P. Scharlemann*. Charlottesville, VA: University Press of Virginia, 1990.

Schillebeeckx, Edward. *Christ the Sacrament of the Encounter with God*. Translated Paul Barrett et al. New York: Sheed and Ward, 1963.

Schmemann, Alexander. *The Eucharist: Sacrament of the Kingdom*. Translated by Paul Kachur. Crestwood, NY: St. Vladimir's Seminary Press, 2003.

———. *For the Life of the World: Sacraments and Orthodoxy*. Rev. ed. Crestwood, NY: St. Vladimir's Seminary Press, 2004.

Schwartz, Regina. "Communion and Conversation." In *The Blackwell Companion to Postmodern Theology*, edited by Graham Ward, 48–68. Oxford: Blackwell, 2002.

———. *Sacramental Poetics at the Dawn of Secularism: When God Left the World*. Stanford, CA: Stanford University Press, 2008.

Seasoltz, R. Kevin, editor. *Living Bread, Saving Cup: Readings on the Eucharist*. Collegeville, MN: Liturgical, 1982.

Sloyan, Gerard S. "The Amen Corner: Presence and Absence in the Eucharist." *Worship* 69.3 (1995) 263–69.

Smit, Peter-Ben. "The Bishop and His/Her Eucharistic Community: A Critique of Jean-Luc Marion's Eucharistic Hermeneutic." *Modern Theology* 19.1 (2003) 30–40.

Sontag, Susan. "The Pornographic Imagination." In *Story of the Eye*, by Georges Bataille, 83–118. London: Penguin, 2001.

Staples, Rob L. *Outward Sign and Inward Grace: The Place of Sacraments in Wesleyan Spirituality*. Kansas City, MO: Beacon Hill, 1991.

Steinberg, Leo. *Leonardo's Incessant Last Supper*. New York: Zone, 2001.

———. *The Sexuality of Christ in Renaissance Art and Modern Oblivion*. 2nd ed. Chicago: University of Chicago Press, 1996.

Steiner, George. *Grammars of Creation*. London: Faber and Faber, 2001.

———. *Real Presences*. Chicago: University of Chicago Press, 1989.

Sturrock, John, editor. *Structuralism and Since: From Levi-Strauss to Derrida*. Oxford: Oxford University Press, 1979.

Taylor, Mark C. *After God*. Chicago: University of Chicago Press, 2007.

———, editor. *Deconstruction in Context: Literature and Philosophy*. Chicago and London: University of Chicago Press, 1986.

———. *Deconstructing Theology*. New York: Crossroads / Chico, CA: Scholars, 1982.

———. *Erring: A Postmodern A/theology*. Chicago: University of Chicago Press, 1984.

———. *Hiding*. Chicago: University of Chicago Press, 1997.

————. "Unending Strokes." In *Theology at the End of the Century: A Dialogue on the Postmodern with Thomas J. J. Altizer, Mark C. Taylor, Charles Winquist, and Robert P. Scharlemann*, edited by Robert Scharlemann, 136–48. Charlottesville, VA: University Press of Virginia, 1990.

Taylor, Mark C., and Esa Saarinen. *Imagologies: Media Philosophy*. London: Routledge, 1994.

Taylor, Mark Kline, editor. *Paul Tillich: Theologian of the Boundaries*. London: Collins, 1987.

Teilhard de Chardin, Pierre. *Le Milieu Divin: An Essay on the Interior Life*. London: Collins / Fontana, 1966.

Templeton, Douglas. *The New Testament as True Fiction: Literature, Literary Criticism, Aesthetics*. Sheffield, UK: Sheffield Academic Press, 1999.

Thompson, Bard, editor. *Liturgies of the Western Church*. Philadelphia, PA: Fortress, 1988.

Thérèse, de Lisieux, Saint. *Story of a Soul: The Autobiography of St. Thérèse of Lisieux*. 3rd ed. Translated by John Clarke, O.C.D. Washington DC: ICS, 1996.

Tillich, Paul. "The Meaning and Justification of Religious Symbols." In *Hermeneutical Inquiry Vol. I: The Interpretation of Texts*, edited by David Klemm, 165–71. Atlanta: Scholars, 1986.

————. "Nature and Sacrament." In *Paul Tillich: Theologian of the Boundaries*, edited by Mark K. Taylor, 82–95. London: Collins, 1987.

————. "The Nature of Religious Language." In *The Essential Tillich: An Anthology of the Writings of Paul Tillich*, edited by F. Forrester Church, 44–56. New York: Collier / Macmillan, 1987.

Torrance, James B. *Worship, Community and the Triune God of Grace*. The Didsbury Lectures. Carlisle, UK: Paternoster, 1996.

Vahanian, Gabriel. *The Death of God: The Culture of Our Post-Christian Era*. New York: Braziller, 1961.

————. *No Other God*. New York: Braziller, 1966.

Vattimo, Gianni. *After Christianity*. Translated by Luca D'Isanto. New York: Columbia University Press, 2002.

————. *Belief*. Translated by Luca D'Isanto and David Webb. Stanford, CA: Stanford University Press, 1999.

Wainwright, Geoffrey. *Doxology: The Praise of God in Worship, Doctrine and Life*. London: Epworth, 1980.

Ward, Graham. *Cities of God*. London: Routledge, 2000.

————, editor. *The Blackwell Companion to Postmodern Theology*. Oxford: Blackwell, 2002.

————, editor. *The Certeau Reader*. Oxford: Blackwell, 2000.

————, editor. *The Postmodern God: A Theological Reader*. Oxford: Blackwell, 1997.

Westhelle, Vítor. *The Scandalous God: The Use and Abuse of the Cross*. Minneapolis, MN: Fortress, 2006.

Williams, Rowan. *On Christian Theology*. Oxford: Blackwell, 2000.

Wright, N. T. *Surprised by Hope: Rethinking Heaven, the Resurrection, and the Mission of the Church*. New York: Harper Collins, 2008.

Yarnold, Edward. *The Awe-Inspiring Rites of Initiation: The Origins of the R.C.I.A.* 2nd ed. Edinburgh: T. & T. Clark, 1994.

Zimmerman, Joyce Ann. *Liturgy and Hermeneutics*. Collegeville, MN: Liturgical, 1999.

Zizioulas, John D. *Being as Communion: Studies in Personhood and the Church.* Crestwood, NY: St. Vladimir's Seminary Press, 1985.

Žižek, Slavoj. *The Puppet and the Dwarf: The Perverse Core of Christianity.* Short Circuits. Cambridge: MIT, 2003.